"Hello?"

"Hi. I saw your ad."

"Yeah?"

"Um. I'm interested in number 88."

"Yeah?"

"Is it sold yet?"

"Let me check . . . . No."

"Could you tell me more about it?"

"It's a floppy thing. From the '60s. Without the stick."

"I see. Could you be a little more specific?"

"What do you mean?"

"Well, what was it for?"

"You know. It was a floppy thing, like from a carnival. It was on a stick and you wave it around. Floppy. Nice piece. Scarce."

"In good condition?"

"Oh, yeah. Great shape. A little repair on the wing. Can't tell, though. Great display piece."

"Can you do any better on the price?"

"No, not really."

"Oh. . . .

Will you take a check?"

"Sure."

Opposite,
FLOPPY THING (missing stick, detail)
(molded black plastic with decal)
4″ tall
1966

BATMAN

COLLECTED

Opposite,

CHILD'S MASK

(black molded plastic, rubber band)

Approx. 7″ tall

1966

Written, Art-Directed and Designed by

Chip Kidd

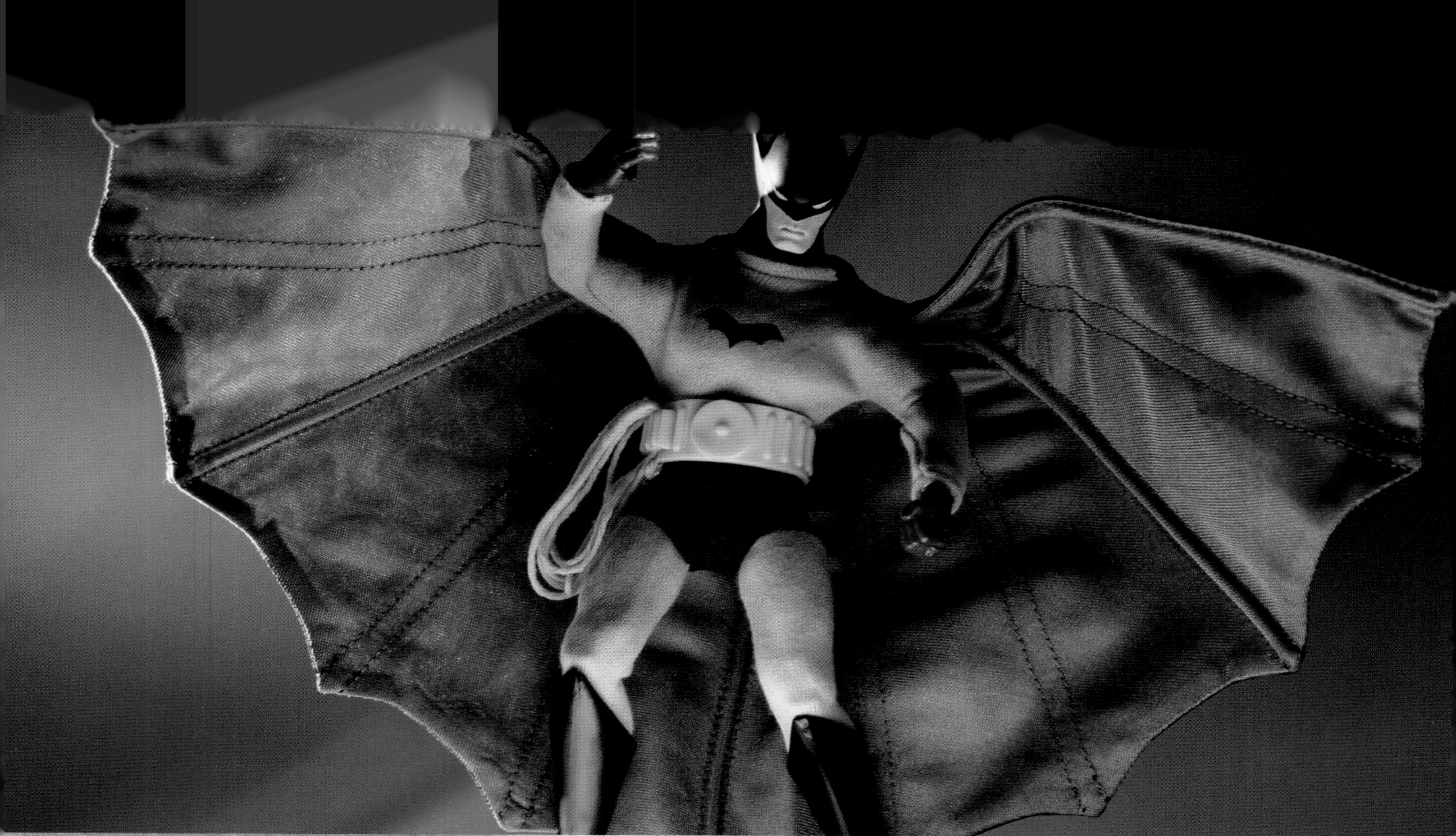

WATSON-GUPTILL PUBLICATIONS • A DIVISION OF BPI COMMUNICATIONS, INC. • NEW YORK

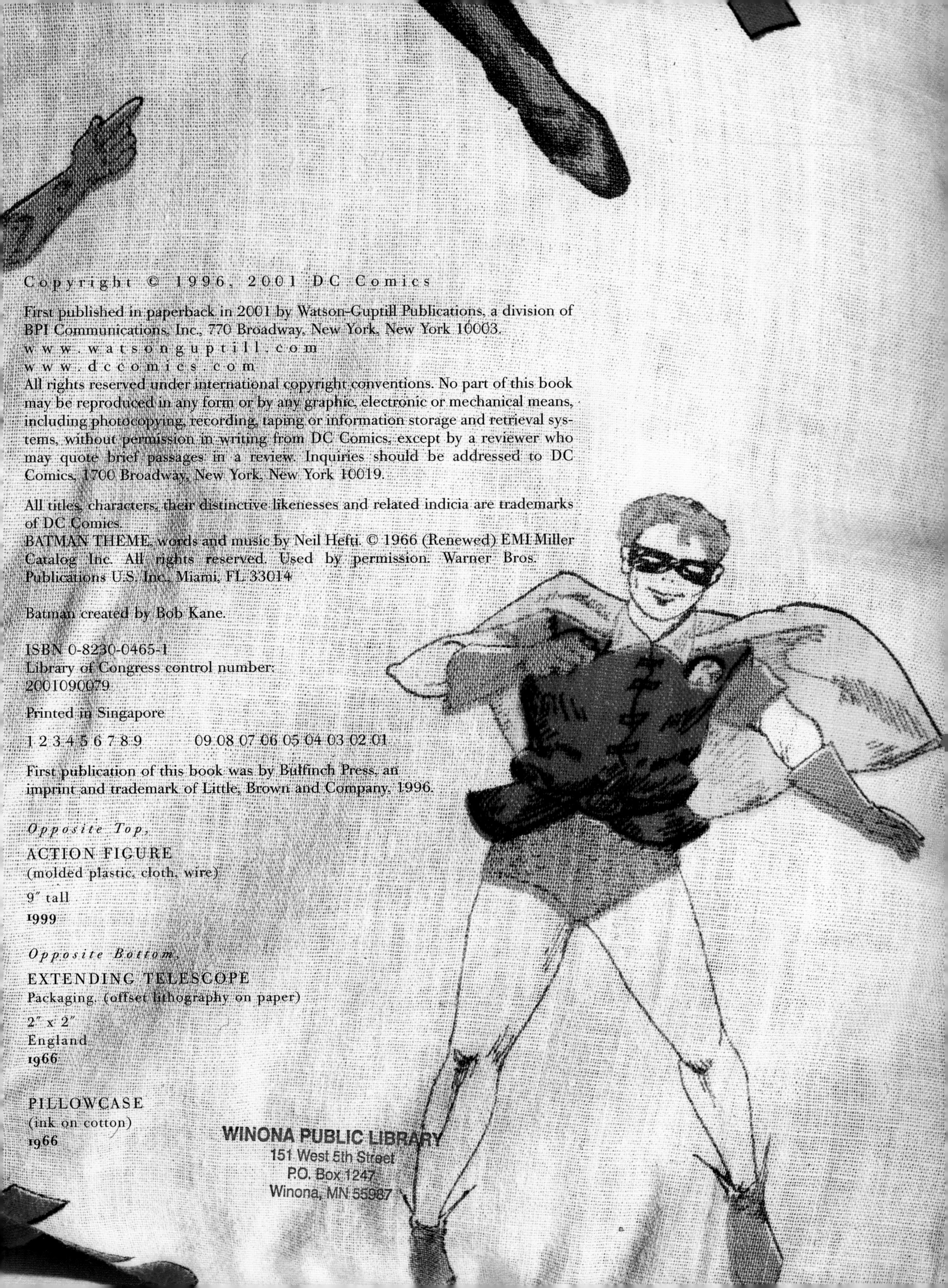

First published in paperback in 2001 by Watson-Guptill Publications, a division of BPI Communications, Inc., 770 Broadway, New York, New York 10003.
www.watsonguptill.com
www.dccomics.com

Batman created by Bob Kane.

ISBN 0-8230-0465-1
Library of Congress control number:
2001090079

Printed in Singapore

1 2 3 4 5 6 7 8 9 09 08 07 06 05 04 03 02 01

First publication of this book was by Bulfinch Press, an imprint and trademark of Little, Brown and Company, 1996.

Opposite Top,

ACTION FIGURE
(molded plastic, cloth, wire)

9″ tall

1999

Opposite Bottom,

EXTENDING TELESCOPE
Packaging, (offset lithography on paper)

2″ x 2″
England
1966

PILLOWCASE
(ink on cotton)
1966

PHOTOGRAPHED BY
GEOFF SPEAR

Camera

POP

BATMAN COLLECTED

CONTENTS

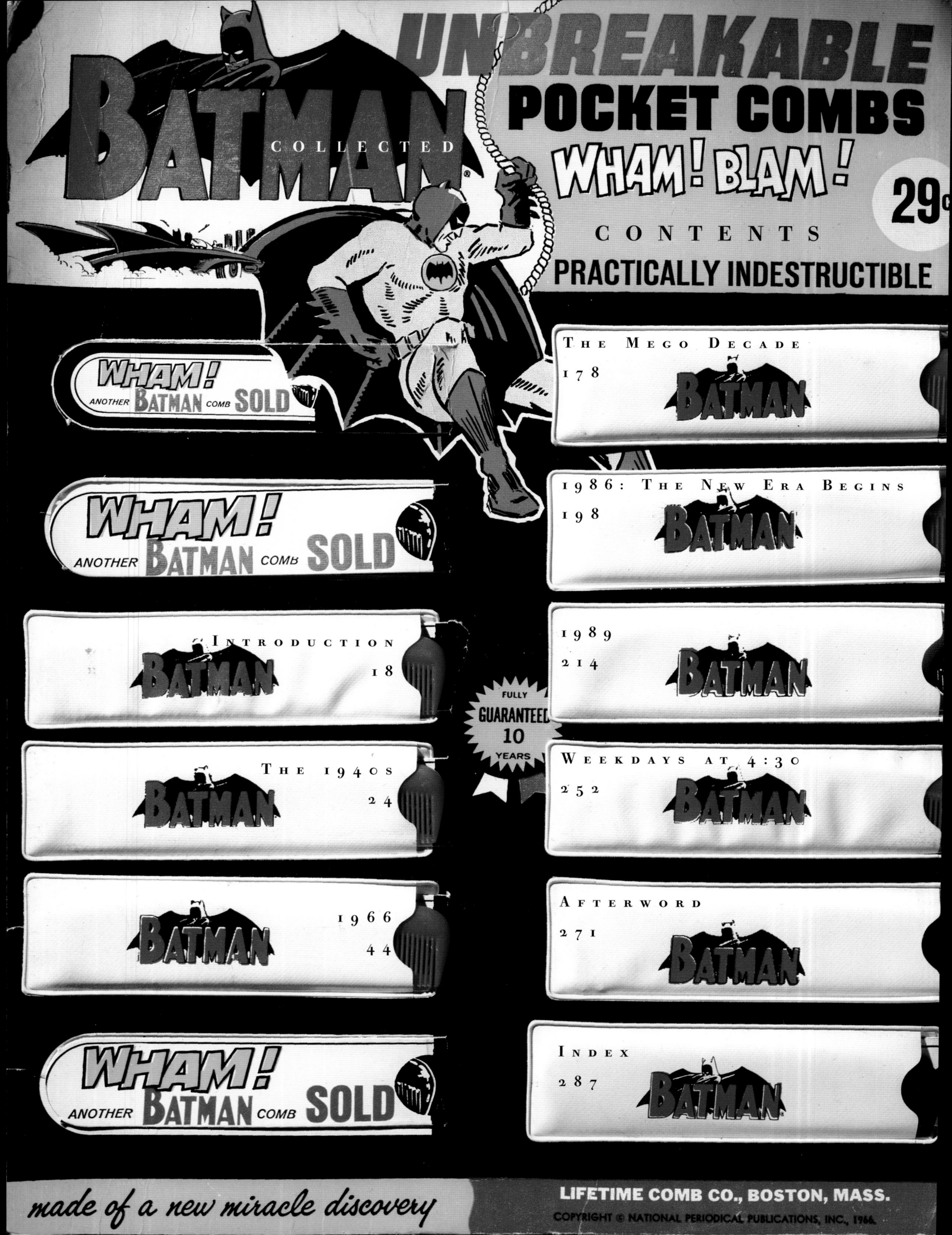

BATMAN
UNBREAKABLE
POCKET COMBS
WHAM! BLAM!
29¢
PRACTICALLY INDESTRUCTIBLE
WHAM! ANOTHER BATMAN COMB SOLD
WHAM! ANOTHER BATMAN COMB SOLD
WHAM! ANOTHER BATMAN COMB SOLD
FULLY GUARANTEED 10 YEARS
made of a new miracle discovery
LIFETIME COMB CO., BOSTON, MASS.
COPYRIGHT © NATIONAL PERIODICAL PUBLICATIONS, INC., 1966.

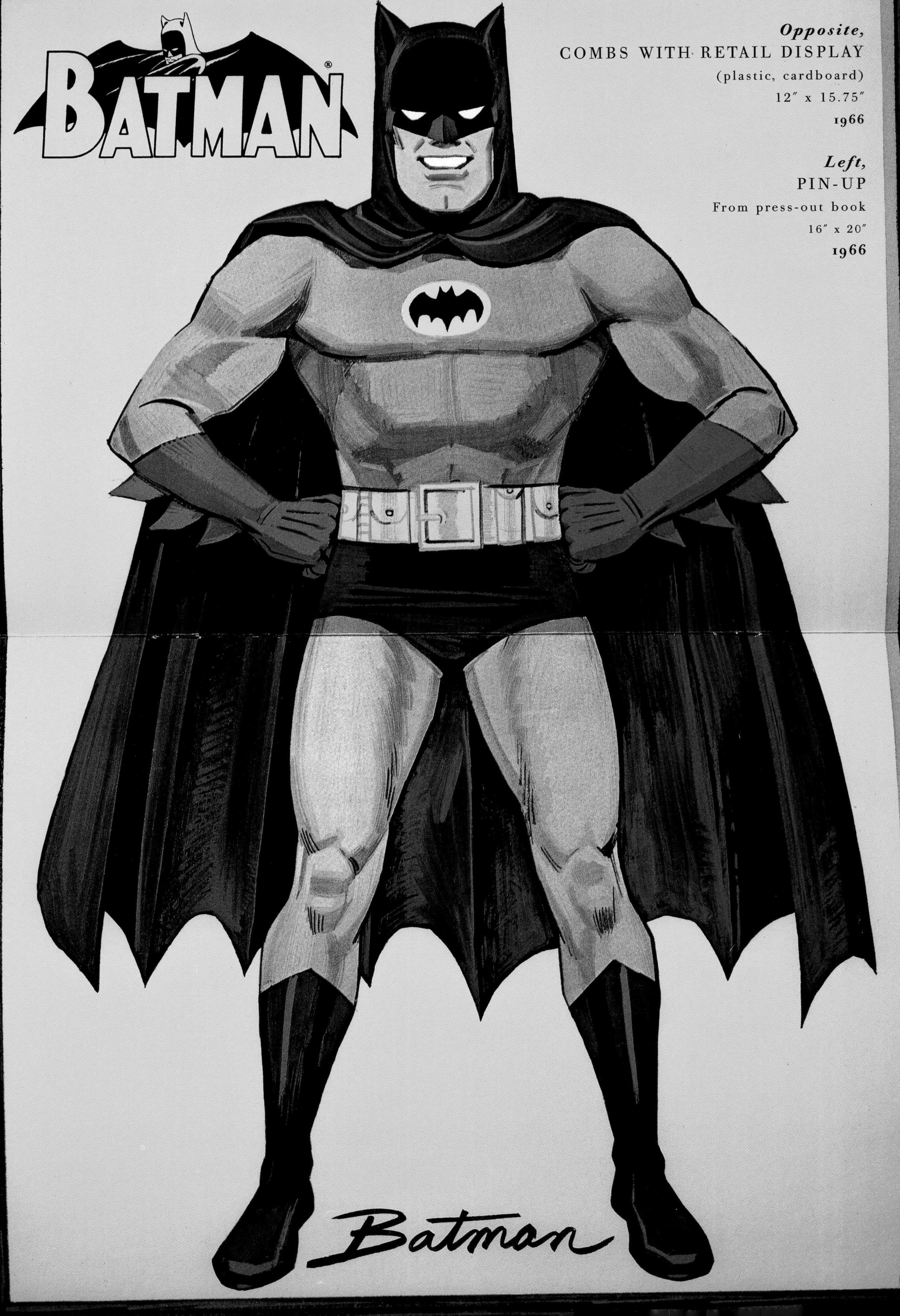

Opposite,
COMBS WITH RETAIL DISPLAY
(plastic, cardboard)
12″ x 15.75″
1966

Left,
PIN-UP
From press-out book
16″ x 20″
1966

This book belongs to :-

My Mom and Dad,

who never made me throw anything away.

And in loving memory of Julia Krug-Smith,
who is looking at it right now.

Above,

JUNE 1966

My brother Walt's fourth birthday. The Batman craze is already in full swing. Notice the puppets my mother made as party favors. I am two, at the head of the table, and my left arm is ready for battle.

OVERLEAF

Left,

ORIGINAL ART FOR
BATMAN AND ROBIN DAILY NEWSPAPER STRIP (detail)

(pen and ink on Craftint board), 3.5″ x 5.75″

Bob Kane and Charles Paris, artists, MAY 27, 1944

PAGE 17

COMIC BOOK PANEL FROM BATMAN #1

Bruce Wayne reacts to the death of his parents. 2″ x 2.8″

Bob Kane, artist, 1940

BANG

"You have taken my companions and my loved ones from me;
The darkness is my closest friend."
–Psalms, 88:18

"Superman is the American dream. Batman is the American truth."
–Bryan Edward Hill

INTRODUCTION

"Every passion borders on the chaotic,
but the collector's passion borders on the chaos of memories."
—Walter Benjamin

In 1968, when I was four, I got the chicken pox. In the midst of a chaos of blankets, Jell-O, soup, Vicks VapoRub, and hot compresses, my father had the wisdom to give me something I could actually use: a Batman night-light. When I woke from my feverish sleep, I had only to turn my head towards the light socket for reassurance that whatever evil might be hiding under my bed would stay there. Whatever harm might be lurking in me would be checked, cured, solved. It occurs to me now that this might be the quintessential Batman object. Just plug it in, and Batman does what he does best: inhabits the night, shows the way, looks cool, and, most important, makes you feel safe.

This, however, was not the start of my interest in Batman. It had begun at least a year earlier, watching Adam West & Co. on TV. Like the rest of the nation's tykes at the time, I was transfixed. Unlike most others, though, I never got over it. This was not a choice, a conscious decision. It just happened. I was, I *am*, obsessed by this character, this American myth. Any book about Batman is by definition also about obsession: Bruce Wayne is unable *not* to fight crime; I am unable not to pursue collecting Batman. It remains an enigma even to me. Why does anyone collect anything? To fill an unknown void? To adore an imagined god? To keep looking for a face in the dark?

The themes at the heart of the Batman mythology are eternal: tragedy, loss of innocence, redemption, and the unending crusade. But what makes it compelling is its reversal of form and content. Batman is a figure that performs good works in the guise of an evil being, a demon. The Joker, his nemesis, dispenses horror and mayhem while assuming the form of someone meant to make us forget our cares, a clown. This message—that things are not what they seem, and therefore one must judge actions, not appearances—has a sense of irony that is closer to classic dramatic traditions than it is to the stereotypes of popular culture. Batman *truly* becomes a modern phenomenon by relying on the twentieth century's two great inventions, mass media and mass production. A myth is nothing if it's not repeated, and the power to do so has never been greater. The variations on a theme that make up this book are proof of that.

Left and Right,
NIGHT LIGHT
(molded plastic, light bulb)
Approx. 2.5″ wide
1966

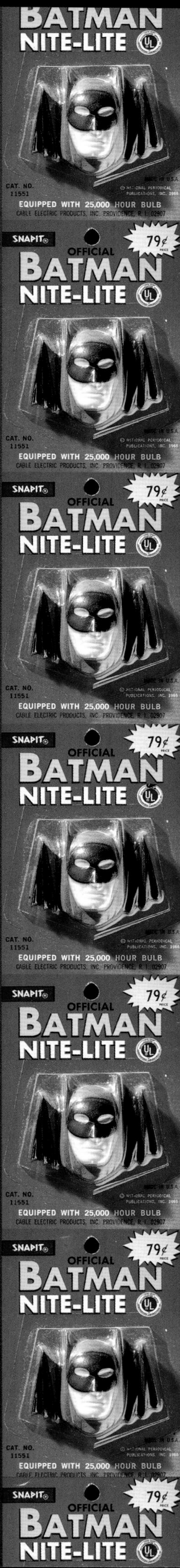

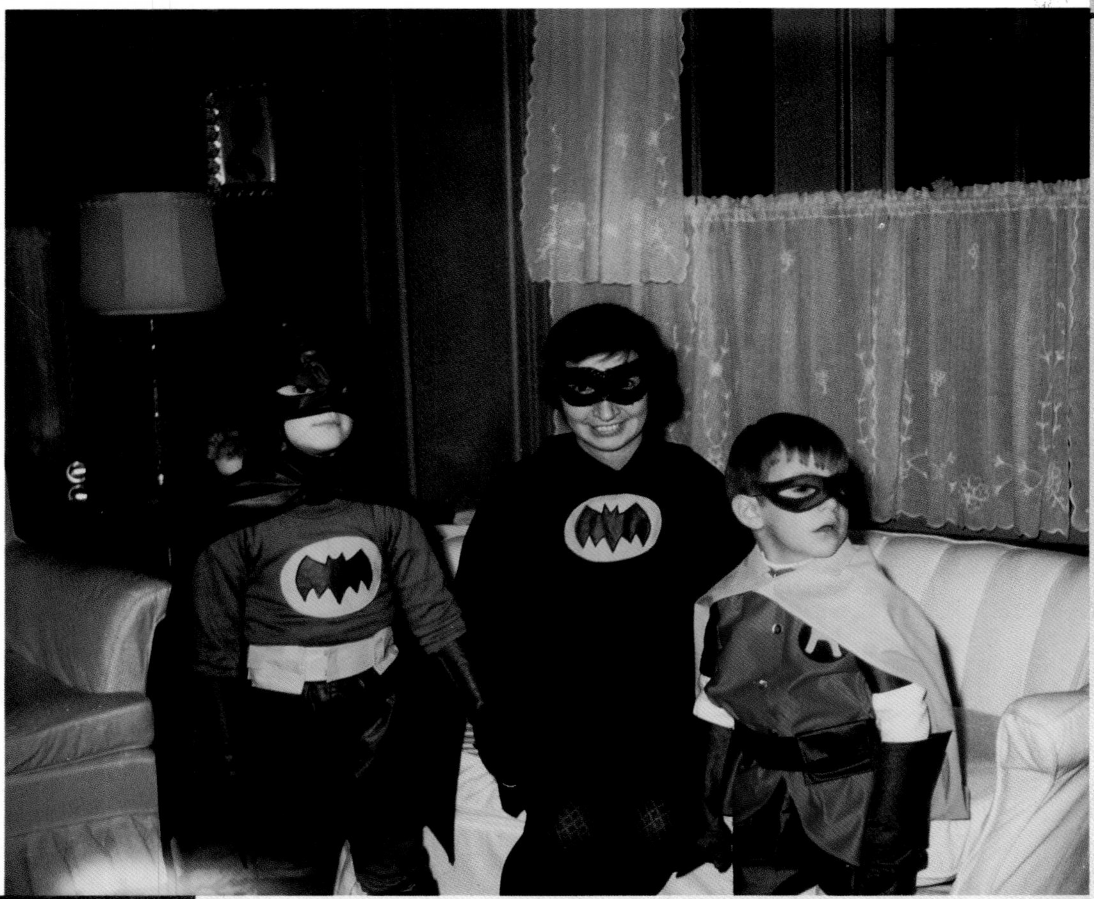

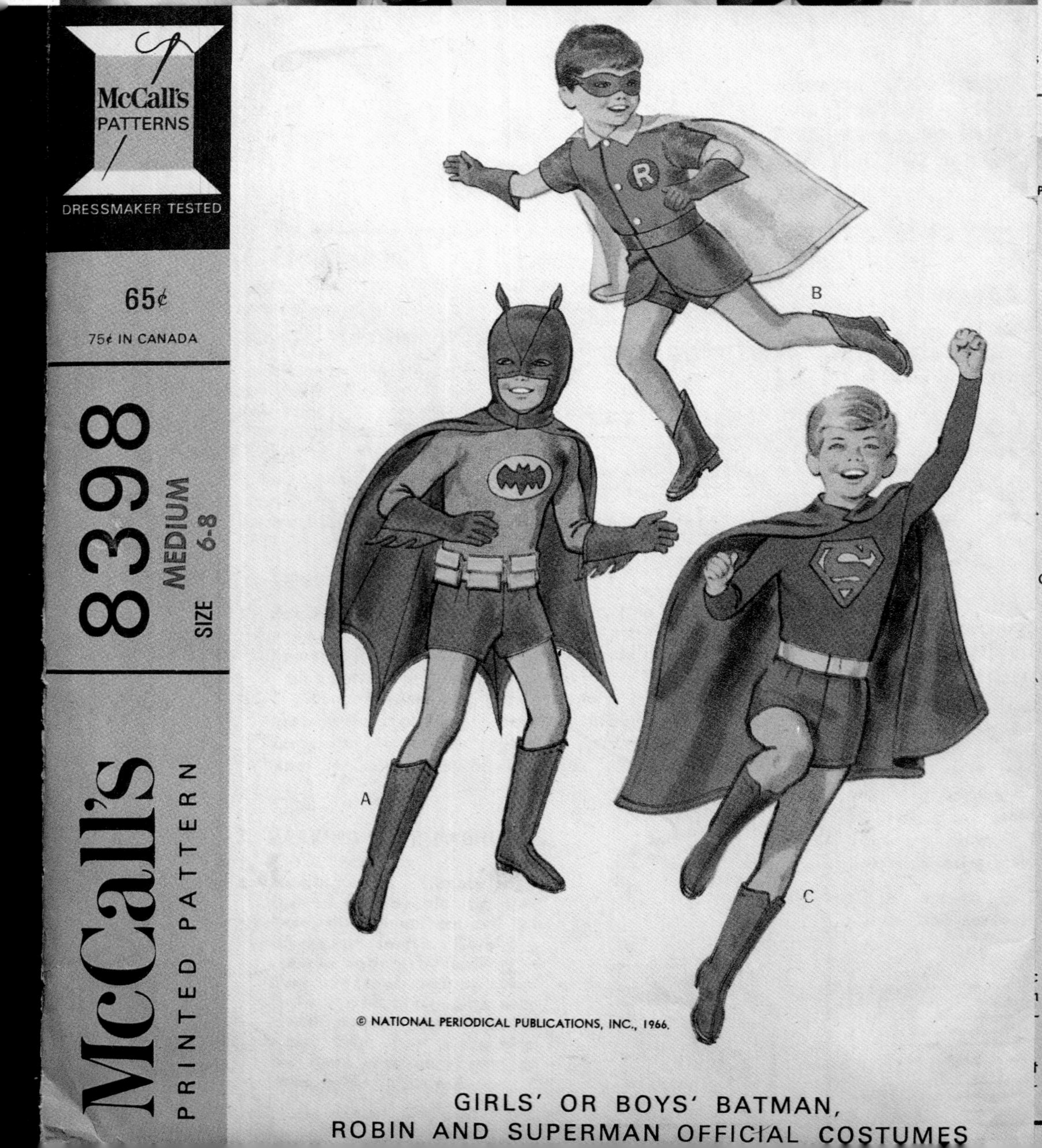

McCall's
PATTERNS
DRESSMAKER TESTED
65¢
75¢ IN CANADA
8398
SIZE MEDIUM 6-8
McCall's
PRINTED PATTERN
B
A
C
© NATIONAL PERIODICAL PUBLICATIONS, INC., 1966.
GIRLS' OR BOYS' BATMAN,
ROBIN AND SUPERMAN OFFICIAL COSTUMES

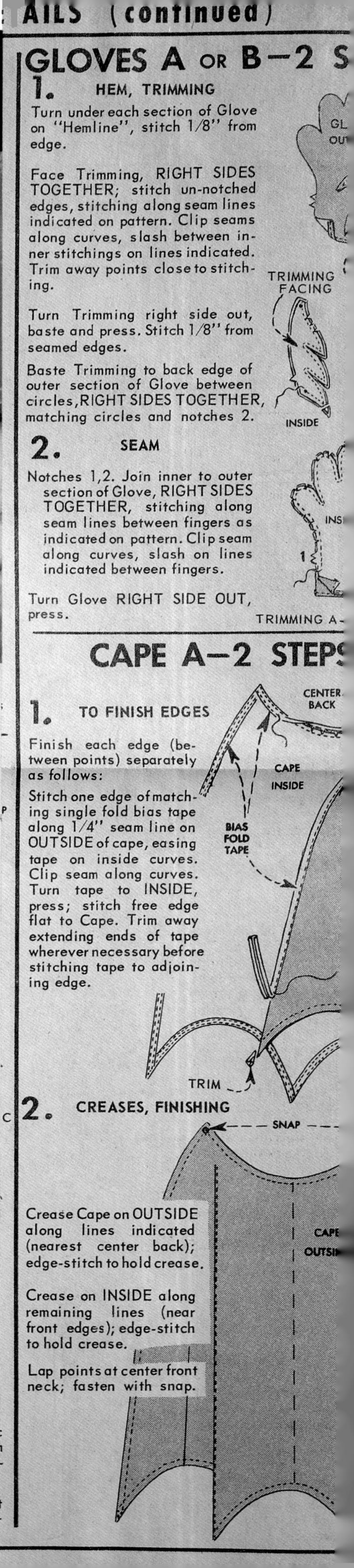

AILS (continued)

GLOVES A OR B–2 S

1. HEM, TRIMMING

Turn under each section of Glove on "Hemline", stitch 1/8" from edge.

Face Trimming, RIGHT SIDES TOGETHER; stitch un-notched edges, stitching along seam lines indicated on pattern. Clip seams along curves, slash between inner stitchings on lines indicated. Trim away points close to stitching.

Turn Trimming right side out, baste and press. Stitch 1/8" from seamed edges.

Baste Trimming to back edge of outer section of Glove between circles, RIGHT SIDES TOGETHER, matching circles and notches 2.

2. SEAM

Notches 1,2. Join inner to outer section of Glove, RIGHT SIDES TOGETHER, stitching along seam lines between fingers as indicated on pattern. Clip seam along curves, slash on lines indicated between fingers.

Turn Glove RIGHT SIDE OUT, press.

CAPE A–2 STEPS

1. TO FINISH EDGES

Finish each edge (between points) separately as follows:

Stitch one edge of matching single fold bias tape along 1/4" seam line on OUTSIDE of cape, easing tape on inside curves. Clip seam along curves. Turn tape to INSIDE, press; stitch free edge flat to Cape. Trim away extending ends of tape wherever necessary before stitching tape to adjoining edge.

2. CREASES, FINISHING

Crease Cape on OUTSIDE along lines indicated (nearest center back); edge-stitch to hold crease.

Crease on INSIDE along remaining lines (near front edges); edge-stitch to hold crease.

Lap points at center front neck; fasten with snap.

Left,

PATTERNS FOR CHILDREN'S COSTUMES

(tissue paper)

1966

The same year I got the chicken pox, my mother made Halloween costumes for my brother and me. Walt, being two years older, got to be Batman; Mom went as Batgirl and I was Robin. Dad joked that he was Alfred the butler, and not just on October 31. The word on my block was that Mr. and Mrs. Schmidt, who lived two doors away, would take your picture and give it to you as a treat instead of candy. This was my first experience of a costume's power to transform, to make someone new (far left). The outfits took quite a beating in the next few years, and only the Batman cape has survived.

Playing Batman with my friends upheld a strong tradition among boys at lunchtime recess everywhere: excluding girls. Nothing alienated the girls more than when we put on masks and screamed our heads off (not that Batman was supposed to do this, but who cared?). I'm still amazed today when I meet a woman who liked Batman as a kid. I certainly didn't know any, and wouldn't have understood them if I did. It was our version of the He-Man Woman Hater's Club from the Little Rascals, another of our major models for social behavior.

I used to watch Batman on TV with Dad, who would guffaw at what seemed to me the most dire of circumstances. I remember watching once when Batman was being pulled up out of the ocean, hanging onto a rope ladder dangling from the Batcopter (piloted by Robin). Just as he was about to clear the surface, a shark attached itself to his leg and wouldn't let go. I was horrified. Robin, apparently oblivious, continued the copter's ascent. By now Batman was a good twenty feet in the air, flailing madly, trying in vain to shake off the shark. I could barely breathe. I was a wreck, frozen with anxiety, and Dad was . . . *laughing*. Sacrilege. I tried to ignore it, to little avail. Then Batman removed an aerosol can labeled "Bat Shark-repellent" from his Utility Belt and sprayed it on his attacker, which immediately dropped into the sea, defeated. Dad was doubled over. I just sat there quietly, overcome with relief and admiration. Imagine having the forethought to bring along shark-repellent.

Above,

CHILD'S CAPE

Sewn by Ann Kidd,
from the patterns pictured to the left,
and depicted in use, above left

Approx. 36″ long

1968

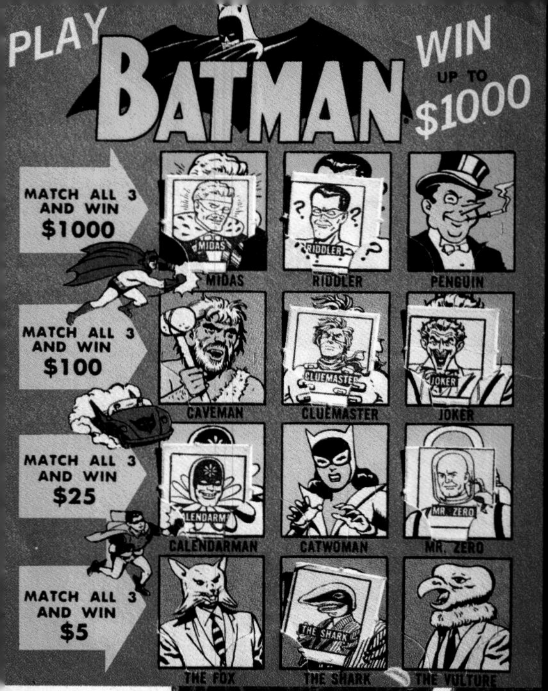

Left,
LOTTERY GAME
(paper)
4″ x 5.5″
1966

Right,
PREPARATORY SKETCH
For
THE DARK KNIGHT RETURNS
Frank Miller, artist
(pen and ink on paper)
4″ x 3″
1985

Below,
PACKAGING FOR SNEAKERS
(detail)
1966

Below Right,
GOGGLES
(molded plastic)
Approx. 6″ wide
England
1966

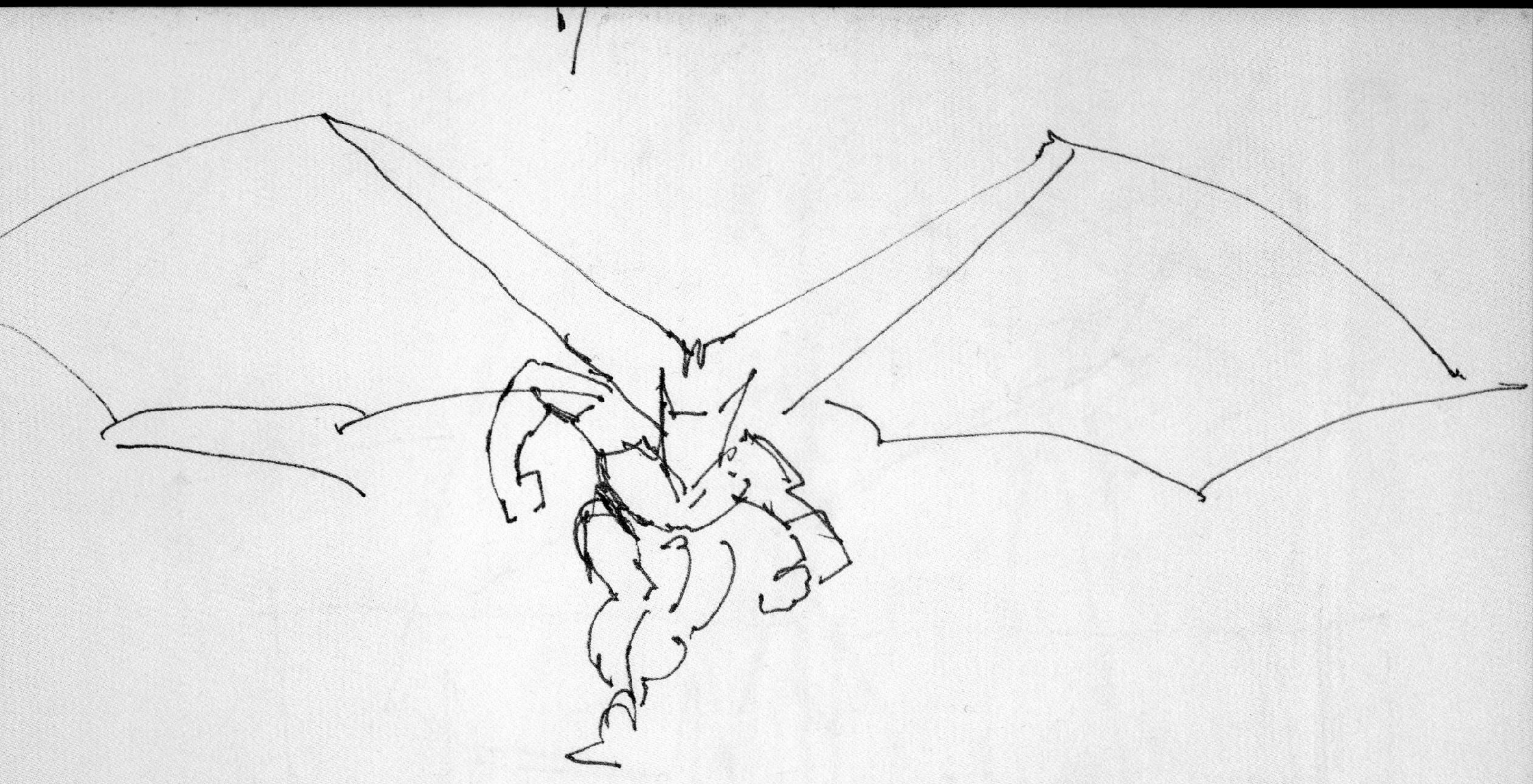

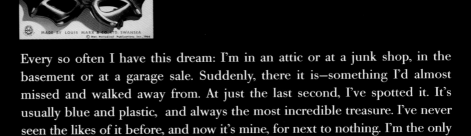

Every so often I have this dream: I'm in an attic or at a junk shop, in the basement or at a garage sale. Suddenly, there it is–something I'd almost missed and walked away from. At just the last second, I've spotted it. It's usually blue and plastic, and always the most incredible treasure. I've never seen the likes of it before, and now it's mine, for next to nothing. I'm the only person who has one. I can't believe how lucky I am.

Then I wake up.

I'd be the first to admit that few things can be as tedious as hearing someone describe a dream. It's like explaining color to a person born blind.

Now, I don't have to *tell* anyone what my dream was like. You're looking at it. You're in it. If some of it is hazy or perplexing or confusing or horrific or a little too good to be true, and if none of it at all is what you were expecting, well, what can I say? That's the way dreams are.

–C. K.

BOB KANE
Yours for bigger and better thrills
Batman
-and that goes double for me.
Robin

Batman was revealed to the world in May of 1939 in the pages of *Detective Comics* #27. It was published by Detective Comics, Inc., who had scored a big hit the previous year with a creation called Superman. Not much about "The Bat-Man" (as he was then called) was disclosed in the first story, but by issue #33 readers were clued in to his motivation to dress as a bat and cause trouble for criminals: When he was a young boy, he had seen his parents killed by a mugger. The first ten stories were eerie, nocturnal, joyless but nonetheless beautifully weird little affairs that featured our hero (looking like the devil himself) dispatching his foes off the tops of tall buildings at the slightest provocation. No doubt about it, though, he had style. The stories were drawn by Bob Kane (then twenty-two years old) and written by Bill Finger. By issue #38, it was decided that Batman had to lighten up, and soon. Shortening his ears and making his cape less winglike diminished the demonic effect, and he actually started smiling, something he had only previously done while watching Dr. Death get burned alive. The major adjustment, however, involved the addition of a partner named Robin who would provide what was thought to be so desperately needed: color and youth. Robin's age (about twelve, give or take a year) provided young readers with the idea that they could be super heroes too; all they needed was training as a circus acrobat and murdered parents.

Sales doubled.

The result was a Batman who was quickly becoming downright joyful, and arguably less interesting. The pin-up at left (the back cover of *Batman* #1) depicts two people who, despite personal tragedies of a devastating magnitude, are beaming with cheer. Soon their adventures took place during the daytime, a concept at war with the very premise of the characters. It would be forty years before the strip's original sensibility was restored.

The question of why there was so little licensing of Batman material from this period could be addressed in terms of the nature of the era. Superman had proved to be a huge licensing success immediately. Why not Batman? Well, one reason might be that he had no superpowers. Of course, that didn't hinder Little Orphan Annie, but remember, she wasn't expected to have any. And let us not forget that Superman and Little Orphan Annie had the added benefits of their own radio shows and newspaper comic strips. Batman had the curious circumstance of originating in a time when big muscle was needed in a world battling Hitler, and Superman more adequately fit the bill. Not to worry. Batman's time would come. And besides, in the meantime, his comic book was doing just fine.

Left,

BACK COVER OF BATMAN #1

Bob Kane, artist

1940

Below,

DETECTIVE COMICS #26 (detail)

The first time Batman is referred to in print

1939

HERE THEY ARE!

BATMAN AND ROBIN

IN A WHOLE FLOCK OF THRILLING, ACTION-PACKED

FULL-COLOR TRANSFERS!

IT'S GREAT SPORT! APPLY THESE THRILLING PICTURES OF YOUR FAVORITE HEROES TO GLASS, METAL, YES, EVEN TO WOOD! EVERY COLORFUL TRANSFER IS DIFFERENT!

A BIG 10¢ VALUE

—SIMPLE DIRECTIONS INSIDE—

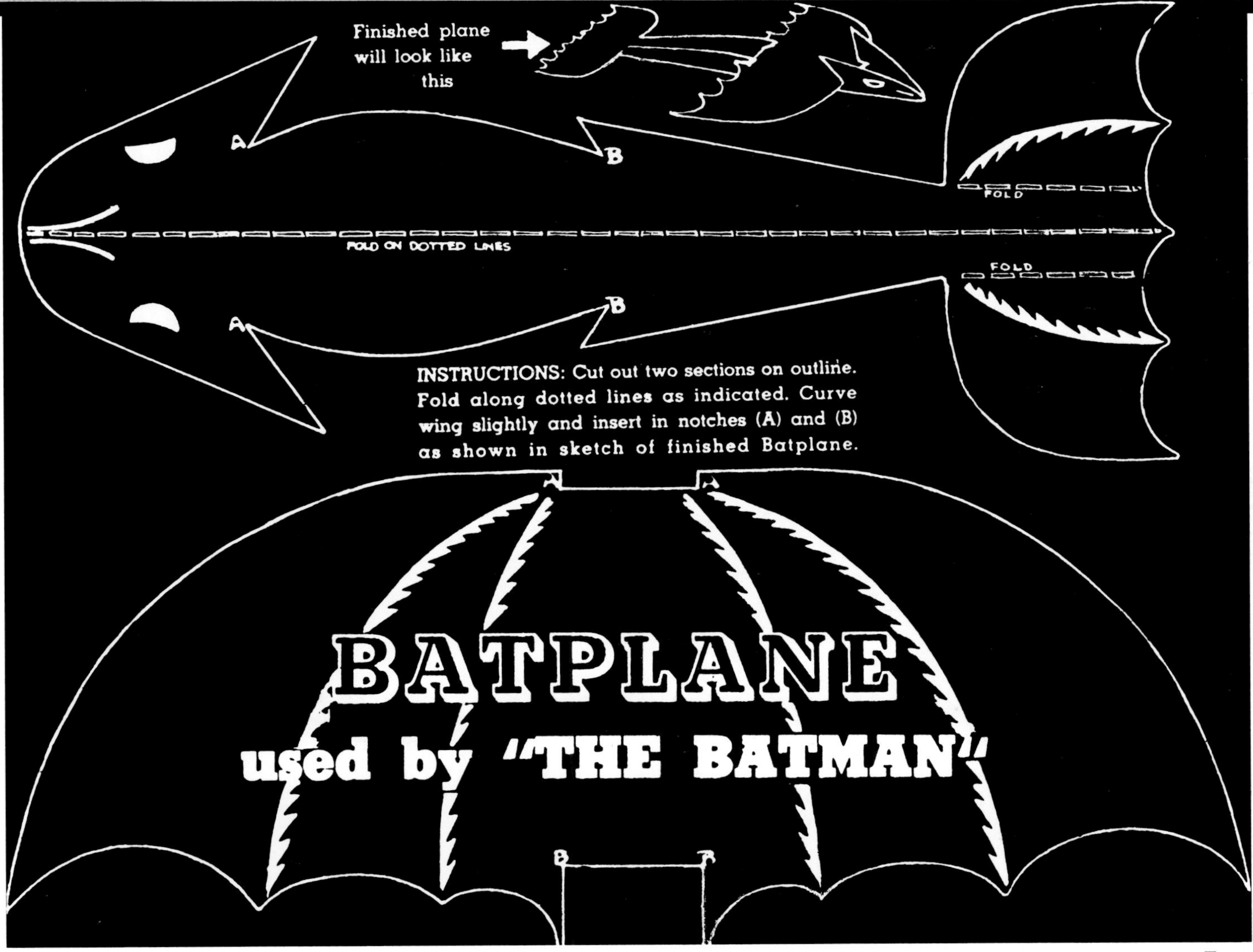

Left,
DECALS
(ink, paper, varnish)
4.5″ x 6″
1944

Above,
BATPLANE
Proposed movie theatre giveaway
11″ wide
1943

Top,
TRADING CARDS
(ink on cardstock)
2.25″ x 3.5″
1949

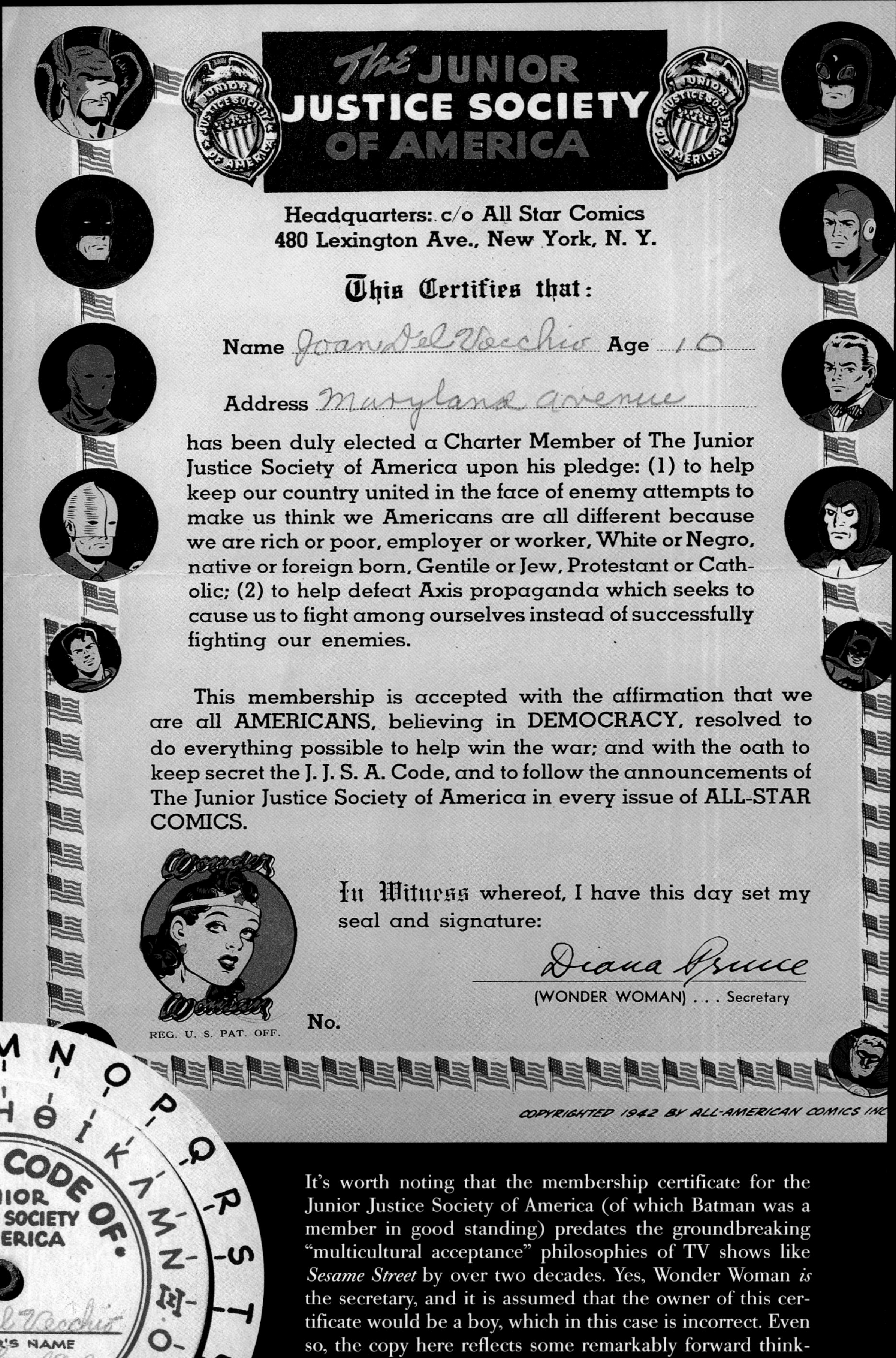
The Junior Justice Society of America

Headquarters: c/o All Star Comics
480 Lexington Ave., New York, N. Y.

This Certifies that:

Name Joan Del Vecchio Age 10

Address Maryland avenue

has been duly elected a Charter Member of The Junior Justice Society of America upon his pledge: (1) to help keep our country united in the face of enemy attempts to make us think we Americans are all different because we are rich or poor, employer or worker, White or Negro, native or foreign born, Gentile or Jew, Protestant or Catholic; (2) to help defeat Axis propaganda which seeks to cause us to fight among ourselves instead of successfully fighting our enemies.

This membership is accepted with the affirmation that we are all AMERICANS, believing in DEMOCRACY, resolved to do everything possible to help win the war; and with the oath to keep secret the J. J. S. A. Code, and to follow the announcements of The Junior Justice Society of America in every issue of ALL-STAR COMICS.

In Witness whereof, I have this day set my seal and signature:

Diana Prince
(WONDER WOMAN) . . . Secretary

No.

It's worth noting that the membership certificate for the Junior Justice Society of America (of which Batman was a member in good standing) predates the groundbreaking "multicultural acceptance" philosophies of TV shows like *Sesame Street* by over two decades. Yes, Wonder Woman *is* the secretary, and it is assumed that the owner of this certificate would be a boy, which in this case is incorrect. Even so, the copy here reflects some remarkably forward thinking for its time.

Opposite Above,
MEMBERSHIP CERTIFICATE
From the Junior Justice Society of America
8.5″ x 11″
1942

Opposite Below,
DECODER
From the Junior Justice Society of America membership kit
4″ in diameter
1942

Above,
ADVERTISEMENT
For the first Columbia Pictures Batman movie serial
8″ x 5″
1943

Left,
DECODER (reverse)
4″ in diameter
1942

OVERLEAF
MOVIE POSTER
(detail)
(three-color traditional lithography on paper)
48″ x 65″
France
1940s

PAGES 32-33
LOBBY CARDS
For the Columbia Pictures Batman movie serials
14″ x 11″
1943, 1949, 1954

TRAPPE
Chapter 4

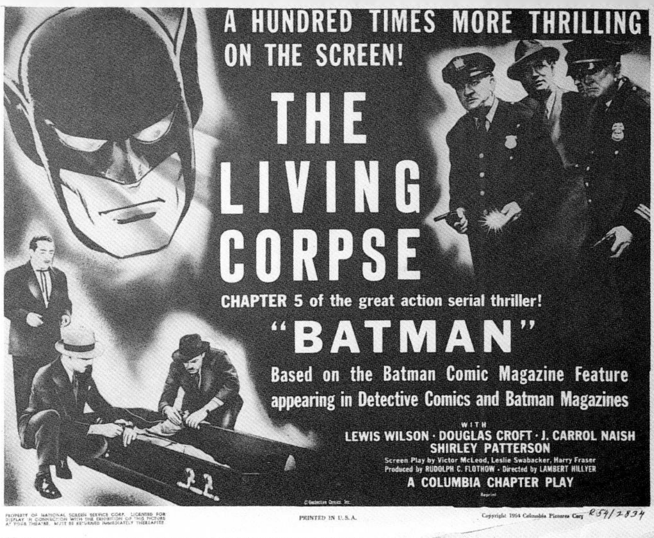

A HUNDRED TIMES MORE THRILLING ON THE SCREEN!
THE LIVING CORPSE
CHAPTER 5 of the great action serial thriller!
"BATMAN"
Based on the Batman Comic Magazine Feature appearing in Detective Comics and Batman Magazines
WITH
LEWIS WILSON · DOUGLAS CROFT · J. CARROL NAISH
SHIRLEY PATTERSON
Screen Play by Victor McLeod, Leslie Swabacker, Harry Fraser
Produced by RUDOLPH C. FLOTHOW · Directed by LAMBERT HILLYER
A COLUMBIA CHAPTER PLAY
PRINTED IN U.S.A.
Copyright 1954 Columbia Pictures Corp.
R54/2834

ALL THE ACTION AND THRILLS OF THE COMIC STRIP MULTIPLIED A HUNDRED-FOLD!
"THE BAT'S CAVE"
CHAPTER 2 of the adventure-packed chapter play!
BATMAN
Based on the Batman Comic Magazine Feature appearing in Detective Comics and Batman Magazines
with
LEWIS WILSON · DOUGLAS CROFT
J. CARROL NAISH · SHIRLEY PATTERSON
SCREEN PLAY BY VICTOR McLEOD, LESLIE SWABACKER, HARRY FRASER
Produced by RUDOLPH C. FLOTHOW · Directed by LAMBERT HILLYER
A COLUMBIA CHAPTER PLAY
COPYRIGHT, DETECTIVE COMICS, INC.
PRINTED IN U.S.A.
R54/2834

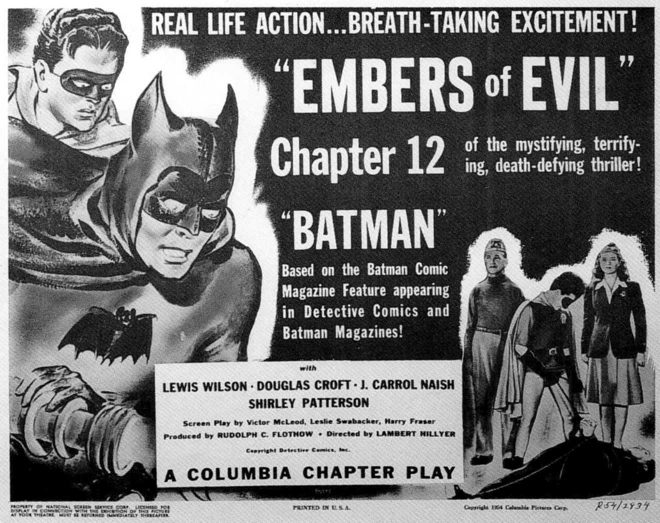

REAL LIFE ACTION...BREATH-TAKING EXCITEMENT!
"EMBERS of EVIL"
Chapter 12 of the mystifying, terrifying, death-defying thriller!
"BATMAN"
Based on the Batman Comic Magazine Feature appearing in Detective Comics and Batman Magazines!
with
LEWIS WILSON · DOUGLAS CROFT · J. CARROL NAISH
SHIRLEY PATTERSON
Screen Play by Victor McLeod, Leslie Swabacker, Harry Fraser
Produced by RUDOLPH C. FLOTHOW · Directed by LAMBERT HILLYER
Copyright Detective Comics, Inc.
A COLUMBIA CHAPTER PLAY
PRINTED IN U.S.A.
Copyright 1954 Columbia Pictures Corp.
R54/2834

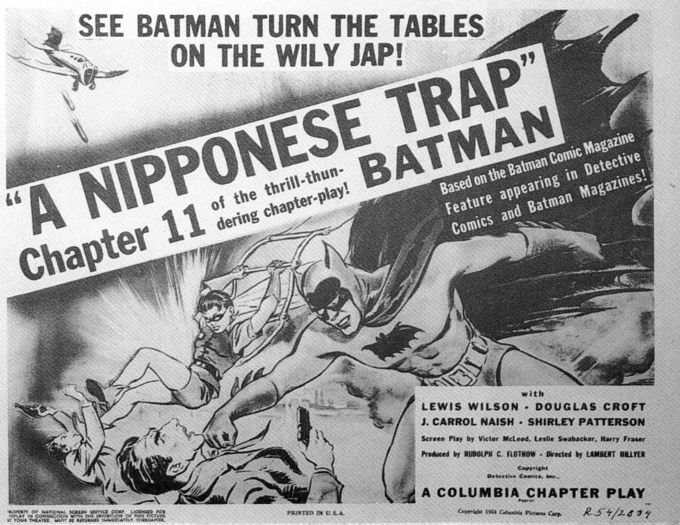

SEE BATMAN TURN THE TABLES ON THE WILY JAP!
"A NIPPONESE TRAP"
Chapter 11 of the thrill-thundering chapter-play!
BATMAN
Based on the Batman Comic Magazine Feature appearing in Detective Comics and Batman Magazines!
with
LEWIS WILSON · DOUGLAS CROFT
J. CARROL NAISH · SHIRLEY PATTERSON
Screen Play by Victor McLeod, Leslie Swabacker, Harry Fraser
Produced by RUDOLPH C. FLOTHOW · Directed by LAMBERT HILLYER
Copyright Detective Comics, Inc.
A COLUMBIA CHAPTER PLAY
PRINTED IN U.S.A.
Copyright 1954 Columbia Pictures Corp.
R54/2834

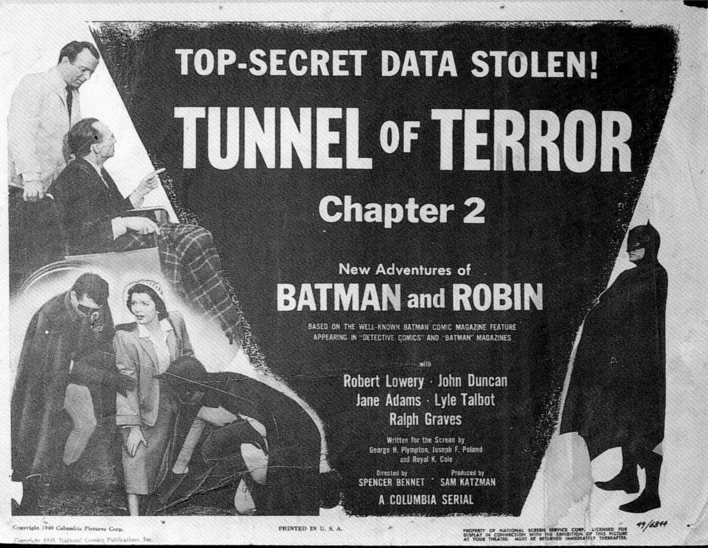

TOP-SECRET DATA STOLEN!
TUNNEL OF TERROR
Chapter 2
New Adventures of
BATMAN and ROBIN
BASED ON THE WELL-KNOWN BATMAN COMIC MAGAZINE FEATURE APPEARING IN "DETECTIVE COMICS" AND "BATMAN" MAGAZINES
with
Robert Lowery · John Duncan
Jane Adams · Lyle Talbot
Ralph Graves
Written for the Screen by George H. Plympton, Joseph F. Poland and Royal K. Cole
Directed by SPENCER BENNET
Produced by SAM KATZMAN
A COLUMBIA SERIAL
Copyright 1949 Columbia Pictures Corp.
PRINTED IN U. S. A.

TARGET —ROBIN!
Chapter 6
New Adventures of
BATMAN AND ROBIN
A COLUMBIA SERIAL

55
THE WIZARD STRIKES BACK!
Chapter 9
New Adventures of
BATMAN AND ROBIN
A COLUMBIA SERIAL

BATMAN VICTORIOUS
Chapter 15
New Adventures of
BATMAN AND ROBIN
A COLUMBIA SERIAL

In 1943, a Batman radio program was proposed to the Mutual Network, to be broadcast from WOR in New York. Only the audition script has survived, the penultimate scene of which appears below. Why the show was never produced remains a mystery, although one could deduce that potential sponsors felt that the concept of Batman fighting the Nazis was a bit hard to swallow. The script's emphasis on death and misery probably didn't help either.

MOVIE POSTER (detail)
(four-color printing on paper)
27″ x 41″
1943

Below,
CHALK CARNIVAL STATUE
Approx. 16″ tall
POSSIBLY LATE 1940S

ROBIN: (*LOW*) Bruce? Mother and Dad . . . they're dead, aren't they?

WAYNE: (*SOFT*) Yes, Robin . . . but thanks to them and Linda and the Batman, a convoy is safe.

ROBIN: (*SLOW*) What am I going to do? Where'll I live?

WAYNE: With me, Robin . . . if you will.

ROBIN: Thanks . . . Batman.

WAYNE: What? What did you say?

ROBIN: The Nazi's face was oily . . . when you hit him, you got oil on your knuckles; it's still there. No! don't wipe it off! That kind of makes you on the same side as my Dad . . . it's kind of like a medal.

WAYNE: I'd rather you hadn't found out, Robin . . . it was my secret; I used the phony accent so that no one would ever associate Bruce Wayne with the Batman. No one must know, Robin!

ROBIN: Not even the girl? This Linda dame?

WAYNE: Especially not her. I work alone, Robin. . . .

ROBIN: Bruce? They killed my Dad and Mother . . . and they tried to kill me! Let me help! Can't I work with you? It's a chance to get even . . . to avenge my parents . . . PLEASE!

(*MUSIC SWELLS, FADES OUT*)

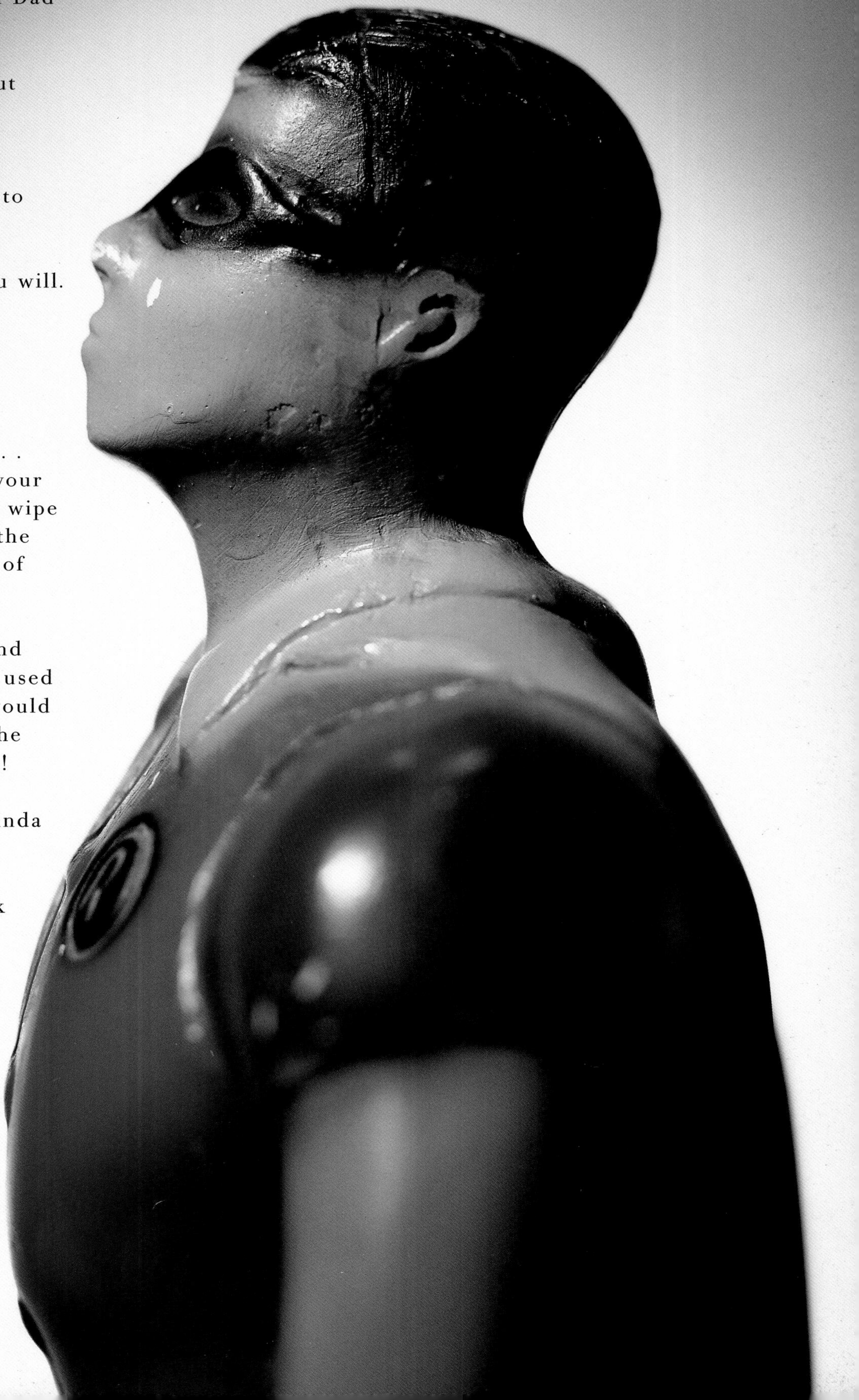

Above,
BELT BUCKLE
(molded brass)
3.5″ x 1.6″
EARLY 1940S

Opposite,
PROMOTIONAL BROCHURE
(cover and first two pages)
For the Batman and Robin newspaper strip
11″ x 17″
1943

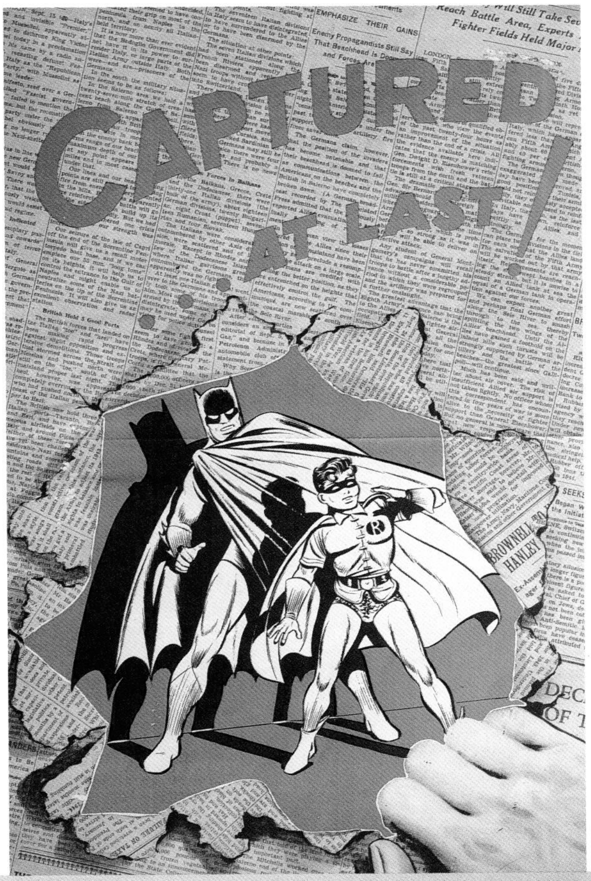

OVERLEAF
ORIGINAL ART
(detail)
For the Batman and Robin Sunday newspaper strip
(pen and ink on illustration board)
Jack Burnley and Charles Paris, artists
14.25″ x 25.5″
FEBRUARY 17, 1946

PAGE 39
DRAWING BOARD USED BY CHARLES PARIS
Featuring a ghosted profile of Batman facing left
(wood)
16″ x 22″
CIRCA 1940S-50S

NOW
BATMAN AND ROBIN
are available as
DAILY AND SUNDAY
COMIC FEATURES
BATMAN AND ROBIN!
LOOK AT THE RECORD

Newsprint has been curtailed . . . WPB forecasts further cuts . . . pages are reduced . . . departments are dropped . . . editors allocate space frugally . . . and every part of every newspaper is judged critically on the basis of its importance to readers. Under stress, READER-POPULARITY is the all-important criterion. BECAUSE of this situation (NOT in spite of it), McClure sought and secured syndication rights to the sensational comic strip, BATMAN and ROBIN . . . a TESTED, PROVEN, audience-builder . . . with many millions of pre-sold faithful fans!

Unlike any other comic strip every syndicated, BATMAN comes to newspapers with a fan-following ranging high into the millions. An estimated 24,000,000 read EVERY ISSUE of the 3,000,000 comic magazines in which BATMAN thrills and entertains; more than 4,000 motion picture theatres will carry BATMAN'S adventures to many millions of serial-fans this year.

A happy combination of many basic human appeals has made BATMAN one of the most sensationally successful strips ever created. Whirlwind action-packed adventure . . . spine-tingling mystery . . . debonaire wit and humor . . . brilliant brainwork and fists of dynamite . . . and just a little (not too much) love interest — all these are woven into the gripping story of BATMAN and Robin!

But see for yourself! Turn the pages and . . .

BATMAN AND ROBIN
by BOB KANE
2-17
BATMAN AND ROBIN HAVE JUST CAPTURED THEIR FAMED FOE, THE PENGUIN—"MAN OF A THOUSAND UMBRELLAS"—WHO HAS JUST FILCHED FROM THE LOCAL POST OFFICE A MYSTERIOUS CARD ADDRESSED TO...
COPYRIGHT 1946 BY DETECTIVE CO ICS, INC.
DIST. BY McCLURE NEWSPA NDICATE
120
POST OFFICE
OSWALD CHESTERFIEL IS IT A NAME OR A STUNT?
WAIT, PENGUIN! YOU FORGOT YOUR OTHER UMBRELLA!
NOW—LET'S SEE WHAT'S ON THIS POST CARD!
THE UMBRELLA BUSINESS, EH? WHY, PENGUIN—THEN YOU MUST BE—
YES! I AM OSWALD CHESTERFIELD COBBLEPOT! AND NO CRACKS!
OH—THIS IS AWFUL! DE AUNT MIRANDA! TO HA BROUGHT ME UP AND BELIEVED IN ME ALL THESE YEARS! THE DISGRACE WILL KILL HER!

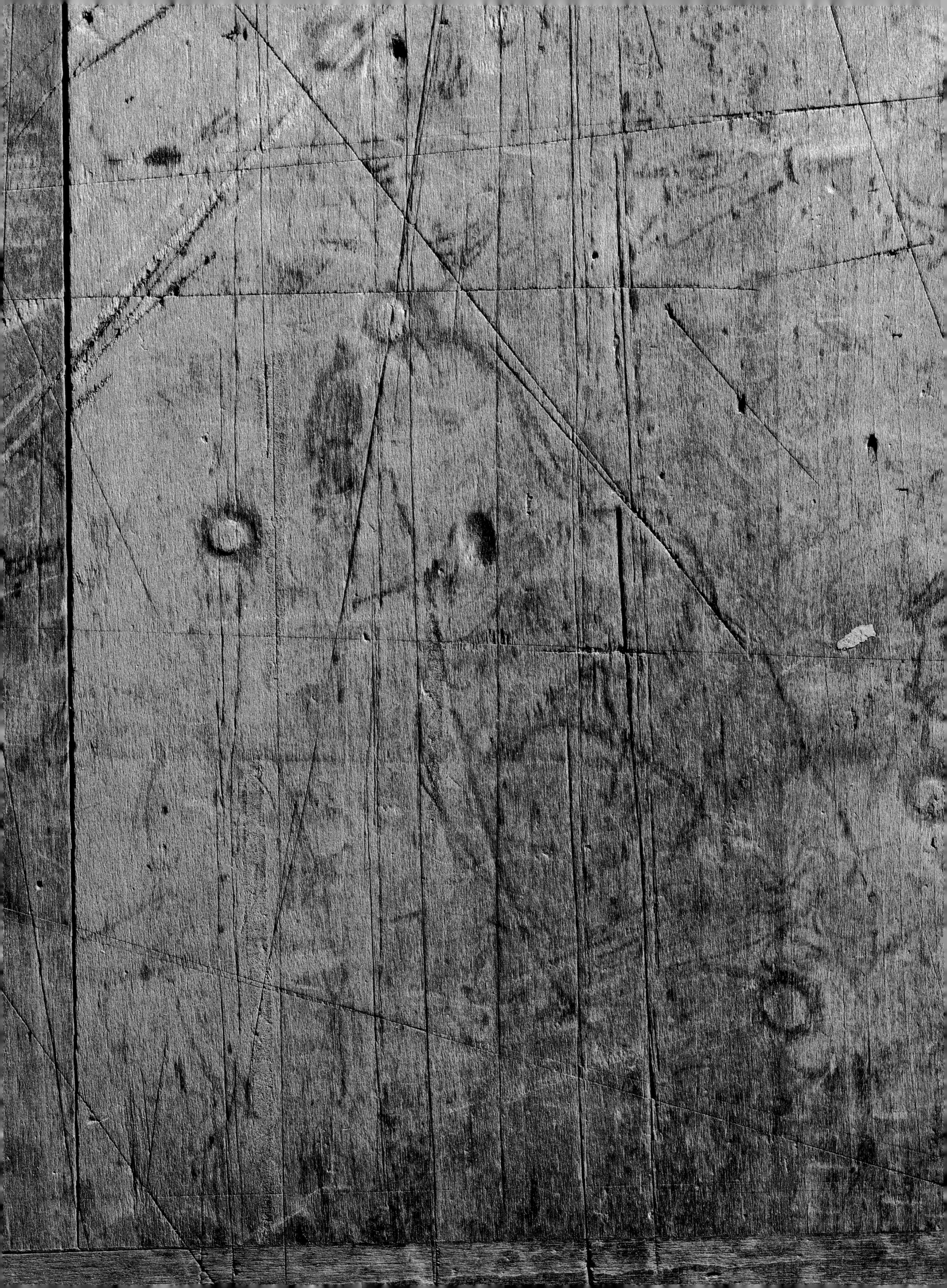

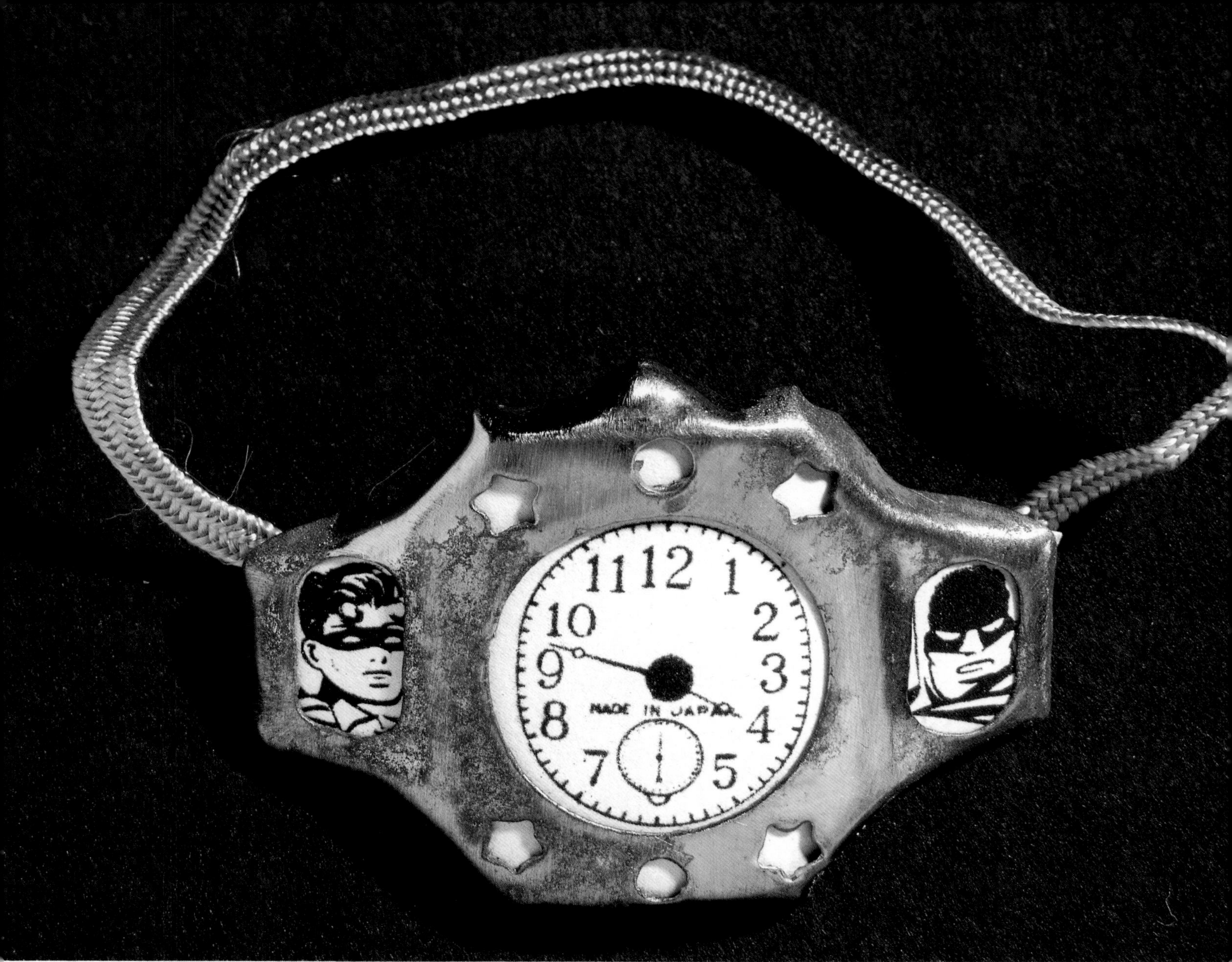

Above,
TOY WATCH
(metal, paper, cord)
1.5″ wide
Japan
POSSIBLY 1950S

Right,
"TIJUANA BIBLE"
(detail)
4″ x 2″
1946

Opposite,
DC COMIC BOOK DISPLAY RACK
(metal, wood)
Approx. 55″ tall
MID 1950S

So-called "Tijuana Bibles" provided subversive amusement during the 1920s, '30s and '40s through the illegal use of copyrighted comic strip characters and their, well, escapades. Above, two panels from a rare example featuring Batman and Robin depict our heroes on a quest to do something that is perhaps best left to the imagination.

In 1954, the U.S. government subjected the comic book industry to intense scrutiny regarding content. Headed by Senator Estes Kefauver, the congressional inquiry focused on comic books and their role in provoking "juvenile delinquency." The outcome caused the ruin of many comic book publishers (including the much-admired EC Comics) and the formation of the Comics Code, a set of rules self-imposed by publishers that put frantic parents (and troublesome feds) at ease. The DC comic book display rack at right is a rare item that shows just how intense the situation had become. The emphasis that all of DC's books are approved by the Code is just as important as who manufactured them.

★ THE LINE OF STARS ★
SUPERMAN DC NATIONAL COMICS
The BEST in COMICS READING
SUPERMAN DC NATIONAL COMICS
No.114
AUG.
TEN CENTS
Detective COMICS
BATMAN and ROBIN vs. The JOKER in "ACROSTIC of CRIME!"
JOKER
ALL DC COMICS approved
by COMICS CODE AUTHORITY

PANEL FROM "FAN-MAIL OF DANGER"
Originally published in BATMAN #92, June, 1955
Sheldon Mofdoff and Charles Paris, artists
Reprinted in a Signet paperback edition, 1966

The image on the right represents the only object in this book that would ever be likely to hang in a museum, be considered critically important, or be taken "seriously." We are told that this image is art, and that the one above is not. We put a higher value on it based on the intent of the artist to make us think differently about his subject matter than we used to, which makes it *ironic;* whereas the image above is sincere and therefore of relatively little worth. Indeed, if someone said that you could choose to own only one object from this book, you'd be smartest to opt for "*Batman*" by Andy Warhol. It would fetch by far the most money at auction (it's a fine example of what art critic Adam Gopnik calls "a formal statement in self-conscious opposition to the painterly looseness of Abstract Expressionism"), and the millions you'd get for selling it would buy all of the other things in this book that you *really* wanted.

OVERLEAF:

Top Left,
TV GUIDE
March 26-April 1 issue
1966

Bottom Left,
SHEET MUSIC (detail)
1966

PAGE 45
ADVERTISEMENT FOR
ZEPEL BATMAN JACKETS (detail)
14″ x 22″
1966

BATMAN
by Andy Warhol
(synthetic polymer paint and crayon on canvas)
30″ x 40″
1960

Private collection

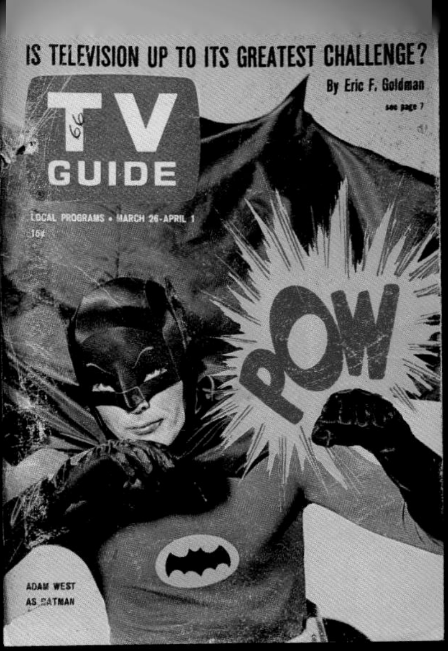

1966

While you are reading this, someone, somewhere, is watching the *Batman* TV show. *Batman* is transmitted in dozens of countries and in as many languages. The first episode was broadcast by ABC on January 12, 1966. The show ran for only two and a half seasons and 120 episodes, but it went immediately into syndication, has aired ever since, and always will be. It spawned a wave of product-licensing that, in its concentration, breadth and scope, had never been seen, not even by Walt Disney. Nowadays, if people say they have a Batman item for sale and it's from the '60s, what they're really saying is that it's from 1966. That's when everything, with very few exceptions, was copyrighted.

Why did Batman work so well as a property in 1966 and not before? Perhaps because the very weaknesses that rendered him useless during the Second World War made him perfect for the Vietnam era. So many people wanted to escape that war—by any means possible. Escape to psychedelia, escape to drugs, escape to Canada, escape to Batman. And what an escape they got. While bearing less resemblance than ever to his somber 1939 image, the Batman on TV in 1966 transported the viewer in the fashion of the best popular art: children were thrilled to take it at face value, while their parents delighted in its irony and sarcasm, and *everybody* loved the way it looked. It didn't last long, but it didn't have to. Its mark will be forever felt, and while dated, therein lies its perennial charm—thirty years later, and counting.

2

BATMAN THEME

FROM "BATMAN"

A Greenway Production in Association with 20th Century-Fox TV for ABC-TV

Words and Music by
NEAL HEFTI

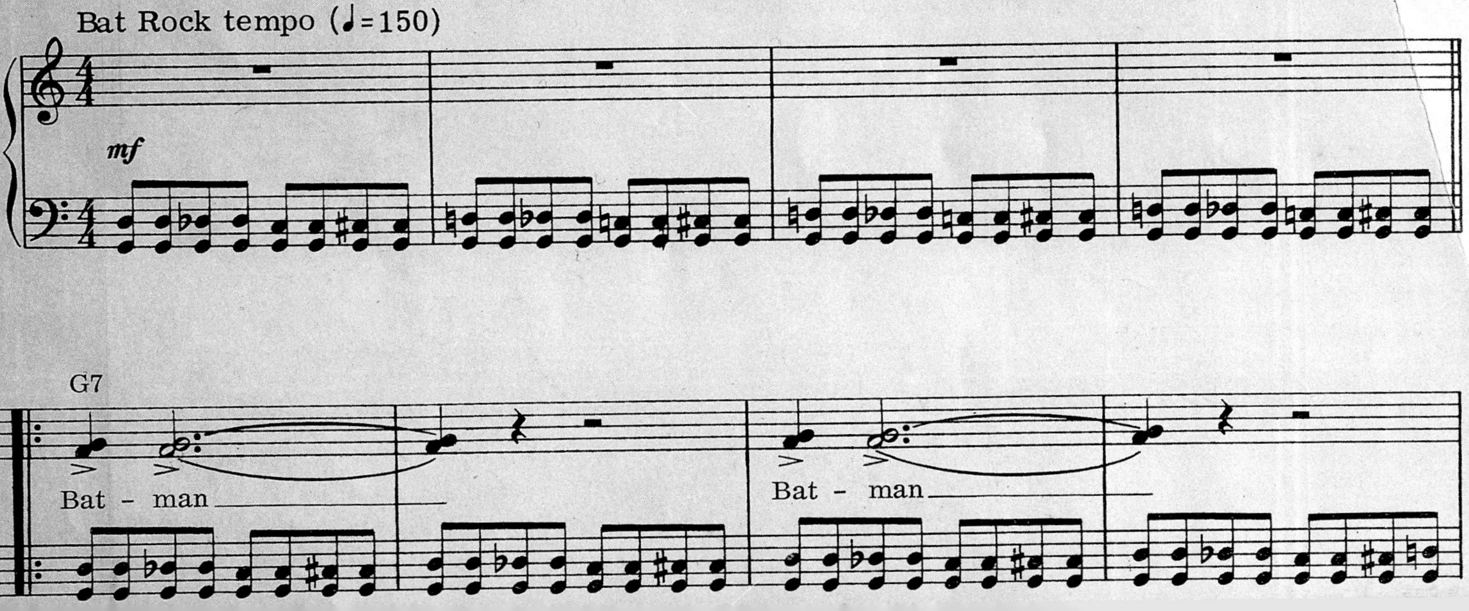

GOSH BATMAN, IT'S A CRIME THE WAY EVERYONE IS CASHING IN ON OUR POPULARITY!
RIGHT BOY WONDER! BUT IN A SOCIETY CHARACTERIZED BY THE COMPETITION OF INDIVIDUALS WHO SEARCH FREELY FOR THEIR INTERESTS IN THE INTERACTION OF ECONOMIC RELATIONSHIPS, WHAT CAN YOU EXPECT?!!!
HOLY FREE ENTERPRISE BATMAN ... YOU DON'T MEAN...???

BATMAN
With ROBIN THE BOY WON
Whitman
EASY TO DO—PIECES JUST PRESS OUT
1928
BATMAN
29c
press-out book
Authorized Edition
WOW!
BATMAN
in selected scenes from the famous Columbia Serials!
PLUS
ARGUS ACTION VIEWER
BOTH ONLY
NOW!
SEE 8mm HOME MOVI
NO NEED FOR PROJECTOR OR SCREEN TO ENJOY A COLUMBIA FILM OR ANY 8mm HOME MOVIE IN FULL ACTION!
ATMA
ROBIN THE BOY WOND
OFFICIAL
BATMAN
BAT CHUTE
HOLY BAT-CHUTES! THIS REALLY GETS US INTO ACTION FAST!
BAT SIZE 27" CHUTE with OFFICIAL BATMAN FIGURE
BALANCED and WEIGHTED for REALISTIC BATMAN ACTION
Whitman
BATMAN
ACTIVITY BOX
PUNCHOUTS TO ASSEMBLE AND SET UP ON PLAY AREA THAT CAN BE COLORED
AGES 5 to 9
© N.P.P., INC. 1966
© N.P.P., INC. 1966

With ROBIN THE Boy WOND
With ROBIN THE Boy WON
BATMAN
CRASH!
CRAP
BOOK
COPYRIGHT © NATIONAL PERIODICAL PUBLICATIONS, INC., 1966.
© N.P.P., INC. 1966
BATMAN
ROBIN
START A COLLECTION
SUCTION CUP BACK WILL STICK TO GLAS
PENGUIN
JOKER
los angeles, calif. 9003
ROBIN

BATMAN
© NAT. PER. PUB. INC., 1966
hot-line
BATPHONE
BATPHONE
© NAT. PER. PUB., INC. - 1966
HOT-LINE

BATMAN AND ROBIN Cartoon Kit
BATMAN AND ROBIN Cartoon Kit
BATMAN
AND ROBIN
Cartoon Kit

The BATMAN
BRUCE WAYNE

Park's No. 284
OFFICIAL
BATMAN SCOPE
OPENS FROM 11 TO 22 INCHES
BATMAN SCOPE
OFFICIAL
BATMAN SCOPE
USE FOR FIGHTING THE FORCES OF EVIL
© NAT. PER. PUB. INC. 1966
PARK PLASTICS CO. LINDEN, N.J.

PAGES 46-47:

Clockwise, from upper left,

NEEDLEPOINT PICTURE
PRESS-OUT BOOK
MOVIE VIEWER
SCRAPBOOK (England)
SUCTION CUPS
NEEDLEPOINT PICTURE
TRASH CAN
ACTIVITY BOX
PARACHUTE FIGURE

Background,
WALLPAPER

ALL 1966

PAGES 48-49:

Clockwise, from upper left,

BATPHONE
COLORFORMS
TIN BUTTON
WRIST RADIOS
PENCIL CASE
ADVERTISEMENT
CAKE DECORATIONS
COLORING BOOK
COMICS PACKAGE CARD
PERISCOPES
LAMP

ALL 1966

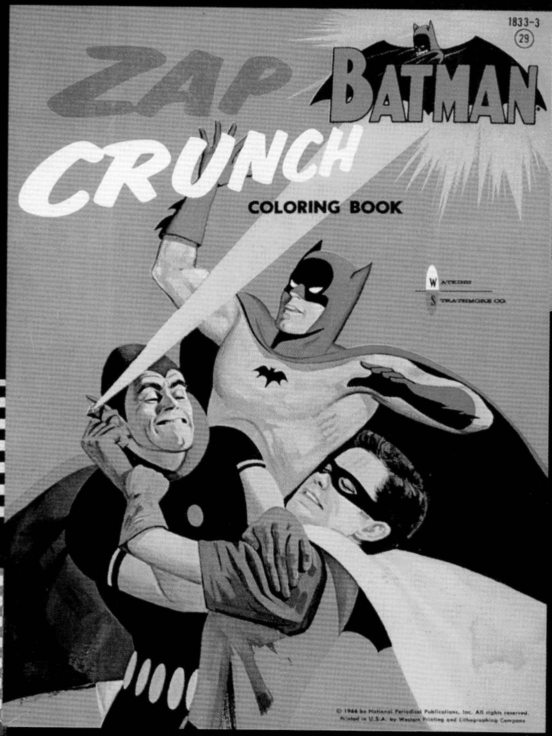

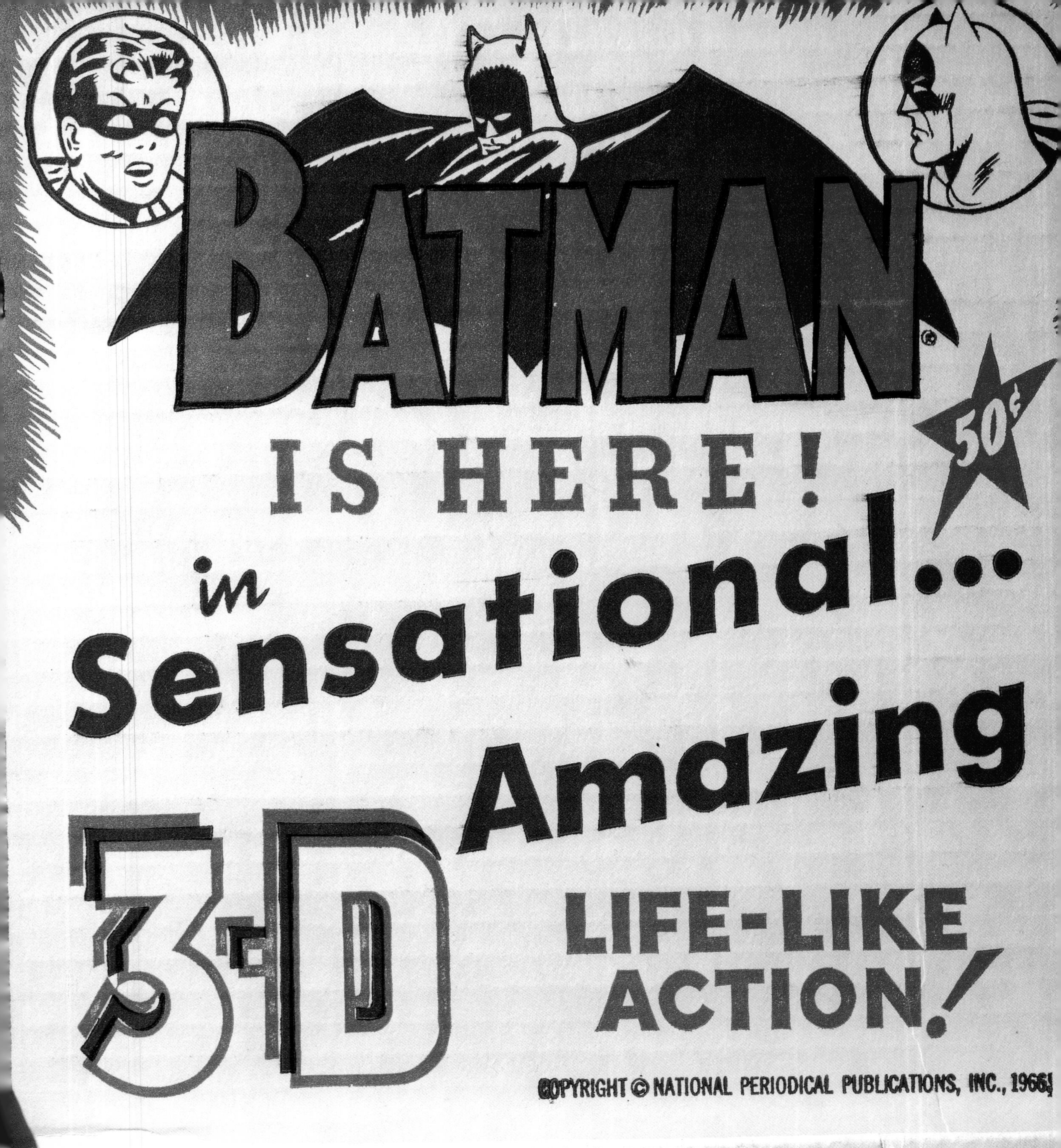
BATMAN®
IS HERE!
50¢
in Sensational...
Amazing
3-D
LIFE-LIKE ACTION!
COPYRIGHT © NATIONAL PERIODICAL PUBLICATIONS, INC., 1966

BATMAN®

Left,
DISPLAY FOR 3-D COMIC BOOKS
9.25″ x 7.25″ x 11″
1966

Left,
INFLATABLE BATMAN ON A STRING
(plastic, cord) Approx. 12″ tall
1966

Below,
SHIPPING BOXES FOR FUN THINGS
1966

POW!
ZOK!
F

D

Opposite,
STICKER BOOK
10.25″ x 12″
England
1966

Left,
LAMP
(vinyl, cloth)
11″ tall
1966

Opposite,
VENDING MACHINE
DISPLAY CARD
5″ x 6.5″
1966

Below,
BATBOAT CARNIVAL RIDE
69″ long
1966

CTION
TMAN
RINGS
BATMAN
ROBIN
BATWOMAN
FFICIAL
OLLECT
ALL
12
RINGS
BATMAN ROBIN
©NATIONAL PERIODICAL PUBLICATIONS INC., 1966
JOKER • BATWOMAN
10c
RIDDLER • PENQUIN
MEMBER
BATMAN RING CLUB
COLLECT ALL
12
BAM!
POW!
Lawson Novelty Co., In
ox 8, Oceanside, N.

THE CAPED CRUSADER
Put on this Mask and become
BATMAN
The Caped Crusader
Just cut on the dotted line and attach string

Above,
SHOE BOX
4.25″ x 3.5″ x 10.5″
1966

Left,
THE FIRST BATMAN HALLOWEEN COSTUME
1965

Right,
BATMOBILE RIDER
(molded plastic)
36.5″ long
1966

Below Left and Right,
TIN BUTTONS
.875″ in diameter
1966

Official BATMAN and ROBIN
BATMOBILE
RIDER
MARX TOYS
NO BATTERIES NEEDED!
JUST BACK UP TO WIND THE POWERFUL SPRING MOTOR AND SET THE BRAKE. RELEASE . . . AND . . . . .
HOLY BLAST OFF
AWAY YOU GO ! ! !
ENDORSED BY BATMAN & RO

BatMan
Water Gun
CAUTION:
NOT RECOMMENDED
FOR CHILDREN UNDER
3 YEARS OF AGE
MADE IN HONG KONG
NO.732

NO.1
BATMAN!
WORLD ADVENTURE LIBRARY
...AND
THE RINGER!
1/-
ANOTHER BREATHTAKING ADVENTURE OF OUR DYNAMIC DUO
NO.2
BATMAN!
WORLD ADVENTURE LIBRARY
MEETS THE JOKER IN
THE LAST LAUGH
1/-
ANOTHER BREATHTAKING ADVENTURE OF OUR DYNAMIC DUO
NO.3
BATMAN!
WORLD ADVENTURE LIBRARY
MEETS
Dr. NO-FACE
1/-
ANOTHER BREATHTAKING ADVENTURE OF OUR DYNAMIC DUO
NO.4
BATMAN!
WORLD ADVENTURE LIBRARY
PENGUIN
GETS
THE BIRD!
1/-
ANOTHER BREATHTAKING ADVENTURE OF OUR DYNAMIC DUO
BATMAN
THE JOKER
GOES NAP!
NO.6
BATMAN!
WORLD ADVENTURE LIBRARY
A ROCKER
FOR
THE RIDDLER
SOCK!
1/-
NO.7
BATMAN!
WORLD ADVENTURE LIBRARY
THE
BOOKWORM'S
BEST SELLER
1/-
ANOTHER BREATHTAKING ADVENTURE OF OUR DYNAMIC DUO
NO.8
BATMAN!
WORLD ADVENTURE LIBRARY
PILE-UP
FOR THE
CATWOMAN
1/-
NO.9
BATMAN!
WORLD ADVENTURE LIBRARY
NO QUACK FOR
THE PENGUIN
1/-
BATMAN
THE ARCHER
AIMS HIGH

Opposite Above,
WATER PISTOL
(molded plastic)
5″ wide
1966

Left,
TIN BUTTON
.875″ in diameter
1966

Opposite Below,
PULP NOVELS
5″ x 7″
England
1966

Below,
ROLYKINS
(molded plastic, ball bearings)
1″ tall
England
1966

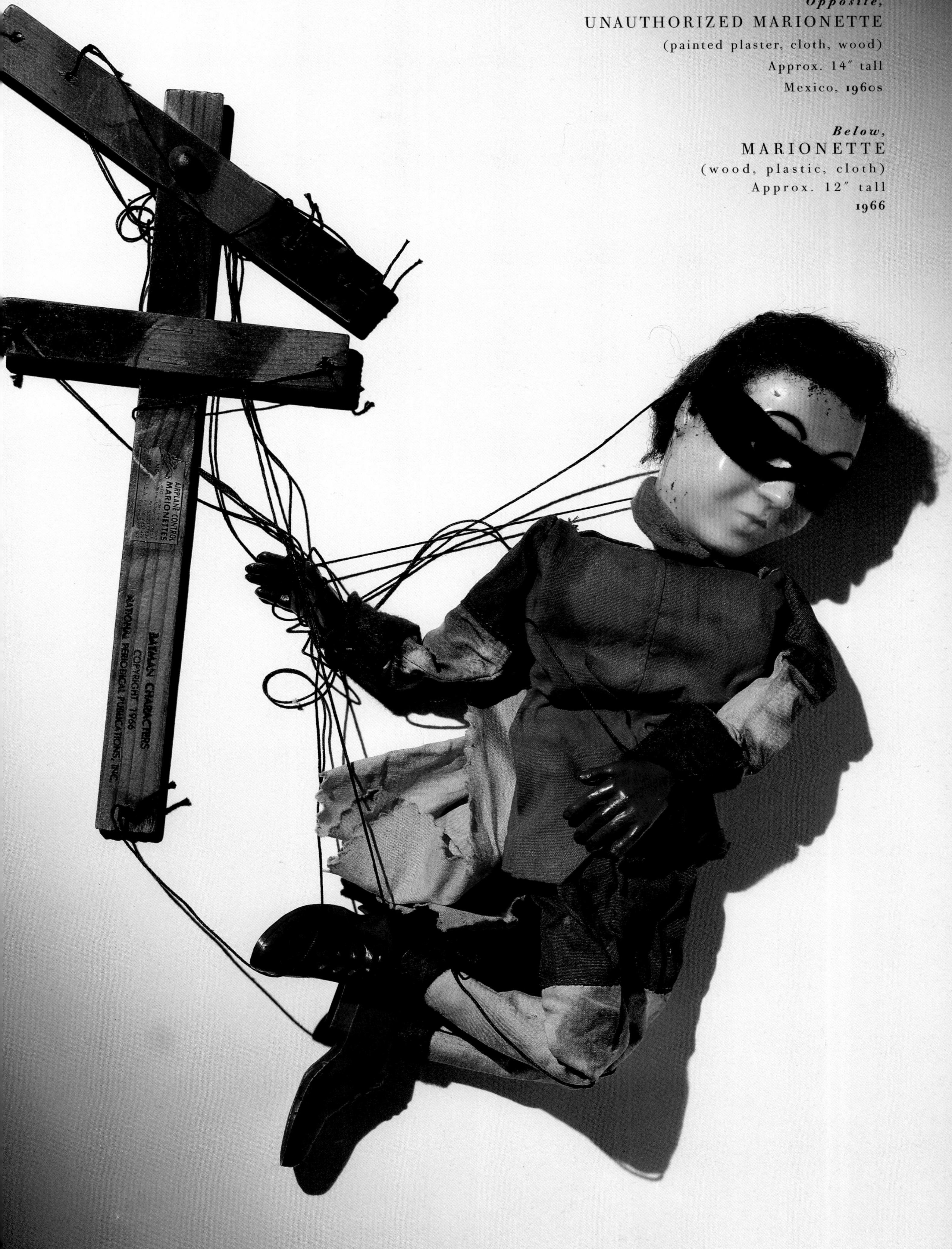

Opposite,
UNAUTHORIZED MARIONETTE
(painted plaster, cloth, wood)
Approx. 14″ tall
Mexico, 1960s

Below,
MARIONETTE
(wood, plastic, cloth)
Approx. 12″ tall
1966

Above,
TIN BUTTON
.875″ in diameter
1966

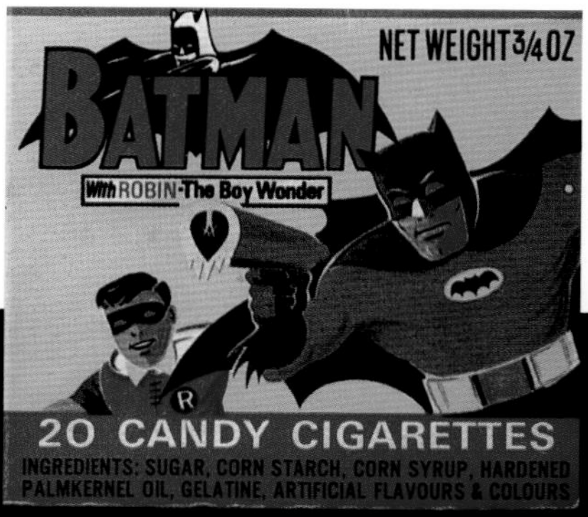

Above,
CANDY CIGARETTES
2.75″ x 2.5″
England, 1966

Above,
ASHTRAY
(painted china)
5.375″ x 5.375″
1966

PAGES 63-65
SECRET SUPER-MICRO RADIO CASE AND INTERIOR
(metal, transistors, satin)
2.125″ x 1.75″
1966

BATMAN ©
SECRET SUPER-MICRO RADIO

BATMAN ©
Super-Micro
BAT RADIO
COPYRIGHT © NATIONAL PERIODICAL PUBLICATIONS, INC., 1966

BATMAN
SUPER
MICRO
RADIO ©

Widely regarded as the artist who ushered in the "Silver Age" of comics, Carmine Infantino became the definitive Batman penciller of the 1960s, beginning in 1964 when he gave the character his "new look" in *Detective Comics* #327 ("The Mystery of the Menacing Mask"). This consisted of a more representational style of drawing, along with a simple but iconic costume modification suggested by DC editor Julius Schwartz: a yellow oval added to the bat symbol on Batman's chest. This gesture finally gave Batman something that Superman had had from the start—a logo. From that moment on, a yellow ellipse with a black bat in it (and any variation thereof) would universally stand for only one thing.

The image at left is classic Infantino (with inks by Murphy Anderson), and while thoroughly unmysterious, it has a strength and solidity that has enabled it to endure many incarnations. It's been a puzzle, a T-shirt, a pin-up, a hardcover book jacket, a paperback book cover (below) and more. Everything, curiously enough, except a comic book cover.

Infantino's work is featured on the packaging for the Captain Action series of dolls (p. 110) and on the box lid for the Aurora Batman model kit (p. 131), two paragons of Batman memorabilia.

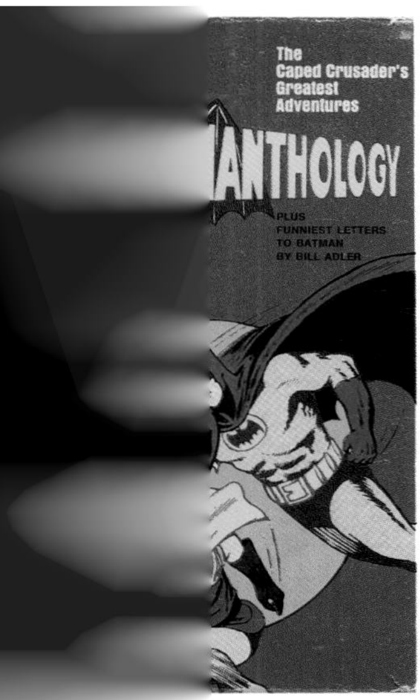

Opposite,
ORIGINAL DRAWING
Carmine Infantino and Murphy Anderson, artists
(pen and ink on illustration board)
11″ x 14″
1966

Above,
BOXED SET OF PAPERBACK BOOKS
4.5″ x 7.25″ x 2.75″
1966

OVERLEAF
PENCIL STUDIES
Carmine Infantino, artist
11.5″ x 17.375″
1966

PALM RESTAURANT MURAL
Carmine Infantino, artist
Approx. 48″ x 60″
New York City
1966

BATSCOPE
DARTLAUNCHER
BATMAN, I HAVE THE EVIL DOER IN THE NEVER-MISS, CROSSHAIR SIGHTS OF MY POWERFUL
(GASP!)
50
FEET
3
BAM
POW
DARTS
FOR EASY REMOVAL BEND DOWN HERE TO BREAK SEAL THEN LIFT UP PLASTIC COVER.
FIENDS LURK ON THE BACK OF THE
RTISED ON TV
MAN
SCOPE

Empire
TARBORO, N.C.
NO. 22
OFFICIAL
BATMAN
BICYCLE
ORNAMENT
RIDE ALONG WITH...
BATMAN
© National Periodical Publications Inc., 1966

Left,
BICYCLE
(molded pl
8″ tall
1966

Opposite,
BAT-CHU
(tin, cloth,
1966

Below,
MINIATU
(tin)
4″ x 2.25″
1966

BATMAN
ROBIN
MINIATURE
LICENSE PLATES
MARX
© NATIONAL PERIODICAL PUBLICATIONS, INC. MCMLXVI
PENGUIN

BAT-CHUTE
BATMAN
BATMAN
BAT-CHUTE
© NATIONAL PERIODICAL PUBLICATIONS, INC. 1966
BATMAN BAT-CHUTE
COPYRIGHT © NATIONAL PERIODICAL PUBLICATIONS, INC. 1966
DRAG-CHUTE FOR BICYCLES
FITS ALL BICYCLES
ATTACH IN SECONDS
VOOOMP

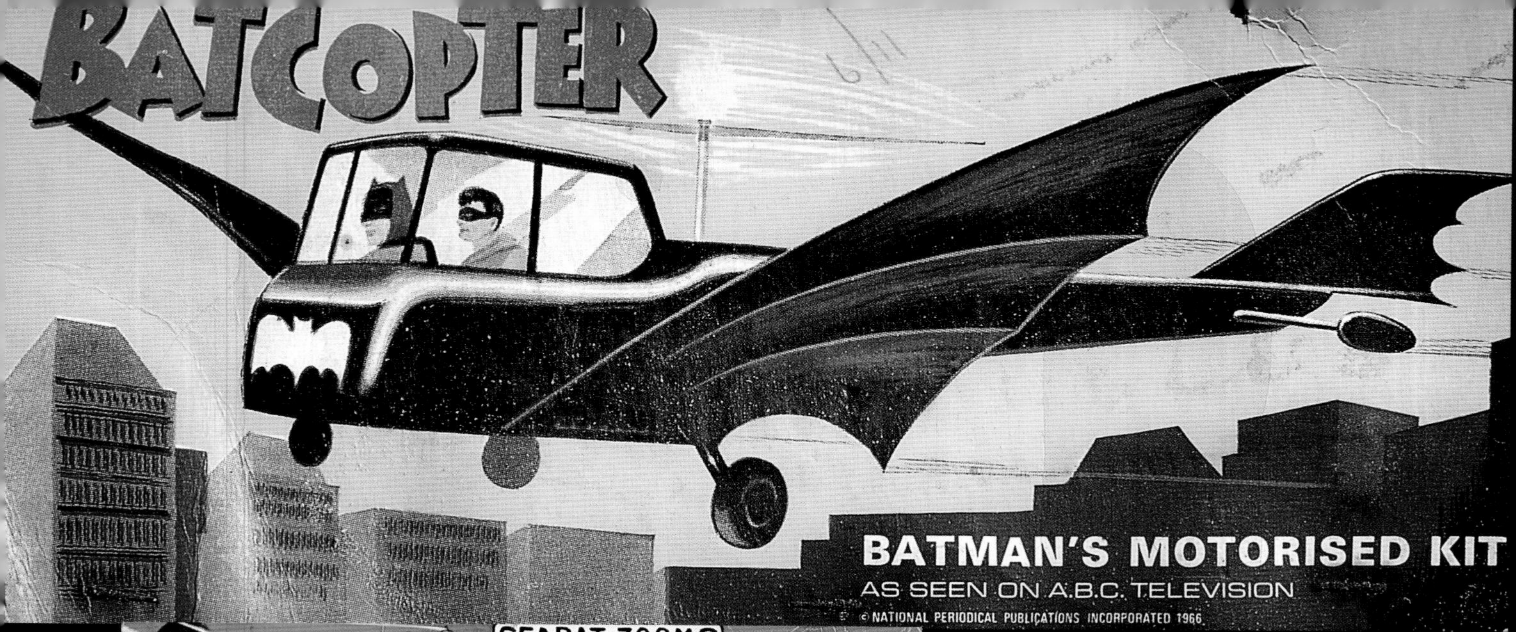

BATCOPTER
BATMAN'S MOTORISED KIT
AS SEEN ON A.B.C. TELEVISION
© NATIONAL PERIODICAL PUBLICATIONS INCORPORATED 1966

SEABAT ZOOMS ALONG ROBIN

LINCOLN INTERNATIONAL
YES BATMAN ITS THE POWERFUL BAT MOTOR
CAT. NO. 3657

Above,
BATCOPTER (packaging)
8.6″ x 4″, England 1966

Left,
SEABAT (packaging)
10″ x 3.8″ x 2.6″, England, 1966

Below,
BATMOBILE (packaging)
4.125″ x 3.6″ x 2.25″, England, 1966

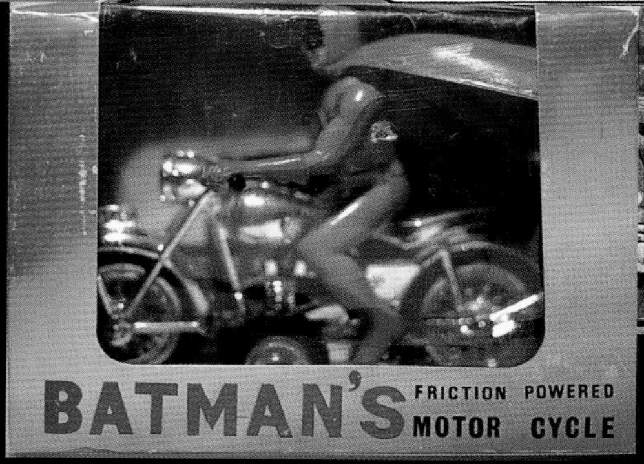

BATMAN'S FRICTION POWERED MOTOR CYCLE

FRICTION BATMOBILE
ONE OF THE MANY MARX TOYS, DO YOU HAVE ALL OF THEM ?

Above,
MOTORCYCLE
5.5″ x 4″
England
1966

Above Right,
BATMOBILE (tin)
12″ long
1966

Right,
BATBOAT CARD
2.25″ x 1″
1966

BATMOBILE
5″ x 2.5″ x 2.5″
England
1966

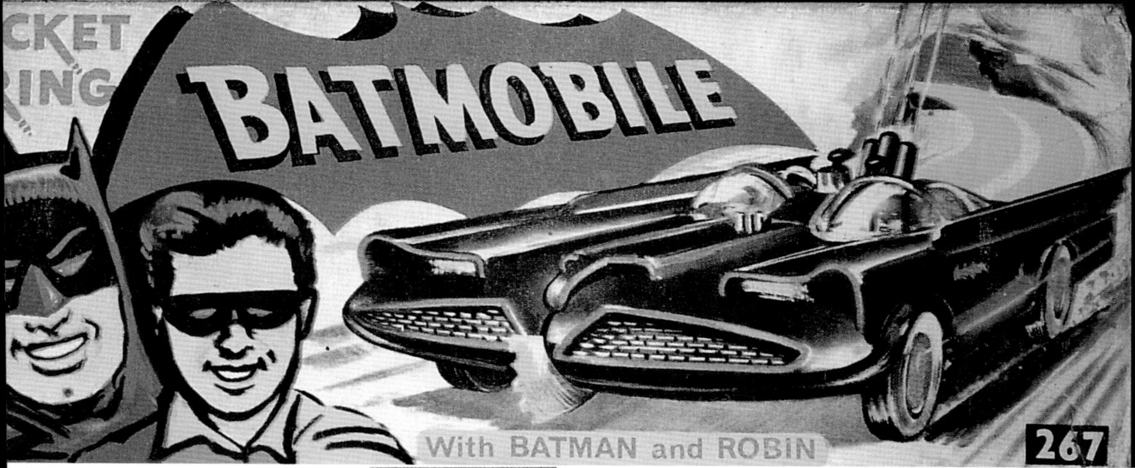
BATMOBILE
With BATMAN and ROBIN
267

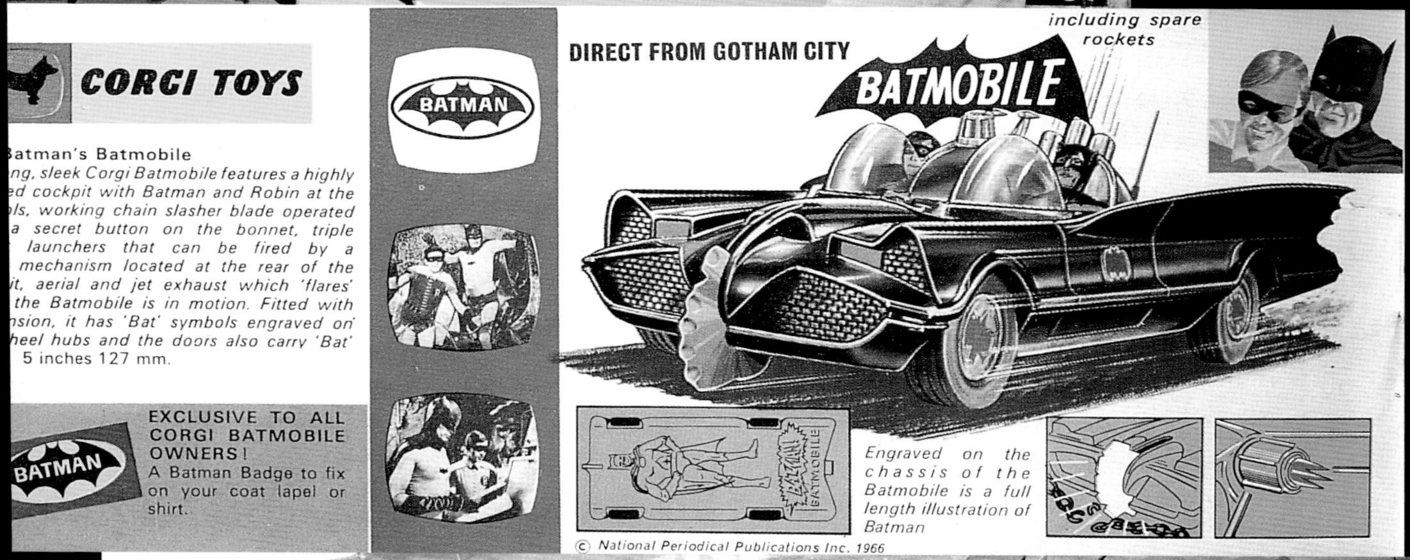
CORGI TOYS
Batman's Batmobile
ng, sleek Corgi Batmobile features a highly
ed cockpit with Batman and Robin at the
ols, working chain slasher blade operated
a secret button on the bonnet, triple
launchers that can be fired by a
mechanism located at the rear of the
it, aerial and jet exhaust which 'flares'
the Batmobile is in motion. Fitted with
nsion, it has 'Bat' symbols engraved on
heel hubs and the doors also carry 'Bat'
5 inches 127 mm.
EXCLUSIVE TO ALL CORGI BATMOBILE OWNERS!
A Batman Badge to fix on your coat lapel or shirt.
BATMAN
BATMAN
DIRECT FROM GOTHAM CITY
including spare rockets
BATMOBILE
Engraved on the chassis of the Batmobile is a full length illustration of Batman
© National Periodical Publications Inc. 1966

ROCKET FIRING
BATMOBILE
BATMAN
OPERATING
TRIPLE ROCKET TUBES
CHAIN SLASHER BLADE
TURBINE JET EXHAUST
SPRING
ROBIN THE BOY WONDE
BATMOBILE OWNERS BADG AND ROCKET
CORGI TOYS
ROCKET FIRING BATMOBILE

United States Patent Office

Des. 205,998
Patented Oct. 18, 1966

205,998

AUTOMOTIVE VEHICLE OR SIMILAR ARTICLE

George Barris, 18035 Medley Drive, Encino, Calif.

Filed Mar. 11, 1966, Ser. No. 1,417
Term of patent 14 years
(Cl. D14—3)

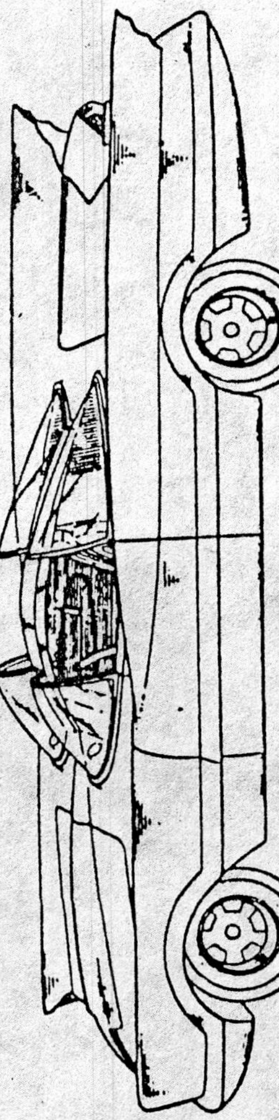
FIG. 1.

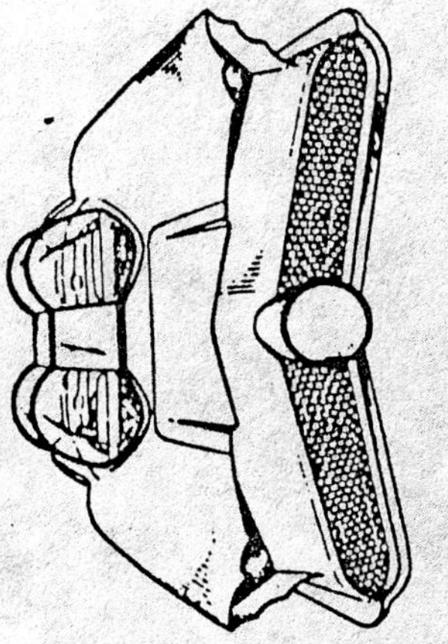
FIG. 3.

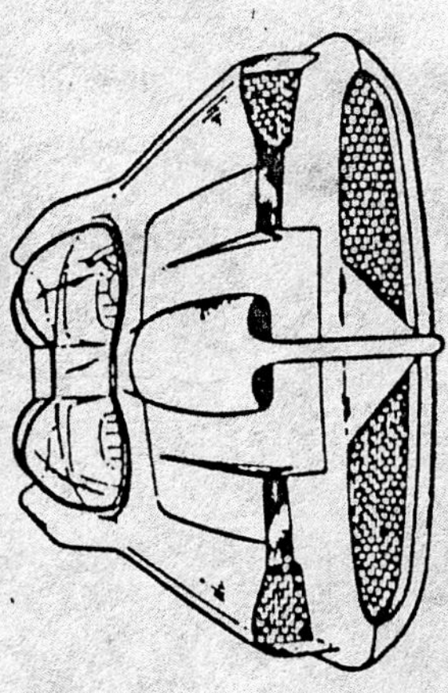
FIG. 2.

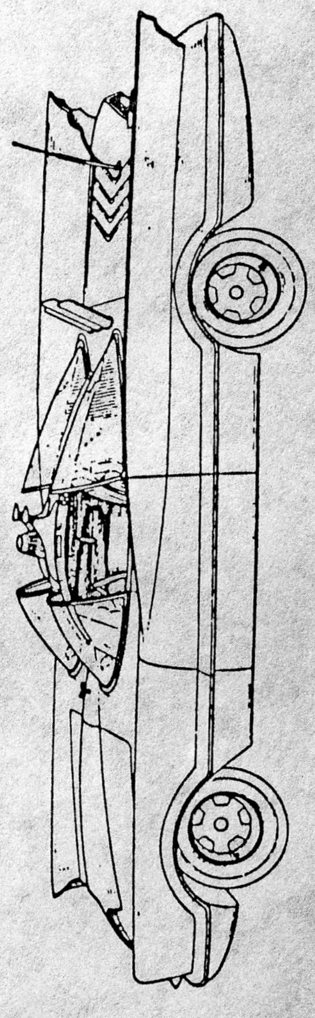
FIG. 4.

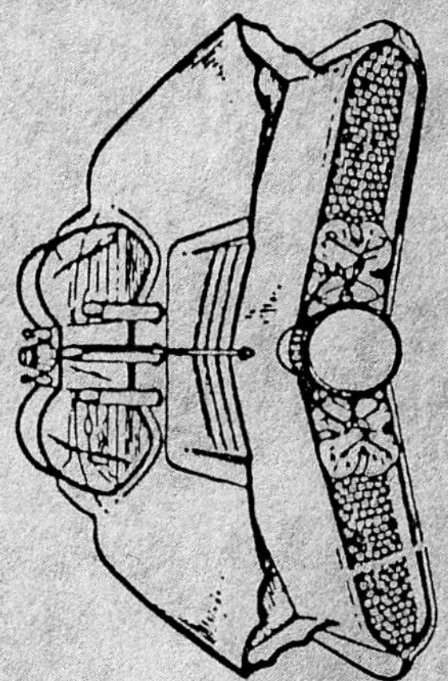
FIG. 6.

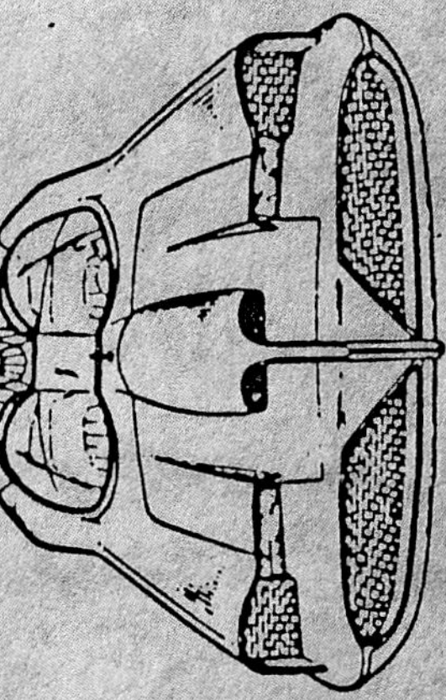
FIG. 5.

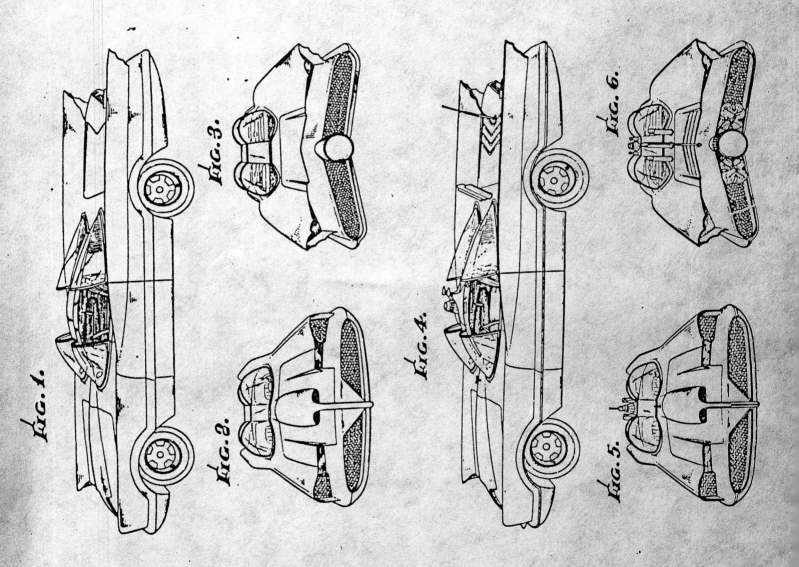

FIGURE 1 is a side perspective view of an automotive vehicle or similar article showing my new design;

FIGURE 2 is a front perspective view of an automotive vehicle or similar article showing my new design;

FIGURE 3 is a rear perspective view of an automotive vehicle or similar article showing my new design;

FIGURE 4 is a side perspective view showing a second embodiment of my new design;

FIGURE 5 is a front perspective view of the automotive vehicle or similar article shown in FIGURE 4; and

FIGURE 6 is a rear perspective view of the automotive vehicle or similar article shown in FIGURE 4.

I claim:

The ornamental design for an automotive vehicle or similar article, as shown and described.

References Cited by the Examiner

UNITED STATES PATENTS

D. 185,843 8/1959 James .... D14—3

WALLACE R. BURKE, *Primary Examiner.*

CONRAD A. BOUSQUET, *Assistant Examiner.*

Left,
PATENT APPLICATION
FOR AN AUTOMOTIVE VEHICLE OR SIMILAR ARTICLE
George Barris, applicant
March 11, 1966

PAGES 77-79
BATMOBILE (detail)
From the BATMAN TV series
1966

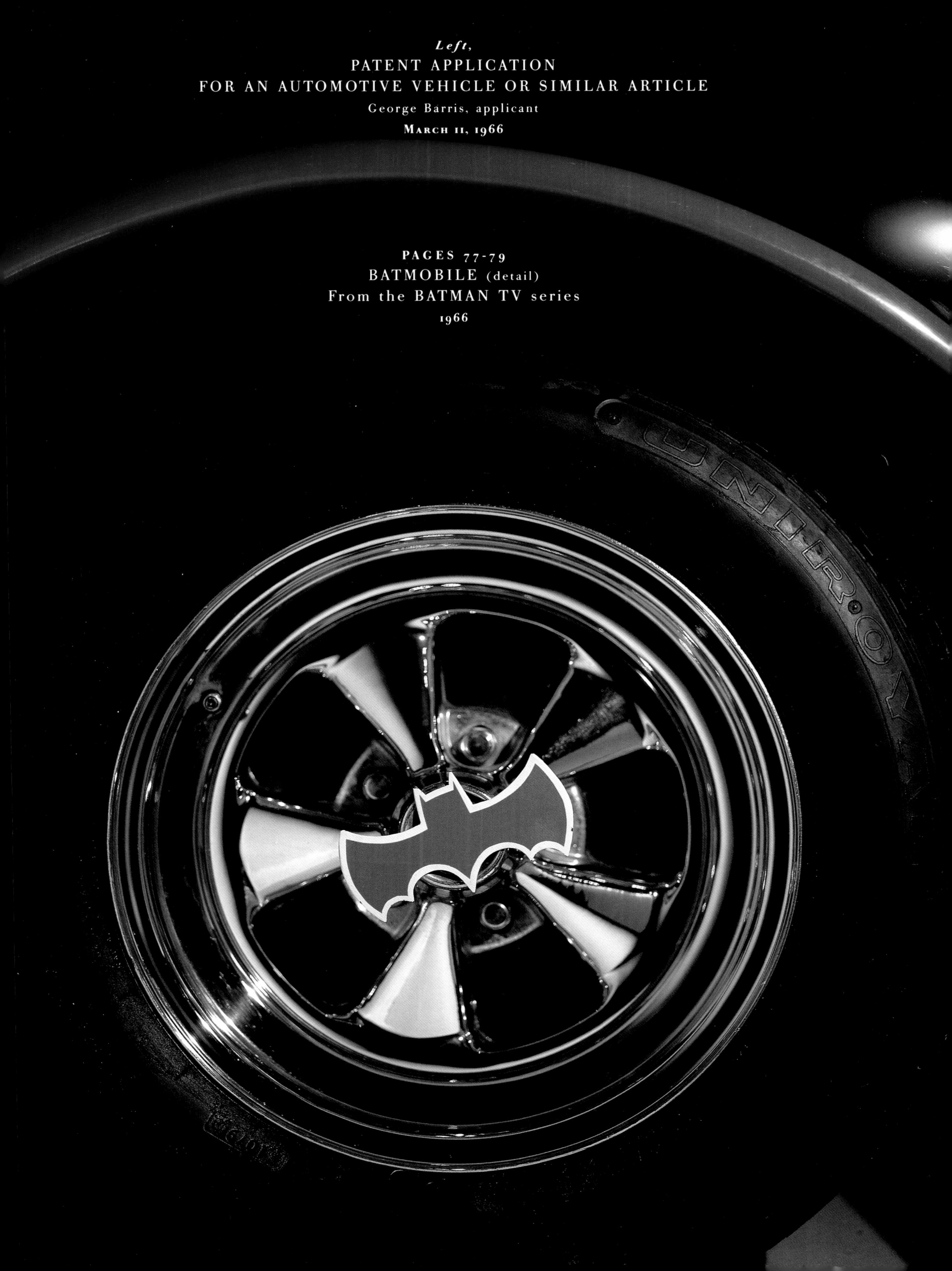

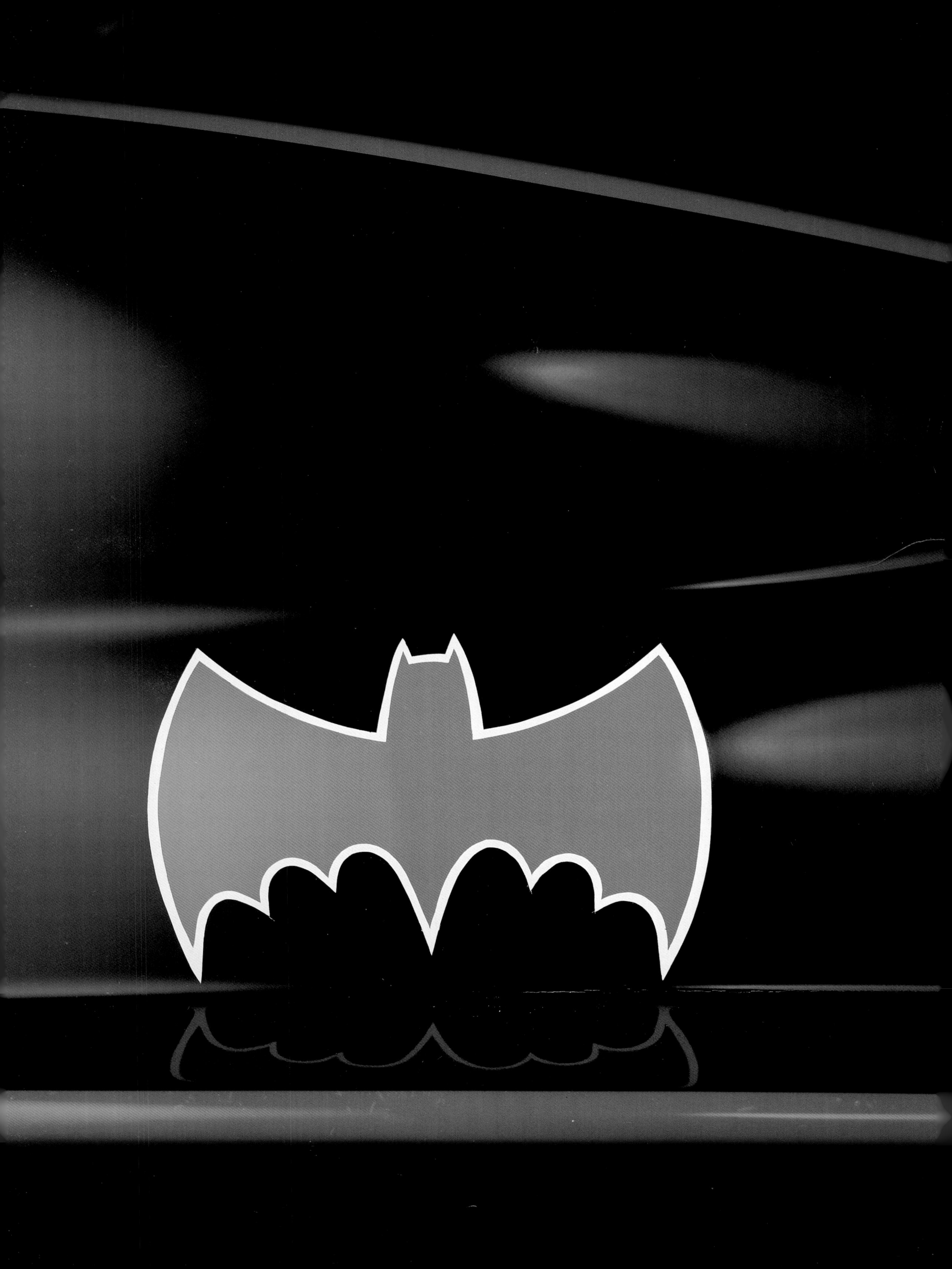

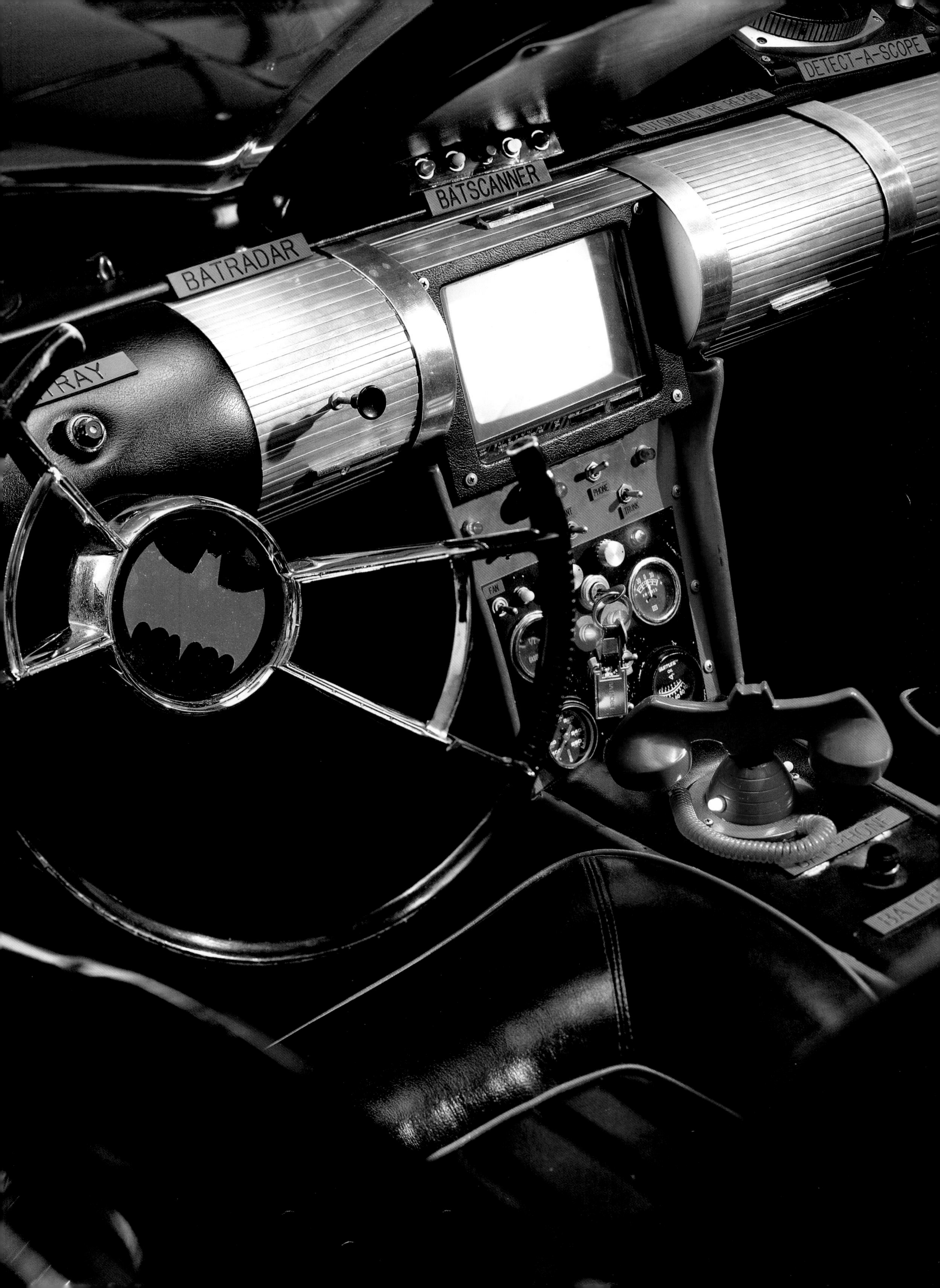
DETECT-A-SCOPE
AUTOMATIC TIRE REPAIR
BATSCANNER
BATRADAR
PHONE
TRUNK
FAN

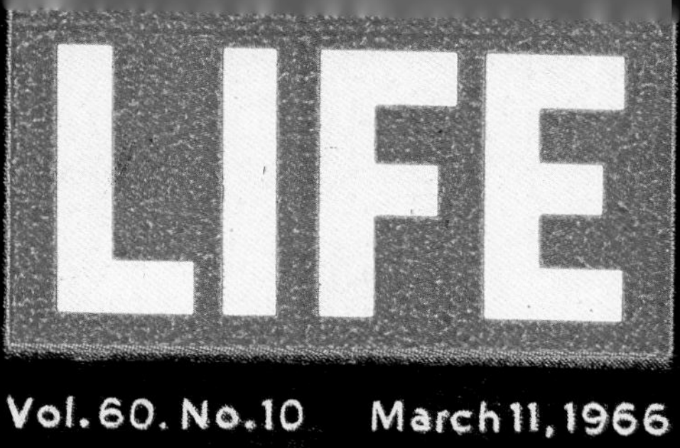

MAD NEW WORLD
of Batman, Superman
and the Marquis de Sade
JUBILEE IN GHANA
Freedom explodes all over
as the tyrant Nkrumah
is overthrown

THE ROMANS
HIGH ROAD
TO GRANDEUR
A mighty empire's
13-century life span
A CITY TESTED
BY TOPLESSNESS
How San Francisco faced up
to restaurant nudity

Shana Alexander
writes about
ADOPTION
MARCH 11 · 1966 · 35¢

Above and Right,
LIFE MAGAZINE
March 11 issue
1966

Below,
FILM MAGAZINES
U.S.A., England
1966

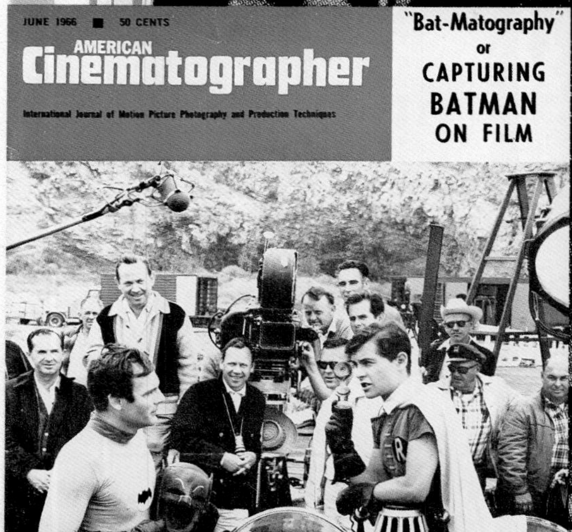

JUNE 1966 50 CENTS
AMERICAN
Cinematographer
International Journal of Motion Picture Photography and Production Techniques
"Bat-Matography"
or
CAPTURING
and filming
october 1966 3s 75c
BATMAN
THE CHASE
BIRDS DO IT
GEORGY GIRL
SEVEN WOMEN
TORN CURTAIN
THE WAR IS OVER
FANTASTIC VOYAGE
RUSSIANS ARE COMING
ON FILM
• EYE-WITNESS REPORT ON RUSSIAN FILM TECHNOLOGY • LIGHTING UNDER DIFFICULT CONDITIONS
• THE CAMERA OF THE FUTURE • A BUILD-IT-YOURSELF 16mm ZOOM-ANAMORPHIC LENS COMBINATION

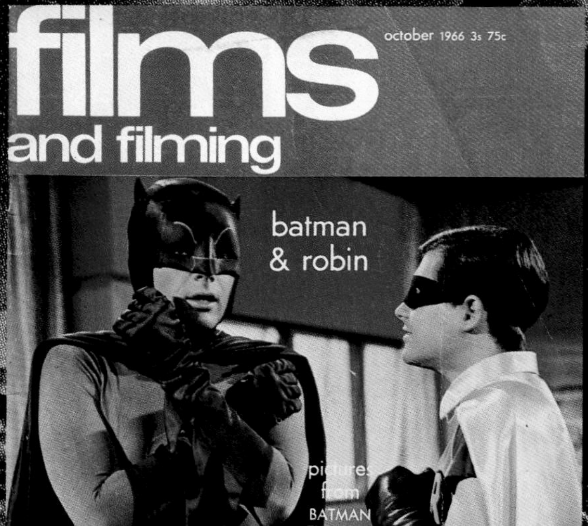

LOCK SET

Left,
MOVIE POSTER (detail)
(offset lithography on paper) 45.6″ x 61.125″
FRANCE, 1966

Below,
ADAM WEST, actor
New York City
JANUARY 7, 1996

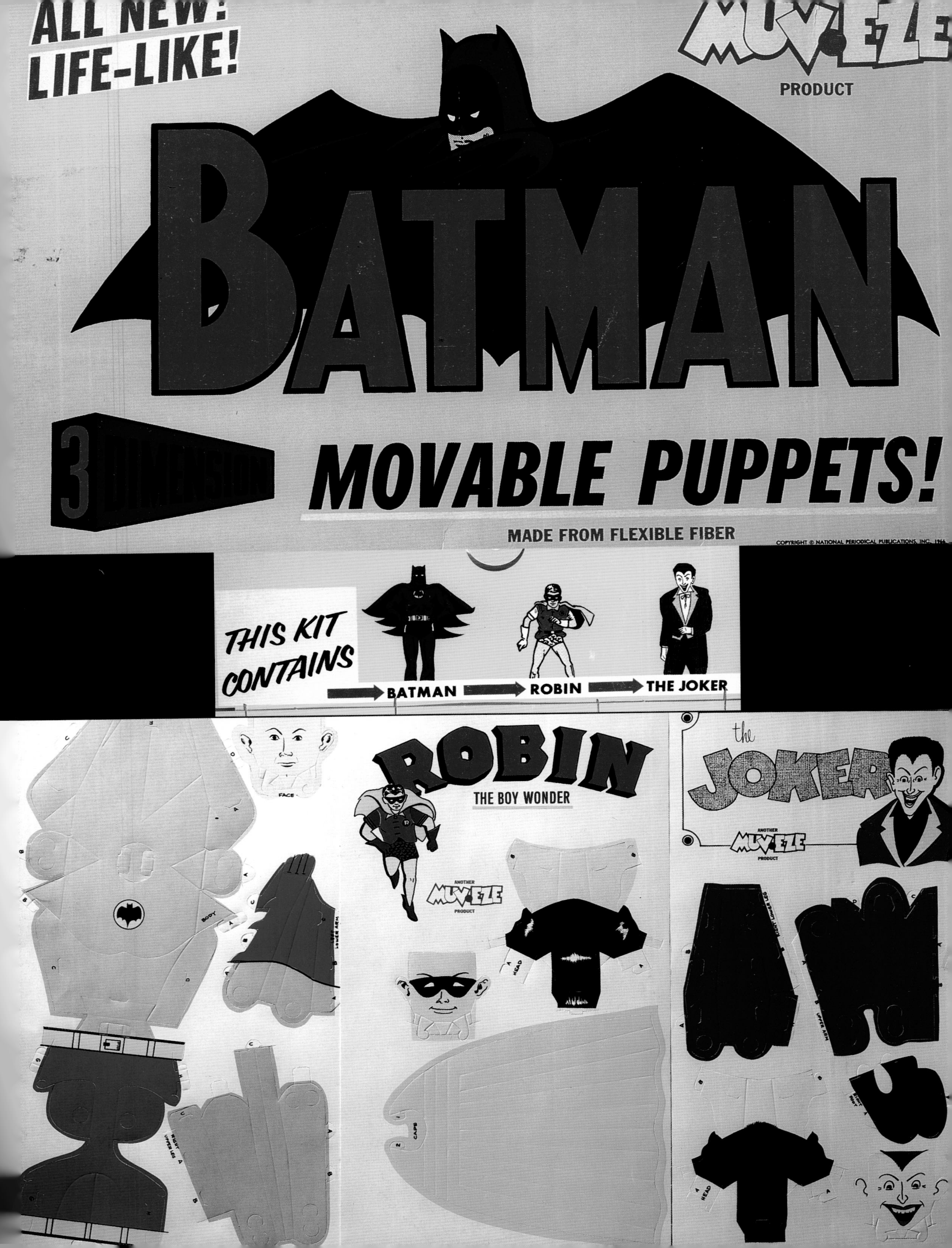

ALL NEW!
LIFE-LIKE!
MUV-EZE
PRODUCT
BATMAN
3 DIMENSION
MOVABLE PUPPETS!
MADE FROM FLEXIBLE FIBER
COPYRIGHT © NATIONAL PERIODICAL PUBLICATIONS, INC. 1966
THIS KIT CONTAINS
BATMAN
ROBIN
THE JOKER
FACE
BODY
ROBIN
THE BOY WONDER
ANOTHER
MUV-EZE
PRODUCT
HEAD
CAPE
the
JOKER
ANOTHER
MUV-EZE
PRODUCT
UPPER ARM
HEAD

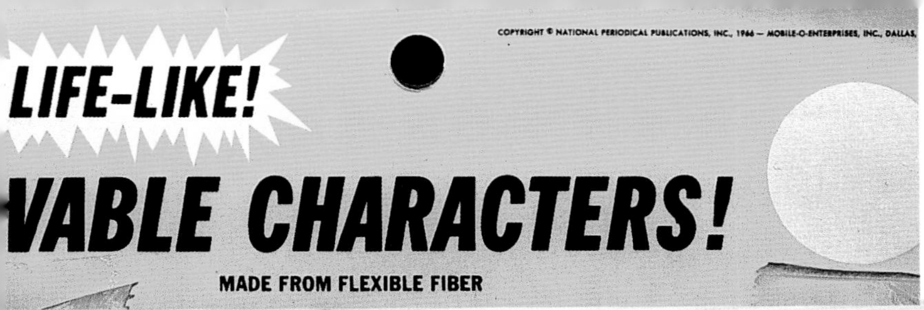

PAPER CUT-OUT FIGURES
(offset lithography on coated paper)
20.825″ x 12″
1966

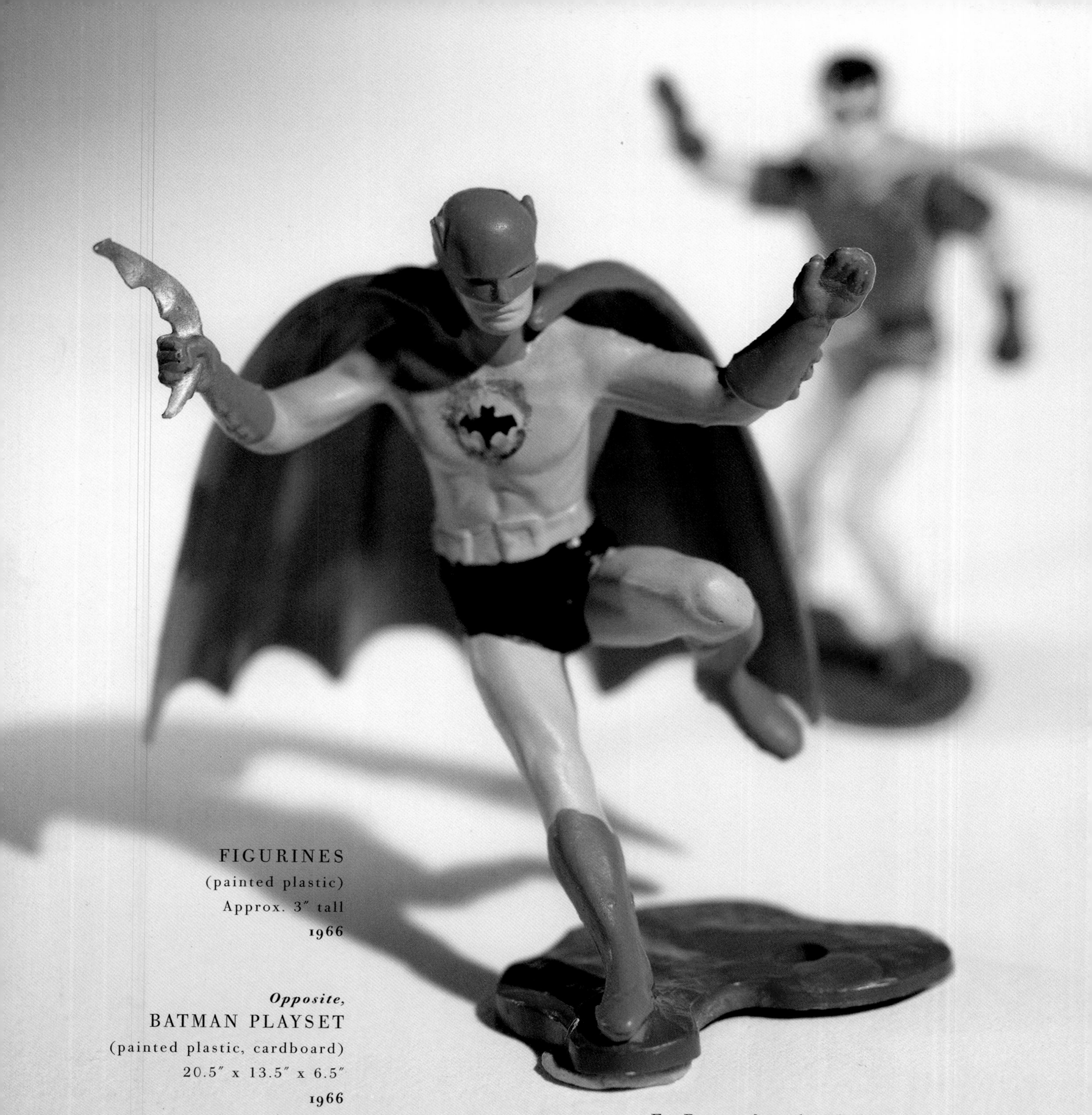

FIGURINES
(painted plastic)
Approx. 3″ tall
1966

Opposite,
BATMAN PLAYSET
(painted plastic, cardboard)
20.5″ x 13.5″ x 6.5″
1966

IDEAL
NO. 3301-9

For Batman fans, the Ideal toy company was aptly named. They were the dominant licensee in 1966, meeting the many caped-crusading needs of the nation's youth with great style and ingenuity, whether tiny figurines to fit in your pocket (above and right), hand puppets, larger dolls to give your best friend's GI Joes a run for their money (see Captain Action, p. 111), or items that actually enabled you to *become* Batman. Their big plastic helmet and cape was a must-have, and the truly lucky received the Utility Belt, a staple of crime-fighting equipment that included the now charmingly low-

Official
BATMAN
© 1966 NATIONAL PERIODICALS PUBLICATIONS
PLAY SET
IDEAL
ROBOT
BAT CAR
BAT CAR
BAT PLANE
BAT PLANE
RAY WEAPON
Superman
Wonder Woman
Robin
FEATURING AUTHENTIC HAND PAINTED FIGURES OF:
BATMAN · ROBIN · WONDER WOMAN · SUPERMAN
Plus ARCH VILLAINS · ROBOT · SOLAR RAY WEAPON

SOFT VINYL
CAPE WITH
DRAWSTRING

Above, HELMET (molded plastic) 11″ tall 1966

Below, IDEAL CATALOG (detail) 1966

Swing along with

The country's going BATTY over the BATMAN TV show get in on the BATCRAZE now!

BATMAN
America's TV Sensation Can Mean Sensational Sales For You!
Full line of Batman equipment
Life-size replicas—as used on the Batman TV show
Action-designed for maximum play
BATMAN is flying high, and your sales will too, when you latch onto IDEAL's action-packed BATMAN equipment.
The BATMAN accessories are full size, realistically detailed versions of the equipment used by the Caped Crusader on his top-rated TV show.
All junior crime-stoppers are sure to want to dress up as their super-idol, so cash in now on the BATMAN excitement.
BATMAN HELMET, BELT AND CAPE SET

Opposite, UTILITY BELT (molded plastic, rope, cardboard) 26″ x 16″ x 2.5″, 1966

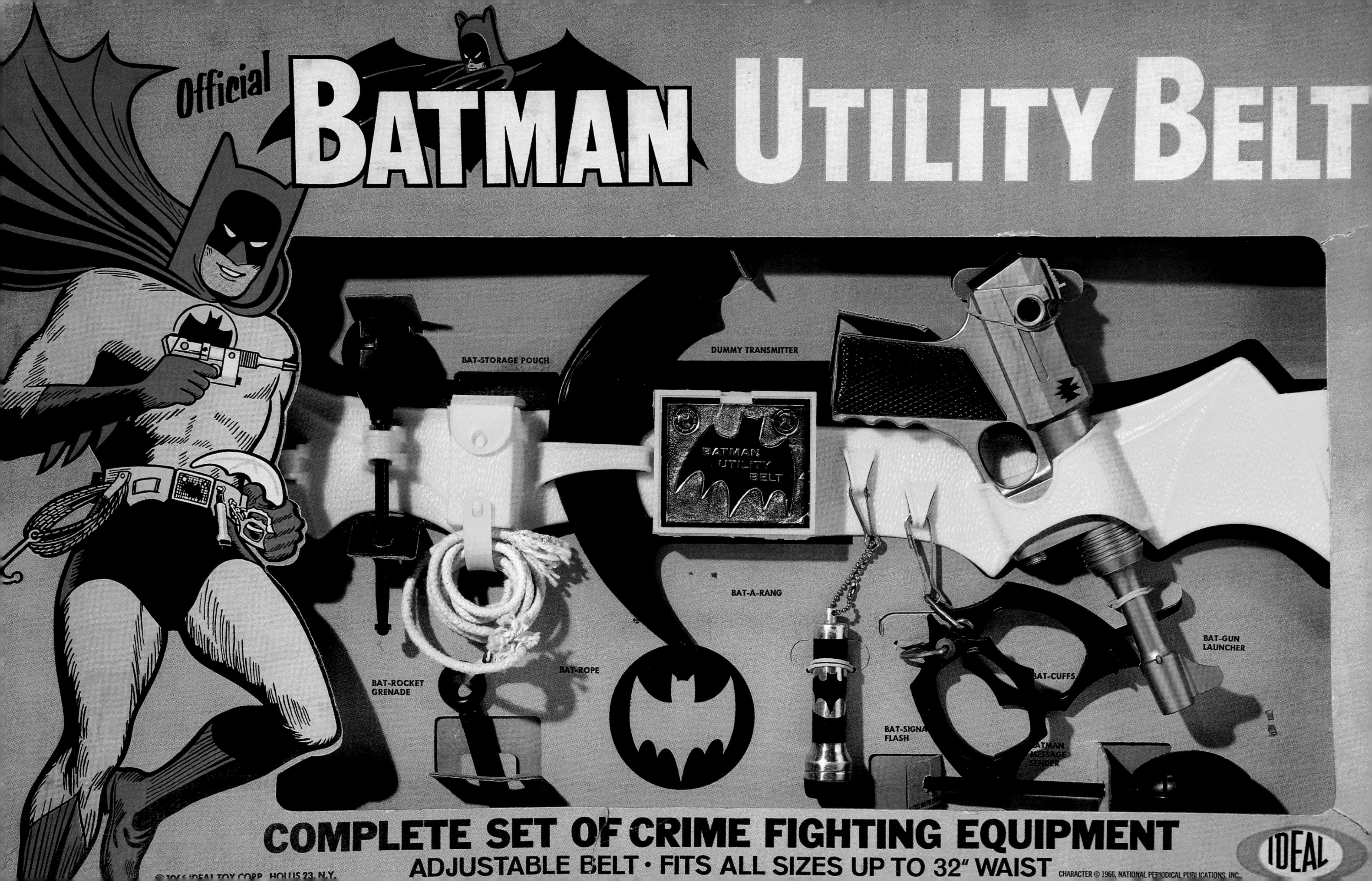
Official
BATMAN UTILITY BELT
BAT-STORAGE POUCH
DUMMY TRANSMITTER
BATMAN UTILITY BELT
BAT-A-RANG
BAT-GUN LAUNCHER
BAT-ROCKET GRENADE
BAT-ROPE
BAT-CUFFS
BAT-SIGNA
FLASH
BATMAN MESSAGE SENDER
COMPLETE SET OF CRIME FIGHTING EQUIPMENT
ADJUSTABLE BELT • FITS ALL SIZES UP TO 32″ WAIST
IDEAL
CHARACTER © 1966, NATIONAL PERIODICAL PUBLICATIONS, INC.

Right,
CARRYING
CASE
(exterior)
(vinyl over
cardboard)
18.2″ x 10.6″
1966

Left,
CARRYING
CASE
(interior)
(vinyl over
cardboard)
18.2″ x 10.6″
1966

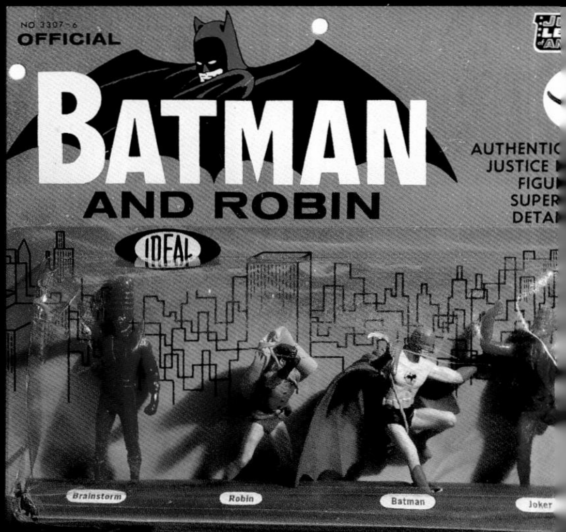

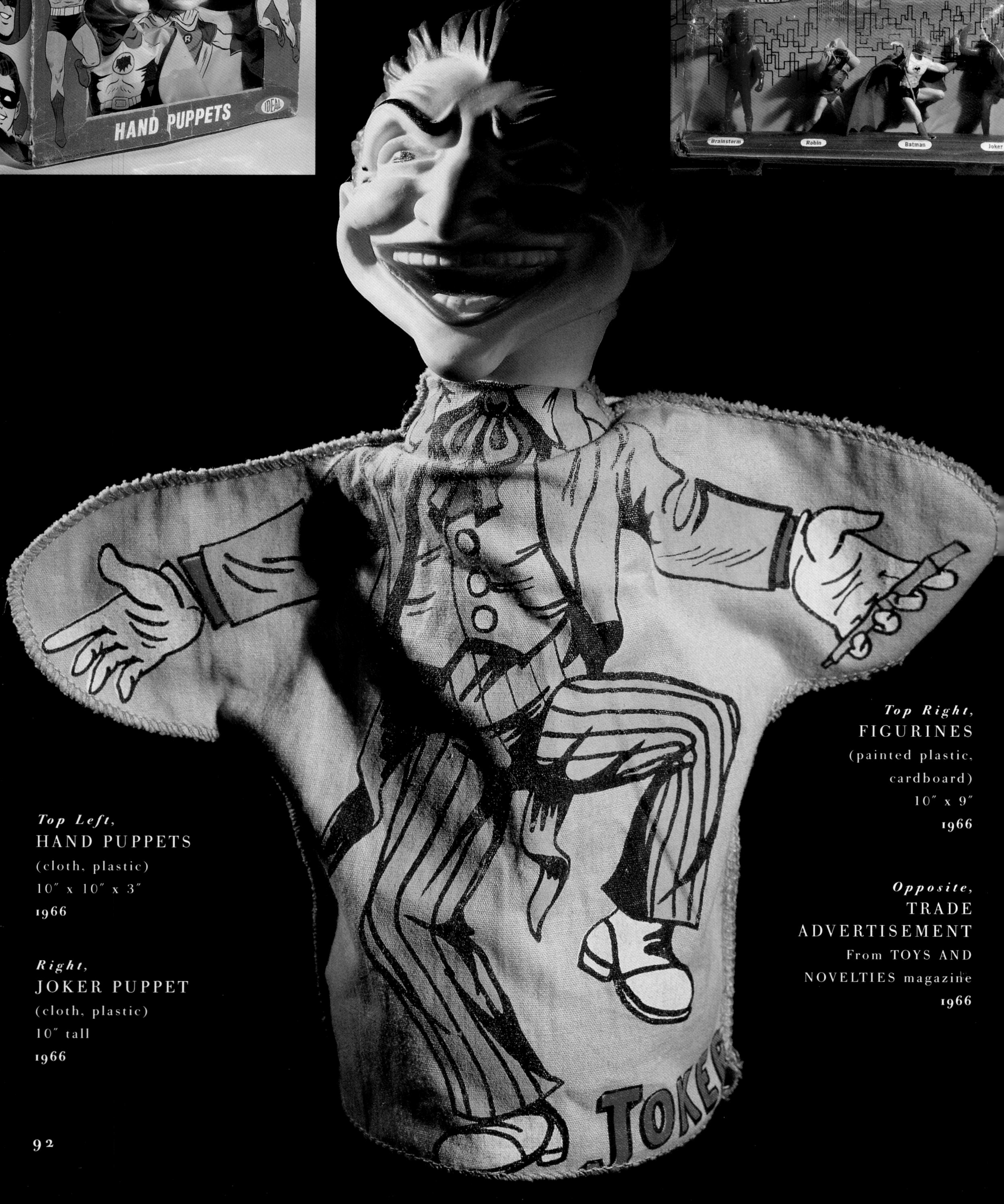

Top Right,
FIGURINES
(painted plastic, cardboard)
10″ x 9″
1966

Opposite,
TRADE ADVERTISEMENT
From TOYS AND NOVELTIES magazine
1966

Top Left,
HAND PUPPETS
(cloth, plastic)
10″ x 10″ x 3″
1966

Right,
JOKER PUPPET
(cloth, plastic)
10″ tall
1966

WARNING!

INFRINGEMENT on BATMAN® MERCHANDISE

National Periodical Publications, Inc. owns and has the sole and exclusive right to use or license the name BATMAN and/or BATMAN and ROBIN and the characters BATMAN and/or BATMAN and ROBIN and the Bat emblem and any likenesses, photographs or facsimiles thereof, in connection with the manufacturing, merchandising, advertising, promotion and/or sale of any merchandise whatsoever, including Tee shirts, Sweatshirts and any other apparel items or toys, games, or novelties. Such names, titles, characters and emblems are protected by copyrights and trade-marks or trade names. We reserve the right to take vigorous legal action both against persons who violate our rights and those dealing with such violators.

Do not do business with any unlicensed persons, firms or corporations. Do not accept imitations. We have already taken steps to institute legal actions against violators.

NATIONAL PERIODICAL PUBLICATIONS, INC.
575 LEXINGTON AVENUE. NEW YORK, N.Y. 10022 / PL 9-5700

If trading cards are the stocks and bonds of the bubblegum set, then Topps Inc. is their Merrill Lynch and Dow Jones combined. The ritual of children (usually boys) bartering illustrated cards with each other has its roots in a gimmick that appeared at the turn of the century, when tobacco manufacturers used to package the cards with cigarettes. This is how baseball cards originated.

Topps knew there was a market for what are now referred to as "non-sports cards," and when *Batman* became a hit the company decided to produce a set of them based on the TV show. For whatever reason, 20th Century-Fox would not provide any photographs, and it was decided that the cards would have to be drawn. Norm Saunders, a veteran illustrator of pulp magazine and paperback covers, worked from pencils by Bob Powell to create 143 gouache paintings (each 3.375″ x 4.75″) for three separate series of cards, and in so doing provided a legacy of some of the oddest Batman art to date. The style was realistic, as if they were attempting to approximate the look of the forbidden photographs, but in most cases the light seemed to be coming from every possible direction, providing an aura of plastic artificiality.

As for the storylines, all the usual Batman themes of the time were taken to an extreme that was just on the other side of comfortable. A gleeful Riddler tried to brand a terrified Robin with a red-hot iron poker in the shape of a question mark; Batman was strapped to a table with knives descending upon him and no hope of escape; heroes and villains alike were routinely bound, gagged, gassed, slapped, kicked, frozen, burned, choked, drowned, crushed, shot at, threatened with circular saws, set upon by giant squids and rats, stretched on the rack, tossed from great heights, smothered with snakes and sprayed with goo. The backs of the cards featured puzzles and little plot summaries that assured anyone interested that everything turned out okay, but I never believed it.

By the fourth series, Fox relented and the cards became photographic and, by comparison, regrettably dull. On TV you weren't allowed to do *half* of that stuff.

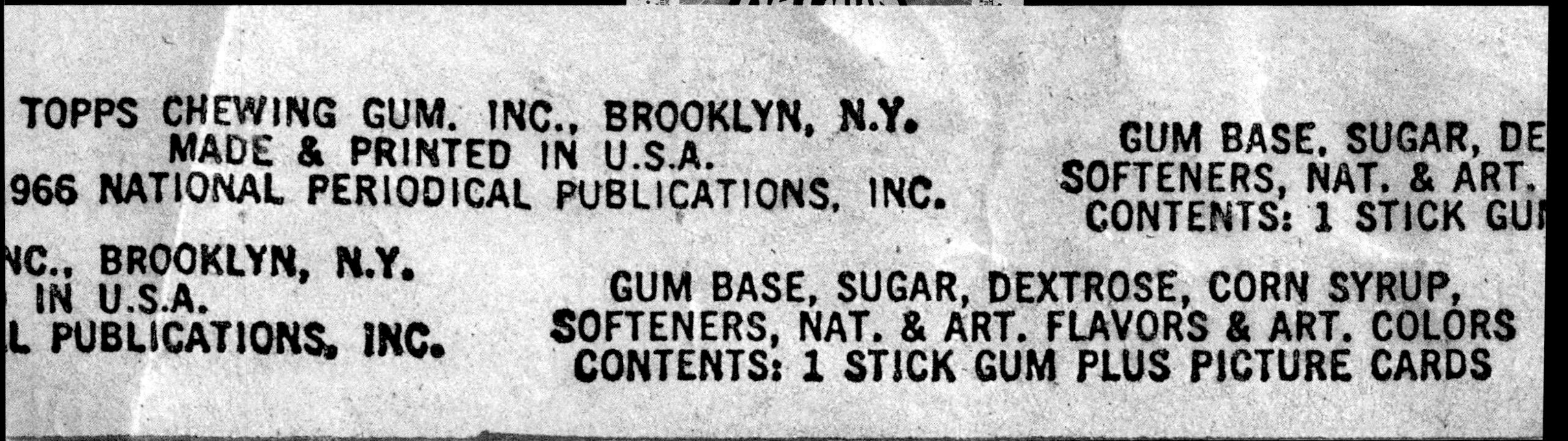

Opposite,
GUM CARD WRAPPER
(3rd series) 5.1″ x 5.8″
1966

Right,
GUM CARD WRAPPER
(1st amd 2nd series) 5.1″ x 5.8″
1966

Below,
SHIPPING CARTON
For Topps gum cards
12″ x 8″ x 16.5″
1966

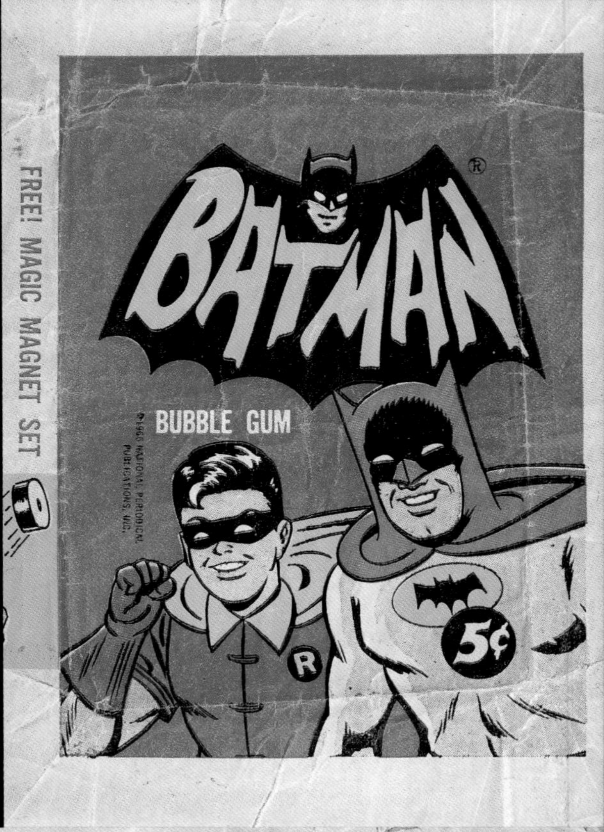

Left,
ORIGINAL ART
Topps trading card
Bob Powell and Norm Saunders, artists
(gouache on illustration board)
3.375″ x 5″, **1966**

Opposite,
TOPPS TRADING CARDS (backs)
Uncut sheet
28.5″ x 43″, **1966**

Below,
UNUSED PENCIL DRAWING
for a Topps trading card
Bob Powell, artist
(pencil on illustration board)
5″ x 3.375″, **1966**

PAGES 99-102
TOPPS TRADING CARDS
Uncut sheets
Norm Saunders, artist
28″ x 42.5″
1966

BATMAN
ROBIN
THE JOKER
BATMAN BUCKS BADMAN
JACK FROST'S JINX
RENEGADE ROULETTE
HYDROFOIL HOTSPOT
PENNED BY THE PENGUIN
FANGS OF THE PHANTOM
A PRESSING POSITION
A WRETCHED RIDDLE
AMPHIBIOUS ATTACKERS
THE PENGUIN PREVAILS
NEANDERTHAL NEMESIS
ROOF TOP VIGIL
THE PENGUIN'S TRAP
THE JOKER IN JAIL
FOLLOWING THE CLUE
INTO THE BATMOBILE
THE CAT WOMAN
THE BATMAN
SPIKES OF DEATH
FIERY ENCOUNTER
CRIME CZAR
"LET'S GO"
BATMAN STRIKES!
ROBIN— BOY WONDER
QUEEN OF CRIME
ROBIN RESCUED
CHLOROFORM VICTIM
BATMAN IN ACTION
DOUBLE-CROSS
THE BAT SIGNAL
POISON PELLET
SINISTER SMILE
GRIM REALIZATION
BAT-A-RANG BULLS-EYE
BEASTLY ENCOUNTER
THE BATARANG
ROBIN TO THE RESCUE
WHIRLPOOL
"TO THE BATCAVE"
THE BAT-GASMASK
THE ENEMIES CLASH
WINGED GIANT
ROBIN IS KIDNAPPED
NIGHTLY PATROL

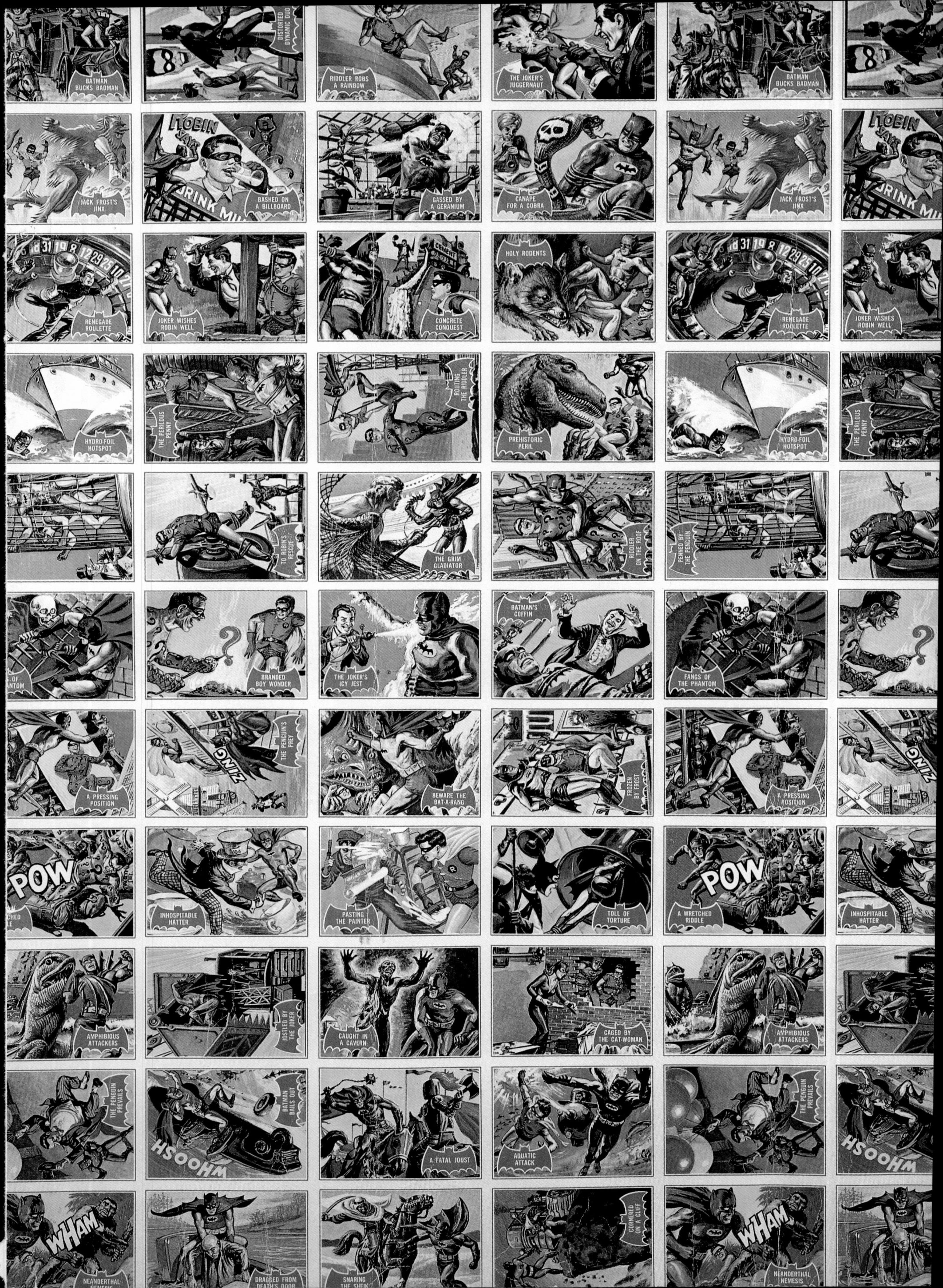
BATMAN BUCKS BADMAN
DISTORTED DYNAMIC DUO
RIDDLER ROBS A RAINBOW
THE JOKER'S JUGGERNAUT
BATMAN BUCKS BADMAN
JACK FROST'S JINX
ROBIN SAYS
DRINK MI
BASHED ON A BILLBOARD
GASSED BY A GERANIUM
CANAPE FOR A COBRA
JACK FROST'S JINX
RENEGADE ROULETTE
JOKER WISHES ROBIN WELL
CEMENT
CONCRETE CONQUEST
HOLY RODENTS
RENEGADE ROULETTE
JOKER WISHES ROBIN WELL
HYDRO-FOIL HOTSPOT
THE PERILOUS PENNY
ROUTING THE RIDDLER
PREHISTORIC PERIL
HYDRO-FOIL HOTSPOT
THE PERILOUS PENNY
TO ROBIN'S RESCUE
THE GRIM GLADIATOR
RIDDLER ON THE ROOF
PENNED BY THE PENGUIN
BRANDED BOY WONDER
THE JOKER'S ICY JEST
BATMAN'S COFFIN
FANGS OF THE PHANTOM
A PRESSING POSITION
THE PENGUIN'S PREY
ZING
BEWARE THE BAT-A-RANG
FROZEN BY FROST
A PRESSING POSITION
ZING
POW
INHOSPITABLE HATTER
PASTING THE PAINTER
TOLL OF TORTURE
POW
A WRETCHED RIDDLE
INHOSPITABLE HATTER
AMPHIBIOUS ATTACKERS
JOSTLED BY THE JOKER
CAUGHT IN A CAVERN
CAGED BY THE CAT-WOMAN
AMPHIBIOUS ATTACKERS
THE PENGUIN PREVAILS
BATMAN BAILS OUT
WHOOSH
A FATAL JOUST
AQUATIC ATTACK
THE PENGUIN PREVAILS
WHOOSH
WHAM
DRAGGED FROM DEATH'S DOOR
SNARING THE SHEIK
CORNERED ON A CLIFF
WHAM
NEANDERTHAL NEMESIS

LANDING A BIG ONE
BOILING BATH
OUT ON A LIMB
DANGER FROM 25TH CENTURY
UNDONE BY AN UMBRELLA
FLYING FOES
CRIME ABOVE THE HARBOR
DANGER IN THE DEPTHS
GOTHAM GALLANTS
PORTABLE BAT SIGNALS
CAPTAIN KIDD'S CAPER
DYNAMITE IN ROBIN'S NEST
THE BATMAN BABY SITTER
INFERNO OF FLAME
THE GHOSTLY FOE
GRAPPLING A GATOR
THE MENACING MUMMY
TARGET OF THE TRAPPER
PENDULUM PERIL
LINK TO LINCOLN
DEATH SPINS A WEB
FACING THE AXE
THE BATLINE LIFE-LINE
TENTACLED TERROR
KNIGHTING A THIEF
CYCLING CRUSADER
SURFING SLEUTHS
BONG
BATMAN WINS A PRIZE
WHOOSH
BATMAN BAILS OUT
JOSTLED BY THE JOKER
INHOSPITABLE HATTER
ZING
THE PENGUIN'S PREY
BRANDED BOY WONDER
TO ROBIN'S RESCUE
A FATAL JOUST
CAUGHT IN A CAVERN
PASTING THE PAINTER
BEWARE THE BAT-A-RANG
THE JOKER'S ICY JEST
THE GRIM GLADIATOR
AQUATIC ATTACK
BATMAN'S COFFIN

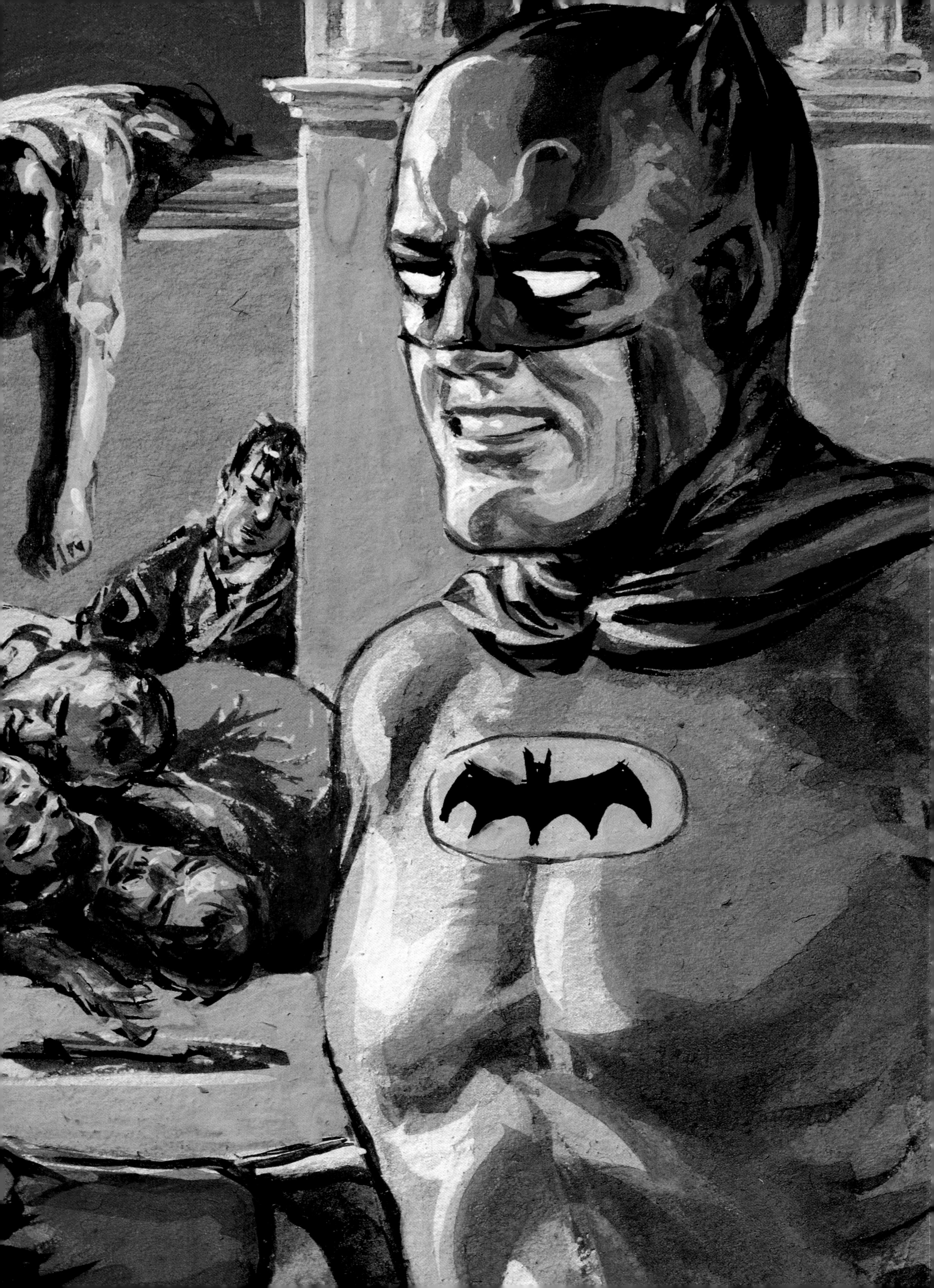

UNDONE BY AN UMBRELLA
FLYING FOES
CRIME ABOVE THE HARBOR
CLIFF HANGERS
WATERY WARFARE
IN THE PATH OF DEATH
DYNAMITE IN ROBIN'S NEST
THE BATMAN BABY SITTER
INFERNO OF FLAME
DUEL OF DEATH
COUNTERFEIT CAPED CRUSADER
POW
MENACE IN FAIRYLAND
PENDULUM PERIL
LINK TO LINCOLN
DEATH SPINS A WEB
LEAP FOR LIFE
BATTLING NATURE'S FURY
TIGHT SQUEEZE
CYCLING CRUSADER
SURFING SLEUTHS
BATMAN WINS A PRIZE
BONG
DEATH SKIS THE SLOPES
THE JOKER'S LAST LAUGH
STRIKING OUT THE COBRA
THE PENGUIN'S PREY
ZING
BRANDED BOY WONDER
TO ROBIN'S RESCUE
THE PERILOUS PENNY
JOKER WISHES ROBIN WELL
BASHED ON A BILLBOARD
ROBIN
BEWARE THE BAT-A-RANG
THE JOKER'S ICY JEST
THE GRIM GLADIATOR
ROUTING THE RIDDLER
CONCRETE CONQUEST
CEMENT
GASSED BY A GERANIUM
RIDDLER ROBS A RAINBOW
BATMAN'S COFFIN
PREHISTORIC PERIL
HOLY RODENTS
CANAPE FOR A COBRA
THE JOKER'S JUGGERNAUT

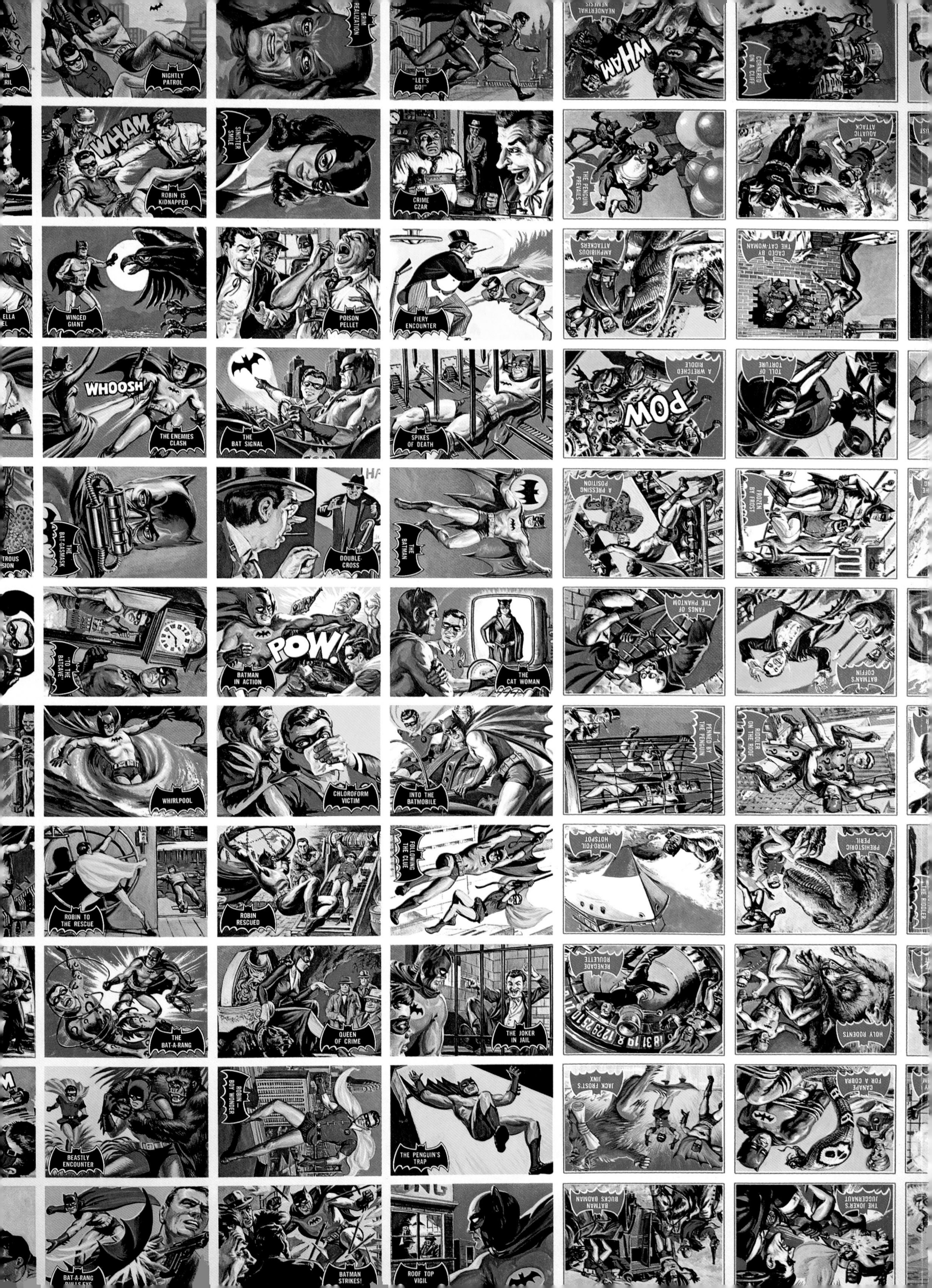
NIGHTLY PATROL
GRIM REALIZATION
"LET'S GO!"
NEANDERTHAL NEMESIS
WHAM
CORNERED ON A CLIFF
WHAM
ROBIN IS KIDNAPPED
SINISTER SMILE
CRIME CZAR
THE PENGUIN PREVAILS
AQUATIC ATTACK
WINGED GIANT
POISON PELLET
FIERY ENCOUNTER
AMPHIBIOUS ATTACKERS
CAGED BY THE CAT-WOMAN
WHOOSH
THE ENEMIES CLASH
THE BAT SIGNAL
SPIKES OF DEATH
A WRETCHED RIDDLE
POW
TOLL OF TORTURE
THE BAT-GASMASK
DOUBLE-CROSS
THE BATMAN
A PRESSING POSITION
FROZEN BY FROST
"TO THE BATCAVE"
POW!
BATMAN IN ACTION
THE CAT WOMAN
FANGS OF THE PHANTOM
BATMAN'S COFFIN
WHIRLPOOL
CHLOROFORM VICTIM
INTO THE BATMOBILE
PENNED BY THE PENGUIN
RIDDLER ON THE ROOF
ROBIN TO THE RESCUE
ROBIN RESCUED
FOLLOWING THE CLUE
HYDRO-FOIL HOTSPOT
PREHISTORIC PERIL
THE RIDDLER
THE BAT-A-RANG
QUEEN OF CRIME
THE JOKER IN JAIL
RENEGADE ROULETTE
HOLY RODENTS
BEASTLY ENCOUNTER
ROBIN BOY WONDER
THE PENGUIN'S TRAP
JACK FROST'S JINX
CANAPE FOR A COBRA
BATMAN STRIKES!
ROOF TOP VIGIL
BATMAN BUCKS BADMAN
THE JOKER'S JUGGERNAUT

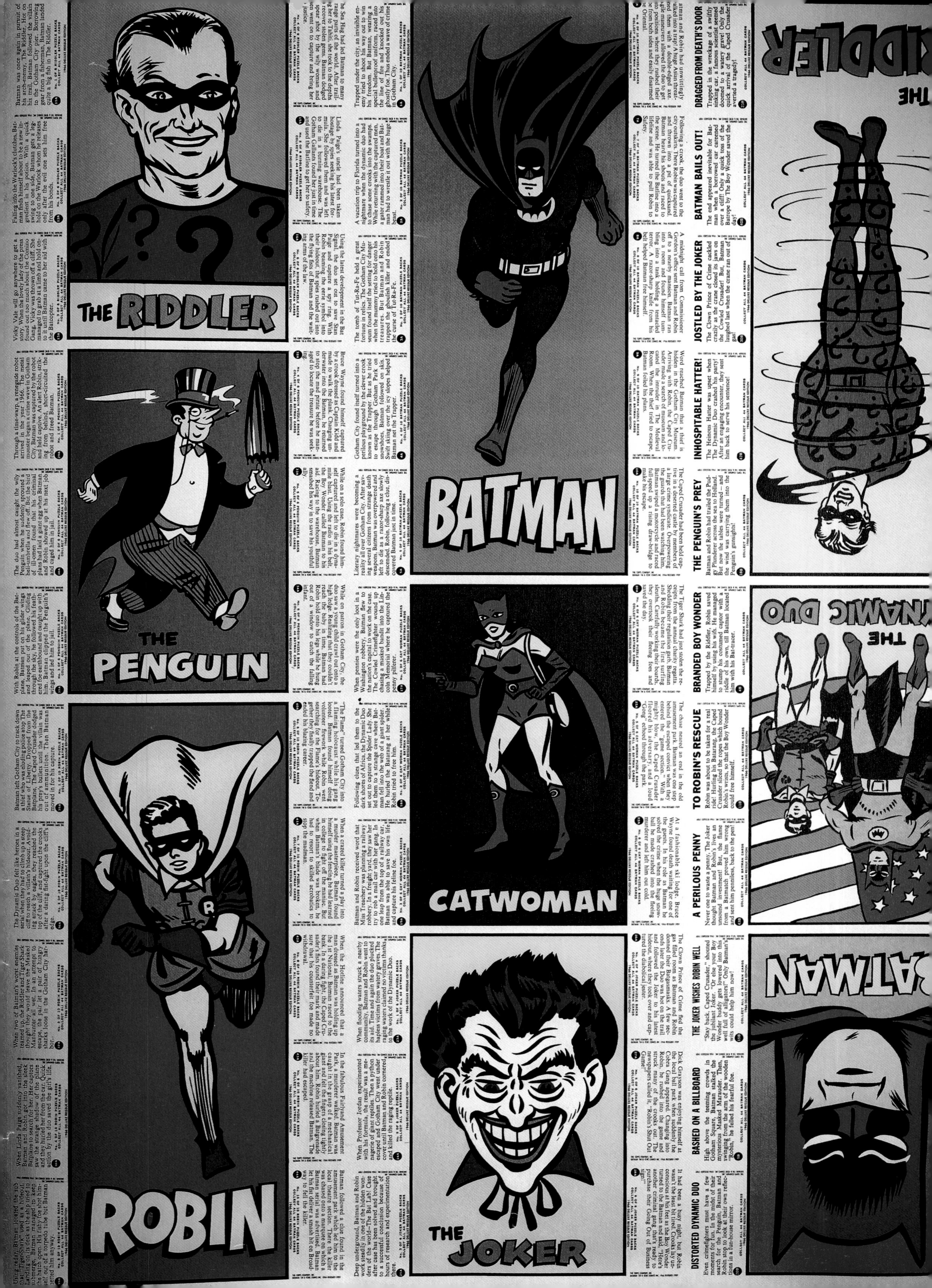
THE RIDDLER
THE PENGUIN
ROBIN
BATMAN
CATWOMAN
THE JOKER

SPECIAL SERIES
BATMAN®
REAL PHOTOS!
SPECIAL 5¢
BATMAN®
BUBBLE GUM
EXTRA
THE RIDDLER'S RIDDLE
IN EVERY PACK

PAGE 104
TOPPS TRADING CARDS
(backs)
Uncut sheet
28″ x 43″
1966

PAGE 105
Top and Bottom,
ORIGINAL ART
For Topps trading cards
Bob Powell and Norm Saunders, artists
(gouache on illustration board)
5″ x 3.375″
1966

Opposite Above,
RETAIL DISPLAY BOX FOR TOPPS TRADING CARDS
5th series
8″ x 3.875″ x 1.5″, **1966**

Opposite Center,
TOPPS TRADING CARD WRAPPERS
5th series
5.125″ x 5.875″, **1966**

Opposite Below,
TOPPS TRADING CARDS
5th series, uncut sheets, 28″ x 42.8″
1966

Below Left,
TOPPS TRADING CARD WRAPPERS
4th series
5.125″ x 5.875″, **1966**

Below Right,
TOPPS TRADING CARDS
5th series, uncut sheets, 28″ x 42.8″
1966

Bottom,
RETAIL DISPLAY BOX FOR TOPPS TRADING CARDS
5th series
8″ x 3.75″ x 1.5″, **1966**

CA
Captain Action
IS HERE
12" TALL FULLY POSEABLE
CHANGE HIS OUTFITS AND CAPTAIN ACTION
BECOMES BATMAN • SUPERMAN • AQUAMAN
LONE RANGER • FLASH GORDON • STEVE CANYON
CAPTAIN AMERICA • SGT. FURY • THE PHANTOM

Captain Action was Ideal's answer to the tremendous success of GI Joe. In fact, the two are related—toy developer Stan Weston contributed significantly to the creation of both. Captain Action was based on an idea known in the toy business as the "razor blade" approach: The consumer bought a basic doll, or "razor," and soon needed accessories ("razor blades") to make it more fun. It was a concept that worked very well for the Barbie doll. Though CA (real name unknown) clearly seemed to belong to some sort of military organization, it was more along the lines of Buck Rogers than the Marines. Instead of assorted army uniforms and equipment, the Captain could transform himself into different comic book characters, such as Batman, Superman, Aquaman, the Lone Ranger, Captain America, Spider-Man and more. He was a hit, but he did not have the staying power of GI Joe, in spite of the addition of Action Boy, the inevitable youthful sidekick who became the Robin to Captain Action's Batman.

Above,
CAPTAIN ACTION

CANYON

Far Left,
POSTER ADVERTISEMENT
(offset lithography on paper)
19.125″ x 12.125″
1966

Left,
CAPTAIN ACTION RETAIL DISPLAY
(printed carboard)
14″ tall
1966

Below Left,
CATALOG PAGE (detail)
1966

CAPTAIN ACTION
T.M.

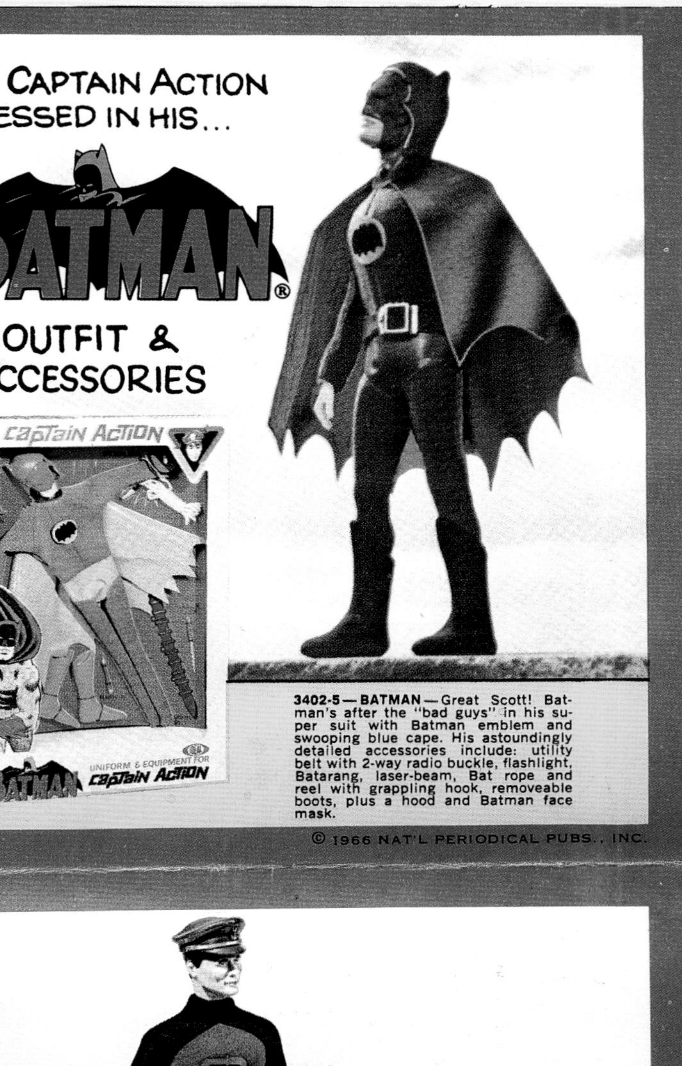
CAPTAIN ACTION
ESSED IN HIS...
ATMAN®
OUTFIT &
CCESSORIES
CAPTAIN ACTION
UNIFORM & EQUIPMENT FOR
CAPTAIN ACTION
3402-5—BATMAN—Great Scott! Batman's after the "bad guys" in his super suit with Batman emblem and swooping blue cape. His astoundingly detailed accessories include: utility belt with 2-way radio buckle, flashlight, Batarang, laser-beam, Bat rope and reel with grappling hook, removeable boots, plus a hood and Batman face mask.
© 1966 NAT'L PERIODICAL PUBS., INC.

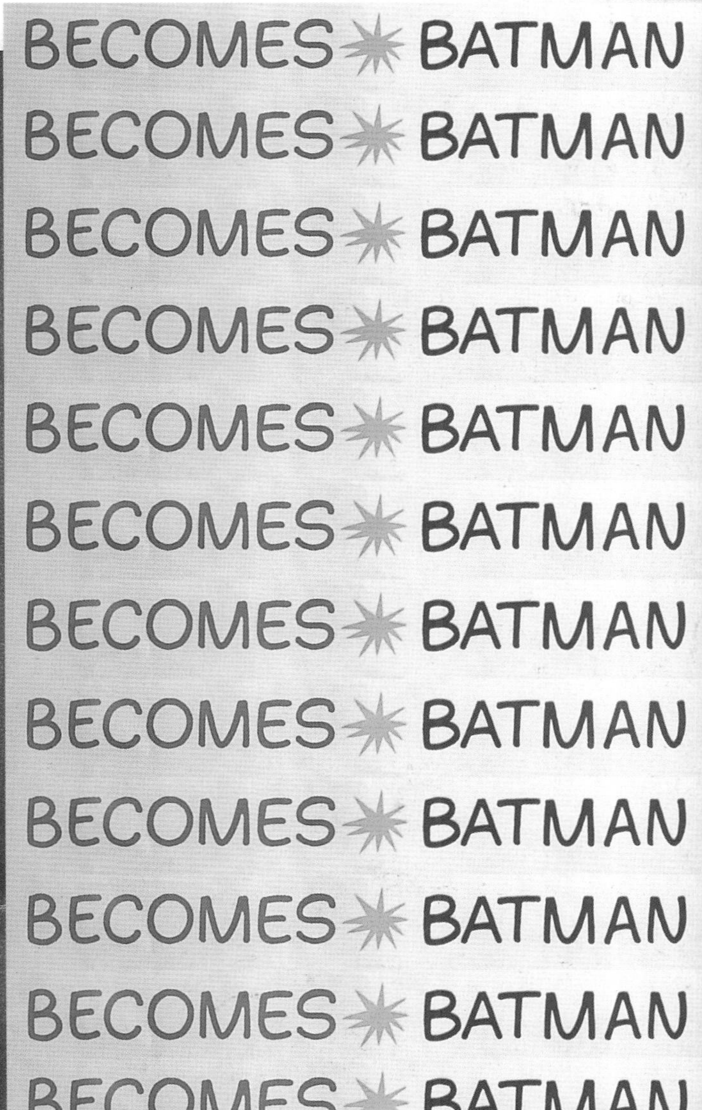
BECOMES BATMAN
BECOMES BATMAN
BECOMES BATMAN
BECOMES BATMAN
BECOMES BATMAN
BECOMES BATMAN
BECOMES BATMAN
BECOMES BATMAN
BECOMES BATMAN
BECOMES BATMAN
BECOMES BATMAN

Above Left and Right,
BATMAN COSTUME
AND CAPTAIN ACTION DOLL
1966

Below Left and Right,
ROBIN COSTUME
AND ACTION BOY DOLL
1967

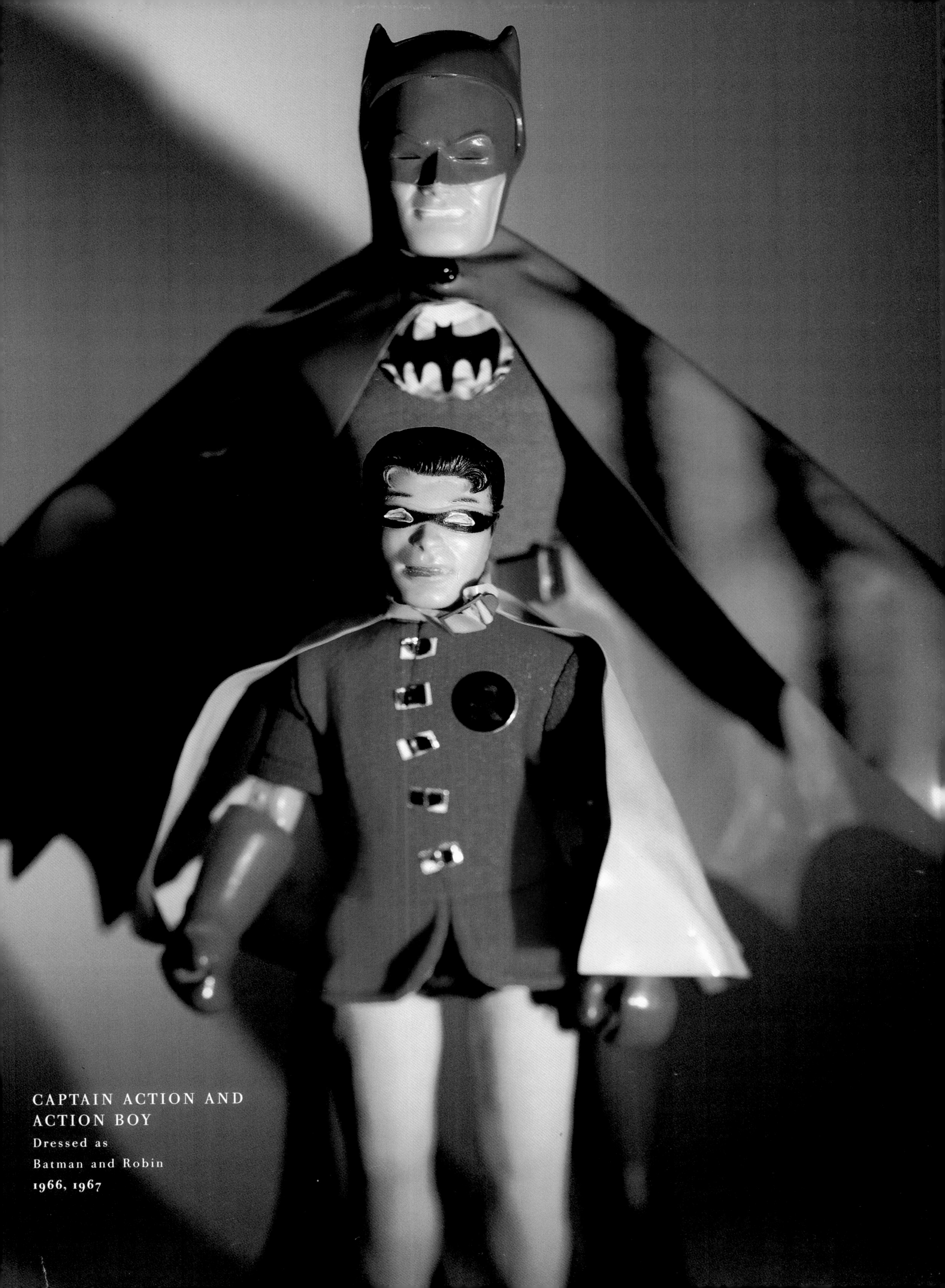

CAPTAIN ACTION AND
ACTION BOY
Dressed as
Batman and Robin
1966, 1967

In 1967, Ideal decided that Captain Action could use a little romance in his life and introduced the Super Queens, Barbie-like versions of four of DC's female characters: Supergirl, Wonder Woman, Mera and Batgirl. Too feminine for boys and too eccentric for girls, they never attracted a large audience and quickly lapsed into obscurity. This has made them something of a Holy Grail for toy collectors, especially when still in the box. The side of the box (below) emphasizes one problem with the Batgirl concept: She'll save the gentleman dangling from the building, but only after she changes her outfit. Even by Batman's standards, this seemed ridiculous.

Dr. Evil was Captain Action's archenemy. On the opposite page, Batman storms his headquarters. This carrying case is possibly the rarest of all CA merchandise.

SUPER QUEEN DOLL
Dressed as Batgirl
12″ tall
1967

DR. EVIL'S
SANCTUARY
(vinyl over cardboard)
16″ tall
1967

BATMAN
ON
OFF

Foreign translations of anything American always fascinate, because they remind us of how different we appear to other cultures than we do to ourselves. If the American styling of Batman in the late '60s seemed appealing but silly, when rendered by the Japanese it became completely insane. The illustrations for the packaging are naive to the point of folk art, as if someone in America was watching Batman on TV and explaining what it looked like over the phone to an artist in Tokyo. That's why I love these so much. I can't help but look at them and wonder what the illustrators thought they were drawing, and what any of it meant.

Today, licensees for DC Comics merchandise are issued "style guides," thick three-ring binders that contain pre-approved art and logos for all the characters. The advantage of this is that it gives a sense of continuity to the products, whoever makes them. The disadvantage is that the products sometimes lack variety. In 1966, no such guides existed, and each company was often left to fend for itself when it came to artwork. The results ranged from the inspired to the ludicrous, but each had its own custom look. An Ideal Batman toy didn't look anything like a Marx, which was distinct from a Corgi and so on. Those days are gone forever.

The true masterworks of the Batman toys made by the Japanese are the tin robots, which they are masters at creating. These exquisite figures manage to evoke sorrow and triumph simultaneously, and seem to be a comment on the mechanization of humanity. If we are all going to become machines, at least we can look like this. . . .

Left,
ROBOT (detail)
(tin, plastic, cloth)
12″ tall
Japan
1966

PAGES 116-17:
Clockwise, from left,
TV BOARD GAME AND PACKAGING
FINGER PUPPETS
CARD GAME
BATBOAT MODEL KIT
Japan
ALL 1966

TV テレビ GAME
遊ぶ時は
取りはずしてください
KOIDE SHINKOSHA
4 5 6 7 8 7 6 5 4
3 2 1 1 2 3
5 4 3 3 4 5
7 6 5 4 3 2 1 1 2 3 4 5 6 7
TV GAME

Bat Man
YANOMAN TOY
MADE IN JAPAN

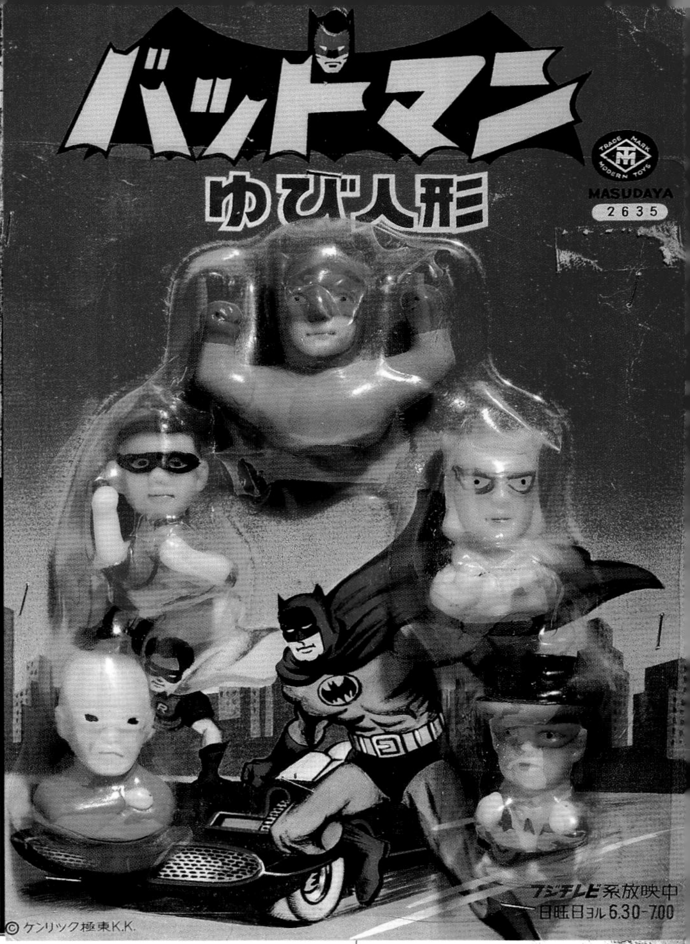
バットマン
ゆび人形
MASUDAYA
2635
MODERN TOYS
フジテレビ系放映中
日曜日ヨル6.30-7.00
© ケンリック極東K.K.

トマン
MAN
こりぞの
えあわせ

ひこうき
ひこうき
ひこうき
1
2
3
20

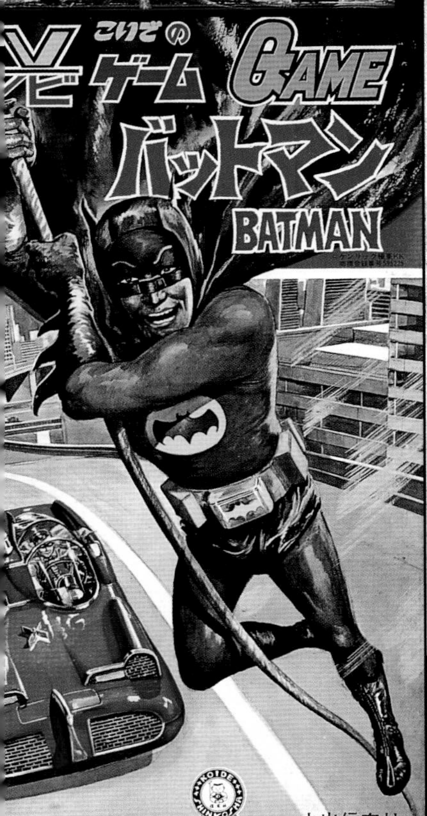
こりぞの
ゲーム
GAME
バットマン
BATMAN
株式会社小出信宏社

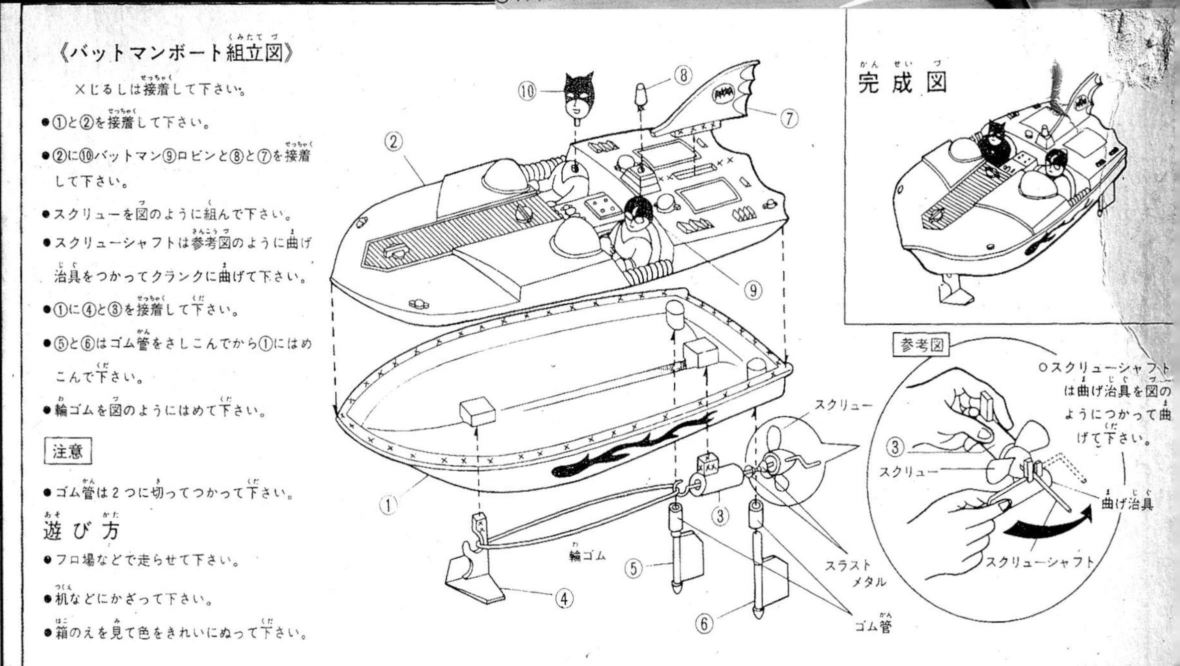
《バットマンボート組立図》
×じるしは接着して下さい。
●①と②を接着して下さい。
●②に⑩バットマン⑨ロビンと⑧と⑦を接着して下さい。
●スクリューを図のように組んで下さい。
●スクリューシャフトは参考図のように曲げ治具をつかってクランクに曲げて下さい。
●①に④と③を接着して下さい。
●⑤と⑥はゴム管をさしこんでから①にはめこんで下さい。
●輪ゴムを図のようにはめて下さい。
注意
●ゴム管は2つに切ってつかって下さい。
遊び方
●フロ場などで走らせて下さい。
●机などにかざって下さい。
●箱のえを見て色をきれいにぬって下さい。
完成図
参考図
○スクリューシャフトは曲げ治具を図のようにつかって曲げて下さい。
スクリュー
曲げ治具
スクリューシャフト
スラストメタル
輪ゴム
ゴム管

IMAI
BATMAN BOAT SERIES
BATMAN BOAT
A
イマイバットマンシリーズNo.4
バットマンボートA

Above and Right,

ROBOT AND PACKAGING

(tin, plastic, cloth)

Approx. 7″ tall

Japan

1966

電動バットマン
BATMAN
胸のバットマークを
ひからせながら歩きます
UM-2
1.5V
BATTERY
日立乾電池
高性能
UM-1(P)/1.5V
Hitachi, Ltd.
単二乾電池二本使用
dai

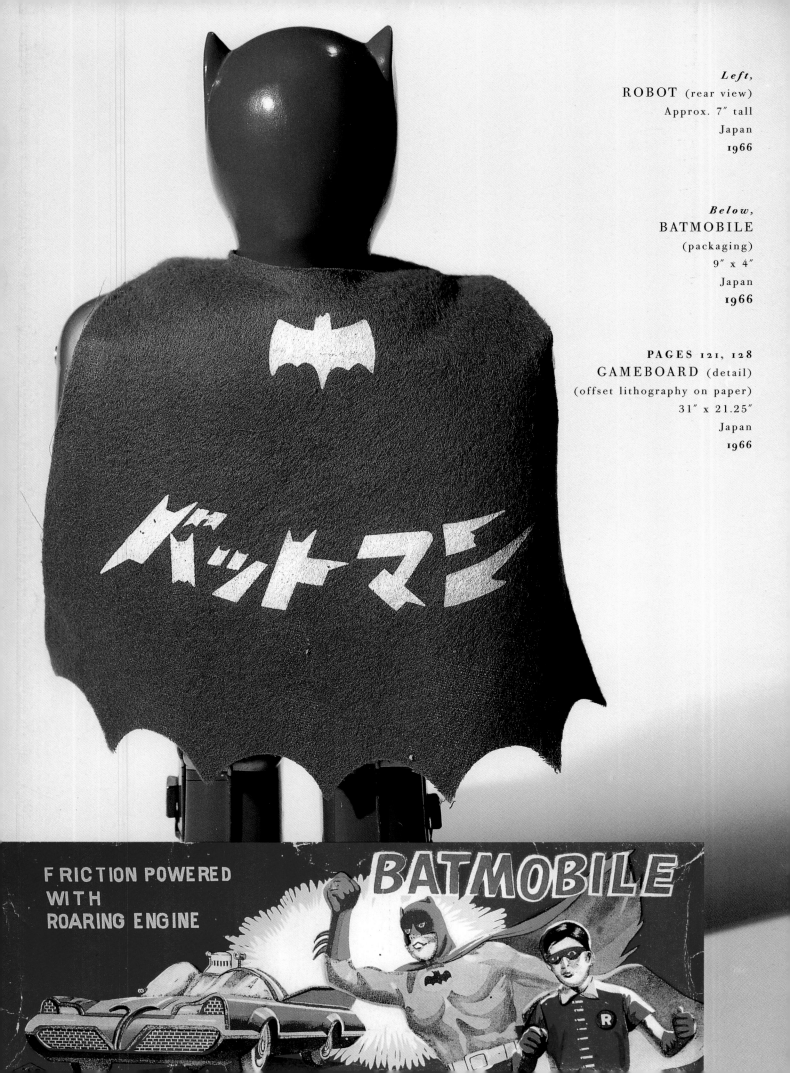

Left,
ROBOT (rear view)
Approx. 7″ tall
Japan
1966

Below,
BATMOBILE
(packaging)
9″ x 4″
Japan
1966

PAGES 121, 128
GAMEBOARD (detail)
(offset lithography on paper)
31″ x 21.25″
Japan
1966

ンすごろく
株式会社 小出信宏社
KOIDE SHINKOSHA
9
電車をとめろ
HASYA!
10
BWEE!
まてっ 百面相めっ
は⑪へ
は⑫へ
は⑨へ
は⑫へ
11
これでもか
SOK!
POW!
は⑬へ
は⑩へ
は⑫へ
は⑤へ
上り
12
GUWAAA!
BABAN
ついせき
は⑨へ
は②へ
は⑪へ
は上り
13
BAM
みんなつかまえたぞ
は上り
は⑥へ
は上り
は⑫へ
2
はやいぞ バットモビル
は④へ
は③へ
は⑥へ
は⑤へ
1
あっ 百面相だっ
は③へ
は④へ
は③へ
は②へ
は⑤へ
は①へ
は②へ
は①へ
は③へ
は④へ

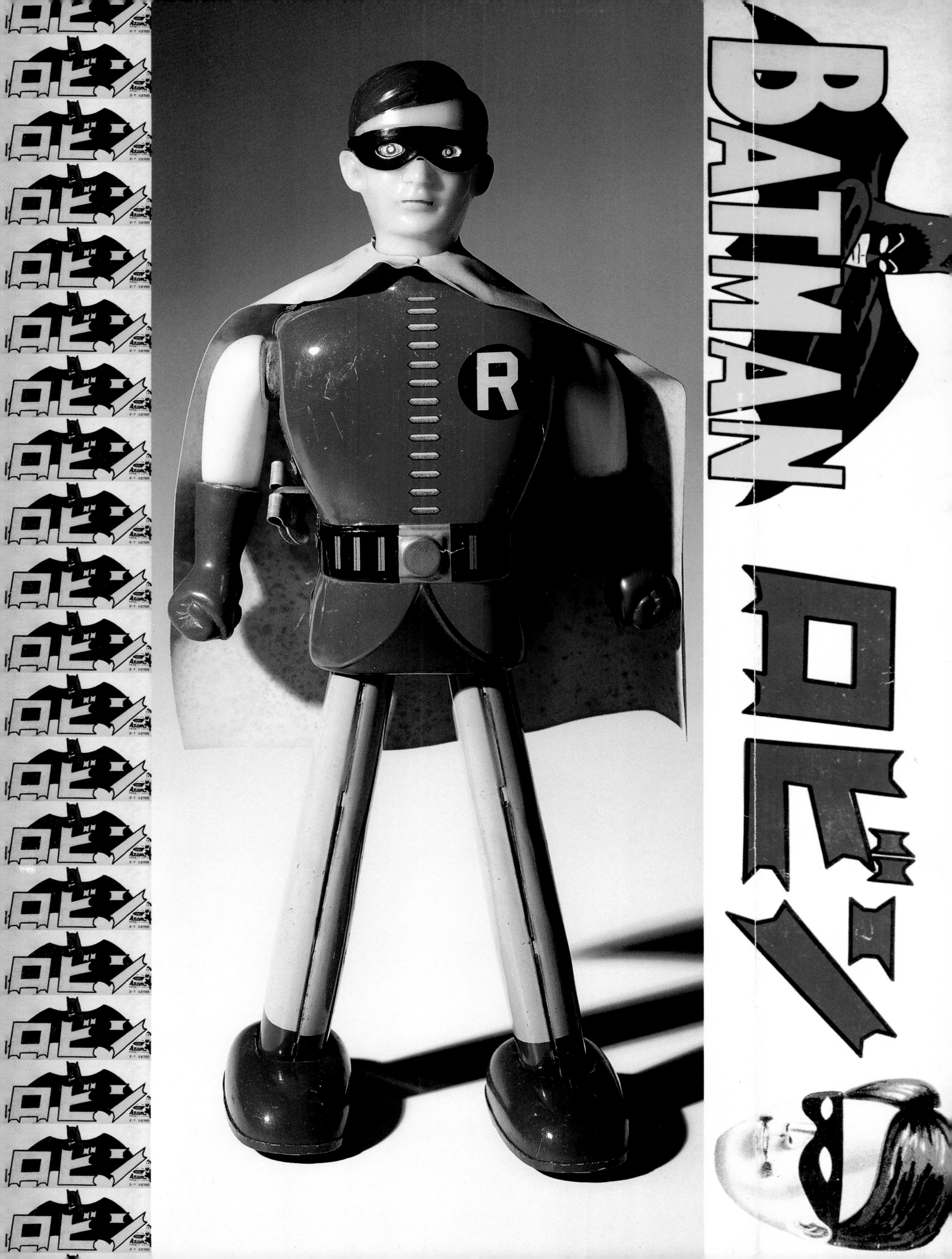
BATMAN
ロビン

Left and Within,
ROBIN ROBOT
AND PACKAGING
(tin, plastic)
Approx. 11″ tall
Japan
1966

Right and Within,
BATMAN ROBOT
AND PACKAGING
(tin, plastic)
Approx. 11″ tall
Japan
1966

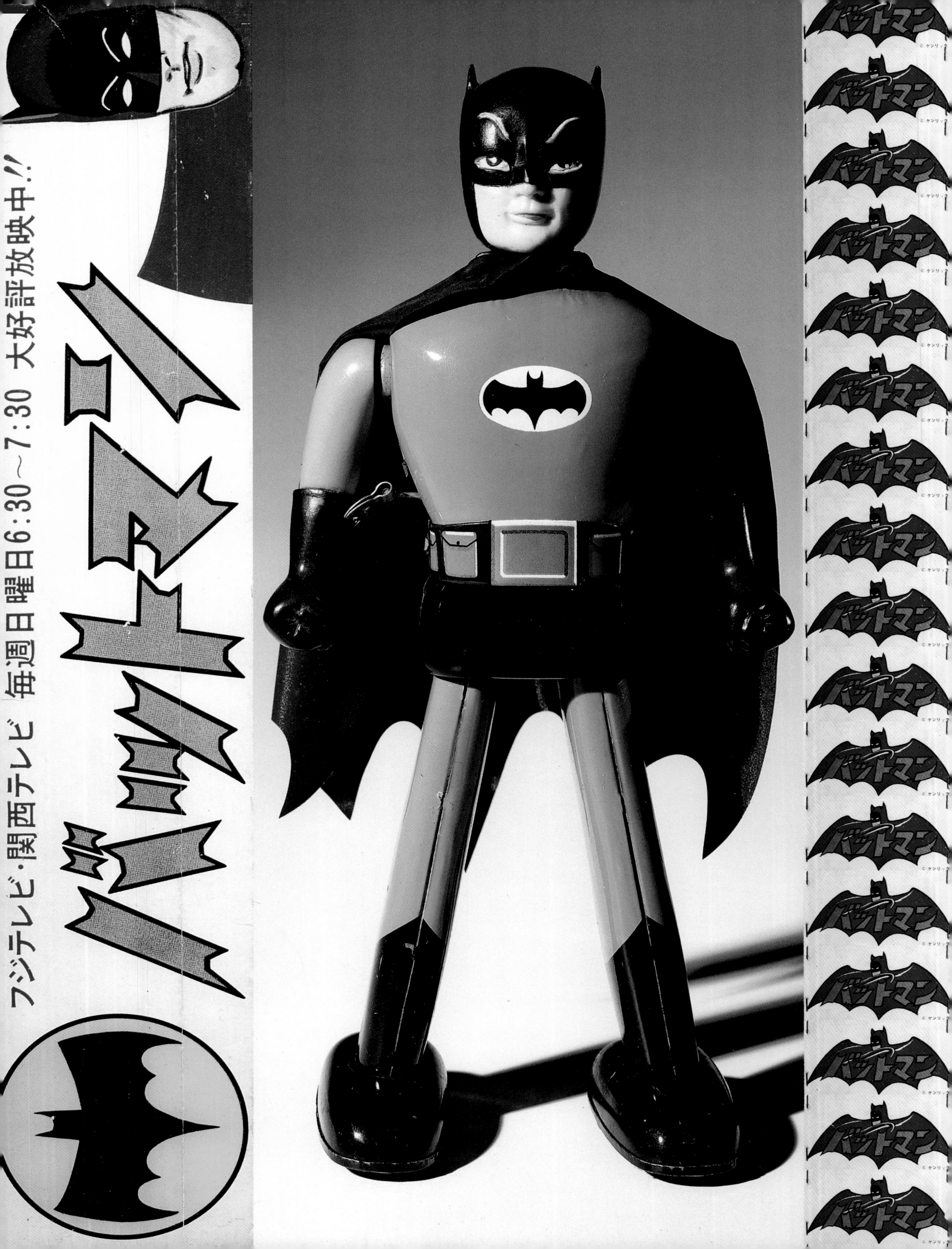
フジテレビ・関西テレビ　毎週日曜日6:30～7:30　大好評放映中!!
バットマン
バットマン

バットマン
ⓒケンリック極東KK
商標登録番号595225
7
ねむりぐすり
SIUUUU
は一回やすみ
は⑩へ
は④へ
は⑧へ
は⑥へ
は⑨へ
は⑩へ
は②へ
GOoooo
バットマンがあぶない
一回やすみ
GAAAAA
8
は⑦へ
は⑩へ
は⑪へ
は⑥へ
CAS
5
やっぱりカーメンだったか
AACH!!
は⑥へ
は①へ
は⑦へ
は②へ
6
ロビン!にがすな
は⑤へ
は⑨へ
は⑦へ
は⑪へ
POLICE
R
4
あっバットマンだ
OWWW
は⑦へ
は⑤へ
は⑥へ
は③へ
3
あやしいぞ
はふりだしへ
は②へ
は⑦へ
2
GOO

BATMOBILE
(tin)
9.5″ long
Japan
1966

Below,
PROMOTIONAL POSTER
14″ x 25.6″
1966

AURORA

Our grandfathers built ships in bottles; our fathers made balsa-wood airplanes; we fell under the spell of Aurora. From the late 1950s through the '70s the Aurora Plastics Corporation produced hundreds of model kits based on subject matter ranging from the usual cars and planes to President Kennedy to movie monsters to a working guillotine. The latter kit—which included a replica of a doomed member of the French aristocracy (in two pieces) and a little basket—was too much for a united front of concerned parents and was quickly yanked from retail shelves.

But the Batman kit thrived, and became one of their all-time best-sellers. In 1964 (two years before the appearance of the *Batman* TV show) someone made the prophetic decision to produce the kit, which is based on the "new look" for the character introduced in the comic books earlier that year. Carmine Infantino and Murphy Anderson drew the art for the box lid, which bore only the faintest resemblance to the actual model and was a reversed image to boot. I always wondered why Batman was removed from his urban setting to swing from a tree, and the bats that were included seemed suspiciously similar to those on Aurora's Dracula model. That didn't stop me, though, from buying and building the kit four times, trying with each attempt to perfect the impossible art of applying just the right amount of glue so that it wouldn't ooze out between the pieces as I squeezed and held them like a vise until they dried. And then came the application of paint, which required a surgeon's patience and steadiness of hand. And the decals, which had to be immersed in water until sticky and fragile as a bee's wings, and gingerly placed exactly where they had to be—you only had one shot.

After the TV show became popular, Aurora followed up with six more kits based on Batman's universe: the Batmobile, the Batboat, the Batplane, the Batcycle, Robin and the Penguin. What better way to feel close to them than to put them together, to give them form, to be able to say we knew them when they were just a heap of colorless pieces?

Right,
ORIGINAL ART
Batman model kit packaging
Carmine Infantino and Murphy Anderson, artists
(ink on photostat paper)
8.5″ x 19.5″
1964

Below,
BATMAN MODEL KIT (box)
13″ x 7.1″ x 2.25″
1964

OVERLEAF
INSTRUCTION SHEET
1964

PAGE 133
BATMAN MODEL KIT (assembled)
{plastic, glue, paint), 10″ tall
1964

FOR SUGGESTED DETAIL PAINTING SCHEME – SEE ILLUSTRATIONS. Paint parts as indicated and allow to dry before assembling.

For best results, use only AURORA'S SPEED-DRY ENAMEL – ONE COAT COVERS – DRIES IN 30 MINUTES – NO BRUSH MARKS.

1

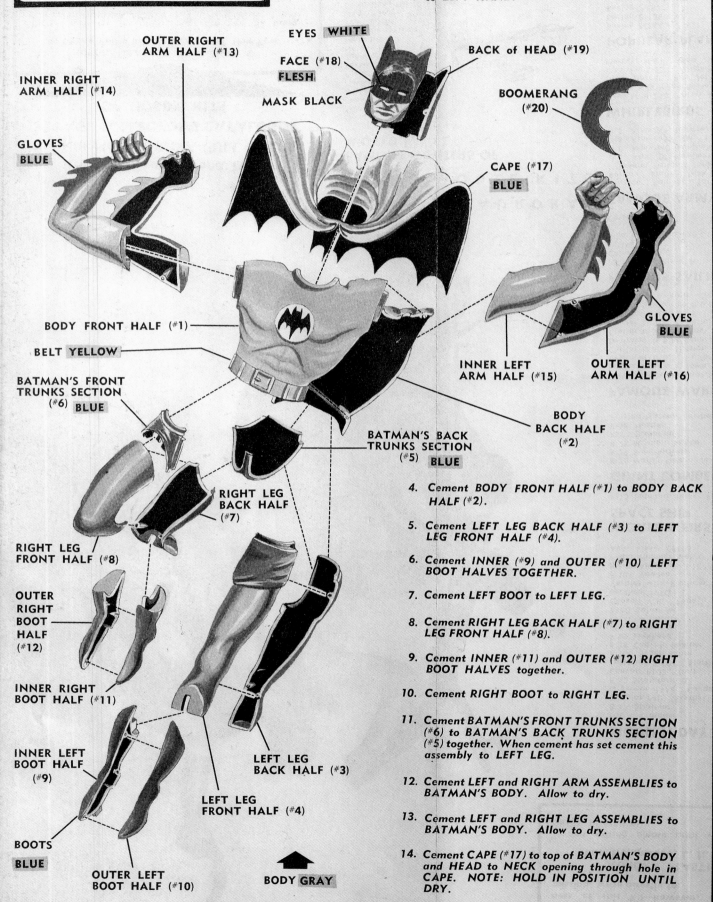

1. *Cement FACE (#18) to BACK of HEAD (#19).*
2. *Cement INNER (#14) and OUTER (#13) RIGHT ARM HALVES together.*
3. *Cement INNER (#15) and OUTER (#16) LEFT ARM HALVES together. Cement SICKLE (#20) to LEFT HAND.*

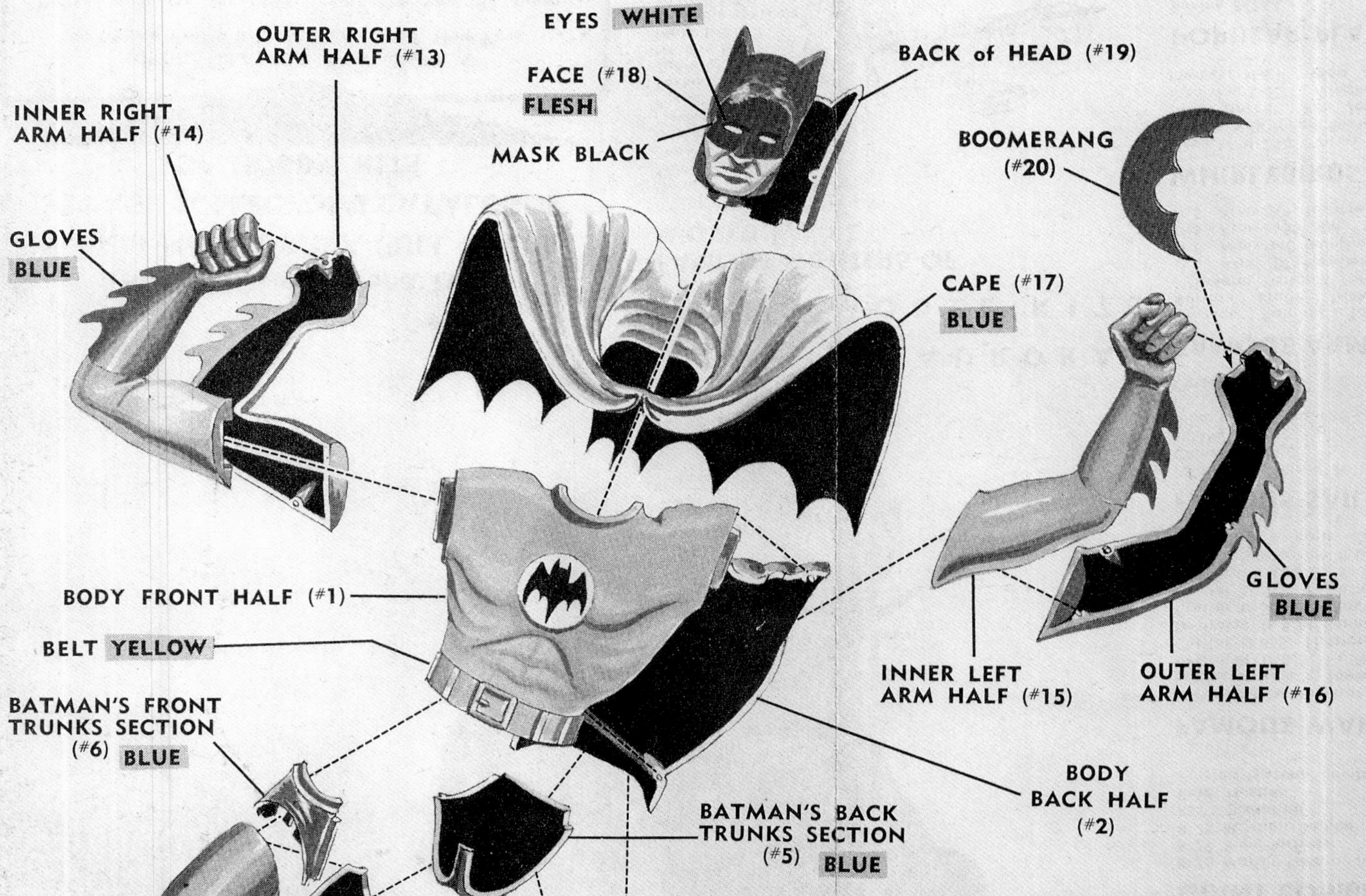

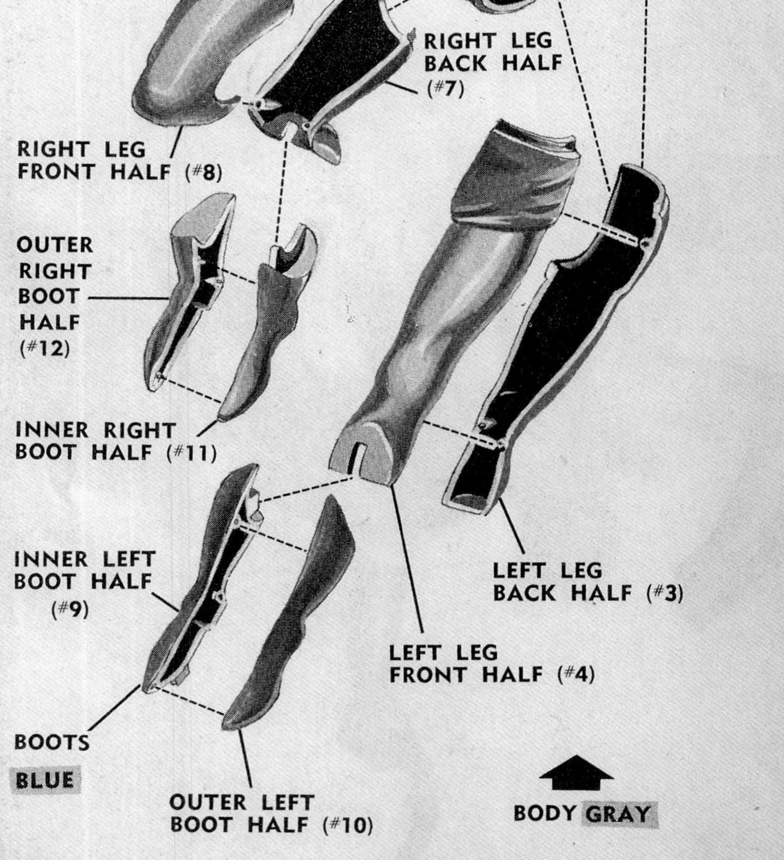

4. *Cement BODY FRONT HALF (#1) to BODY BACK HALF (#2).*
5. *Cement LEFT LEG BACK HALF (#3) to LEFT LEG FRONT HALF (#4).*
6. *Cement INNER (#9) and OUTER (#10) LEFT BOOT HALVES TOGETHER.*
7. *Cement LEFT BOOT to LEFT LEG.*
8. *Cement RIGHT LEG BACK HALF (#7) to RIGHT LEG FRONT HALF (#8).*
9. *Cement INNER (#11) and OUTER (#12) RIGHT BOOT HALVES together.*
10. *Cement RIGHT BOOT to RIGHT LEG.*
11. *Cement BATMAN'S FRONT TRUNKS SECTION (#6) to BATMAN'S BACK TRUNKS SECTION (#5) together. When cement has set cement this assembly to LEFT LEG.*
12. *Cement LEFT and RIGHT ARM ASSEMBLIES to BATMAN'S BODY. Allow to dry.*
13. *Cement LEFT and RIGHT LEG ASSEMBLIES to BATMAN'S BODY. Allow to dry.*
14. *Cement CAPE (#17) to top of BATMAN'S BODY and HEAD to NECK opening through hole in CAPE. NOTE: HOLD IN POSITION UNTIL DRY.*

Shoot all art

3" matt 2 wp

5 5/16" matt 2 wp

12 15/16" matt 2 wp

Shoot all art

Shoot all art

Opposite Above,
COOKIE BOX
Burry Products
10.5″ x 5″ x 4″
1966

Opposite Below,
ORIGINAL ART
Batmobile model kit packaging
(acrylics on canvas)
21.25″ x 9.25″
1966

Below,
BATMOBILE MODEL KIT
Factory-assembled
(plastic, glue, paint)
6.5″ wide
1966

Bottom,
BATMOBILE MODEL KIT (box)
13.125″ x 5.25″ x 1.5″
1966

NATIONAL PERIODICAL PUBLICATIONS I
"BATCYCLE"
ALL PLASTIC ASSEMBLY KIT
AURORA
WITH ROBIN'S DETACHABLE GO KART

Left,
BATCYCLE MODEL KIT
(plastic, glue, paint)
Approx. 5″ tall

Above,
TRADE ADVERTISEMENT

The curious thing about models is that the process of making them, which drives you crazy, must be the whole *point* of making them, because the end product is totally useless. You can't play with them, because of their fragility. You shouldn't even touch them, except to dust them, which isn't exactly a thrill, and they just get dusty all over again. They sit forlornly on the shelf in your room—heroes without a crusade, villains with no despicable deeds to hatch. So you look at them and say, "Hmm. I really didn't do such a great job on *that* one. I think I'll build it one more time. . . ."

Above and Right,
ROBIN MODEL KIT
(plastic, glue, paint)
9″ tall
1966

START
STOP
ROBIN
THE BOY WONDER

Published by
THE WATKINS-STRATHMORE COMPANY
RACINE, WISCONSIN

The longing for toys that do not exist has motivated a new generation of hobbyists to create them for themselves. Once part of an underground movement whose increasing popularity has forced it to the surface, these self-named "Resin Heads," "Toy Geeks" and "Garage Kit Mechanics" are often comics fans who are good with their hands and impatient with toy manufacturers. They invent the toys they always wanted and never got. One of the best of these is Michael Stutelberg, who sells hotel furniture by day and designs and builds tiny planes, cars, boats and helicopters by night, in his basement. One of Michael's obsessions is obscure Bat-vehicles. The Whirly Bat (below) is one of Batman's less practical contraptions from the late '50s, seen at left on a coloring book title page. The Batmobiles of 1950 and the early '60s (next two pages) both exhibit a faithfulness to their source material and a high level of sophisticated craftsmanship.

Left,
COLORING BOOK TITLE PAGE (detail)
8″ x 10.8″
1966

Below,
WHIRLYBAT
Customized by Michael Stutelberg
(molded plastic, paint, model glue), Approx. 3″ tall
1995

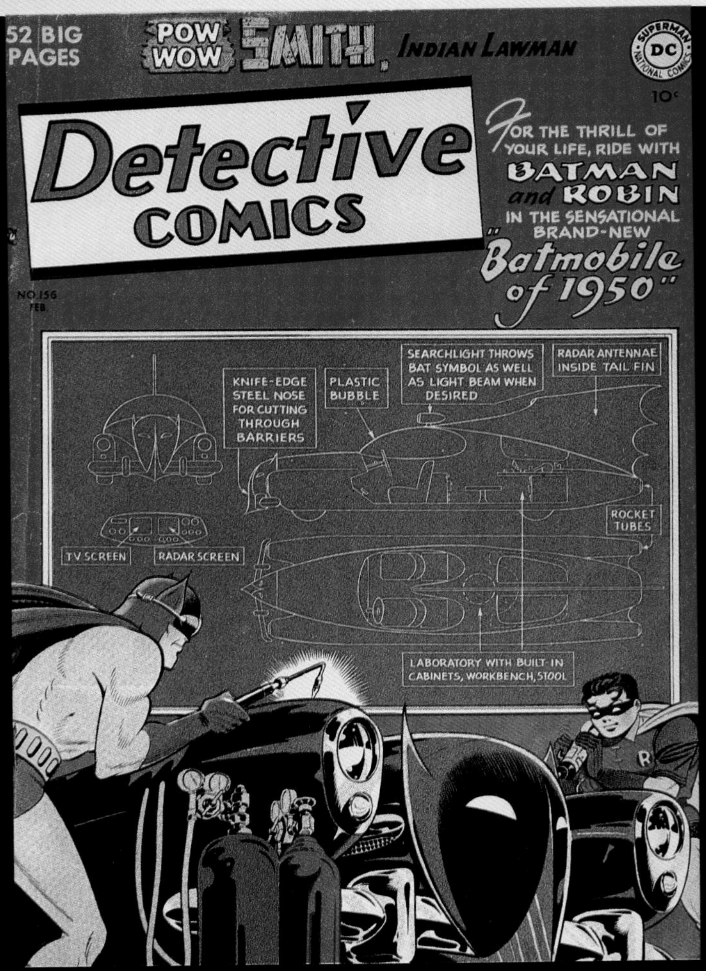

Top,
BATMOBILE (1950 model)
Customized by Michael Stutelberg
(plastic, paint, glue) Approx. 10″ long
1995

Above,
DETECTIVE COMICS #156
Dick Sprang, artist
7.375″ x 10.125″
1950

(plastic, paint, glue) Approx. 8″ long

1996

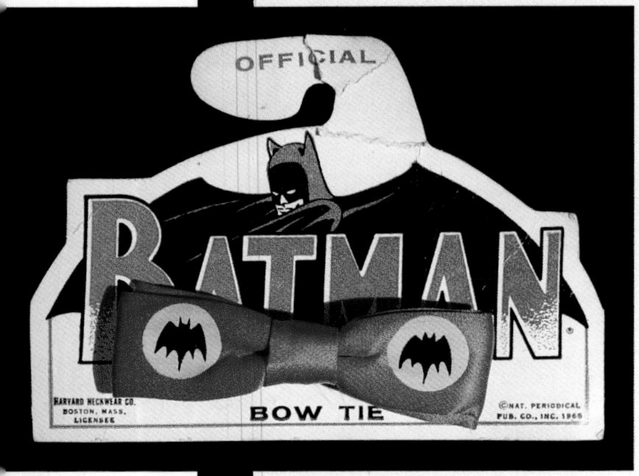

Above,
BOW TIE
Approx. 3.5″ wide
1966

Right,
SNEAKER
Approx. 8″ long
1966

Opposite,
SHORT PANTS
1966

from THE BAT-CAVE
Best Wishes, Batman and Robin
BATMAN
100% COTTON
WASHABLE
SIZE 3
MADE IN U.S.A.

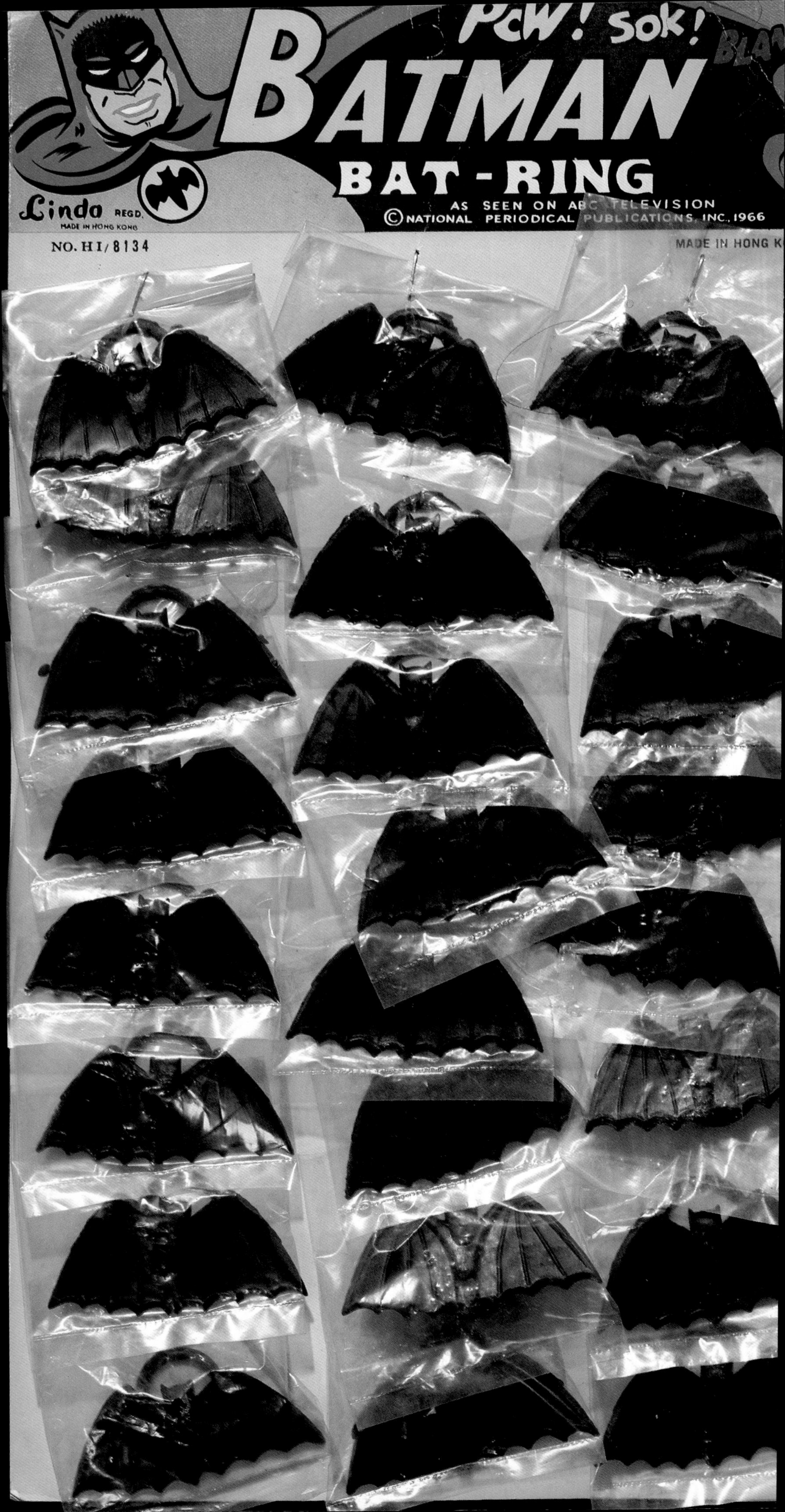

Right,
BAT-RINGS
(black rubber)
2.5″ wide
1966

Left,
WRIST WATCH
Approx. 2.5″ wide
1966

Below,
BAT CYCLE
From the
BATMAN TV series
Customized by
Dan Magiera
1966

Opposite,
BEACH TOWEL
(terry cloth)
36″ x 72″
1966

Opposite Inset,
BUTTON
(unauthorized)
1.5″ in diameter
1968

Below,
EYEGLASS CASE
(cloth over cardboard)
5.5″ wide
1966

Bottom,
CHARM BRACELET
(painted metal)
6.5″ wide
1966

ONCE AGAIN.....
HAVE A BELT ON ME, CHUM!
KAPOW!
© NATIONAL PUB. INC.
PERIODICAL REG. U.S. PAT. OFF.
Send Batman
to Viet-Nam

COLGATE
soaky
THE FUN BATH

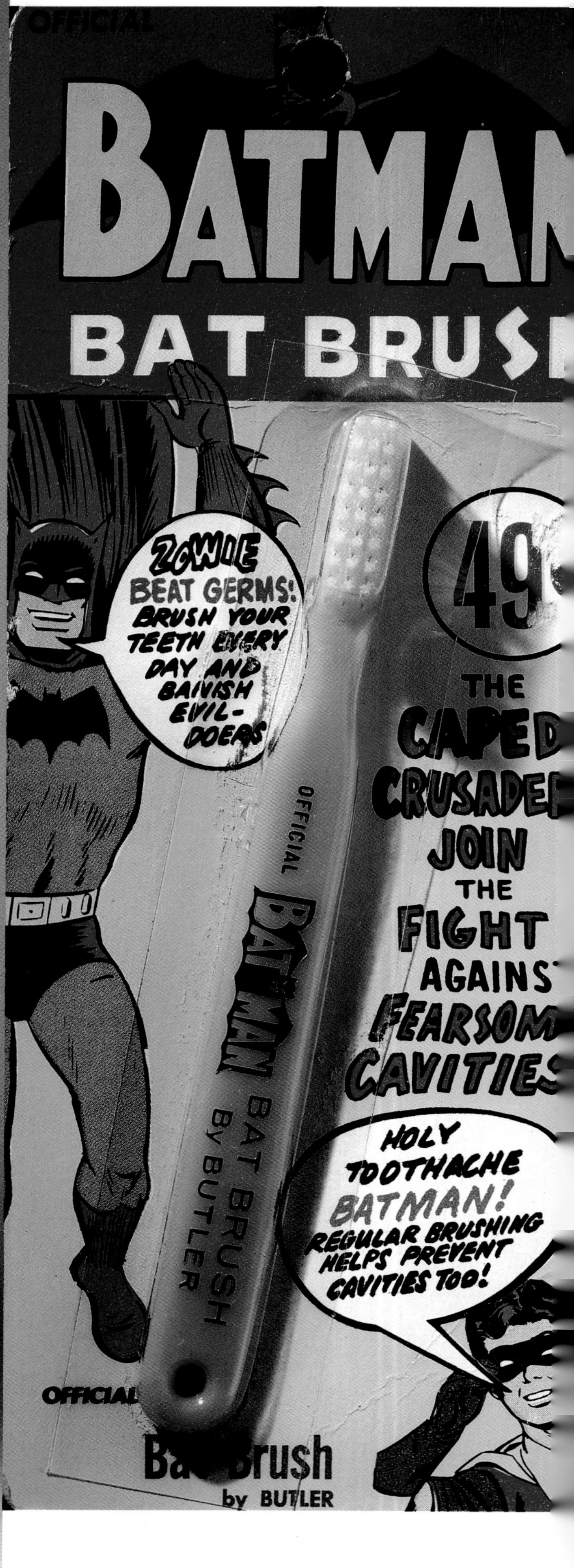
OFFICIAL
ZOWIE
BEAT GERMS!
BRUSH YOUR TEETH EVERY DAY AND BAIVISH EVIL-DOERS
THE
JOIN
THE
FIGHT
OFFICIAL
BATMAN BAT BRUSH
By BUTLER
HOLY TOOTHACHE BATMAN!
REGULAR BRUSHING HELPS PREVENT CAVITIES TOO!
OFFICIAL
Bat Brush
by BUTLER

Below,
TOOTHPASTE AND POSTER OFFER
6″ wide
1966

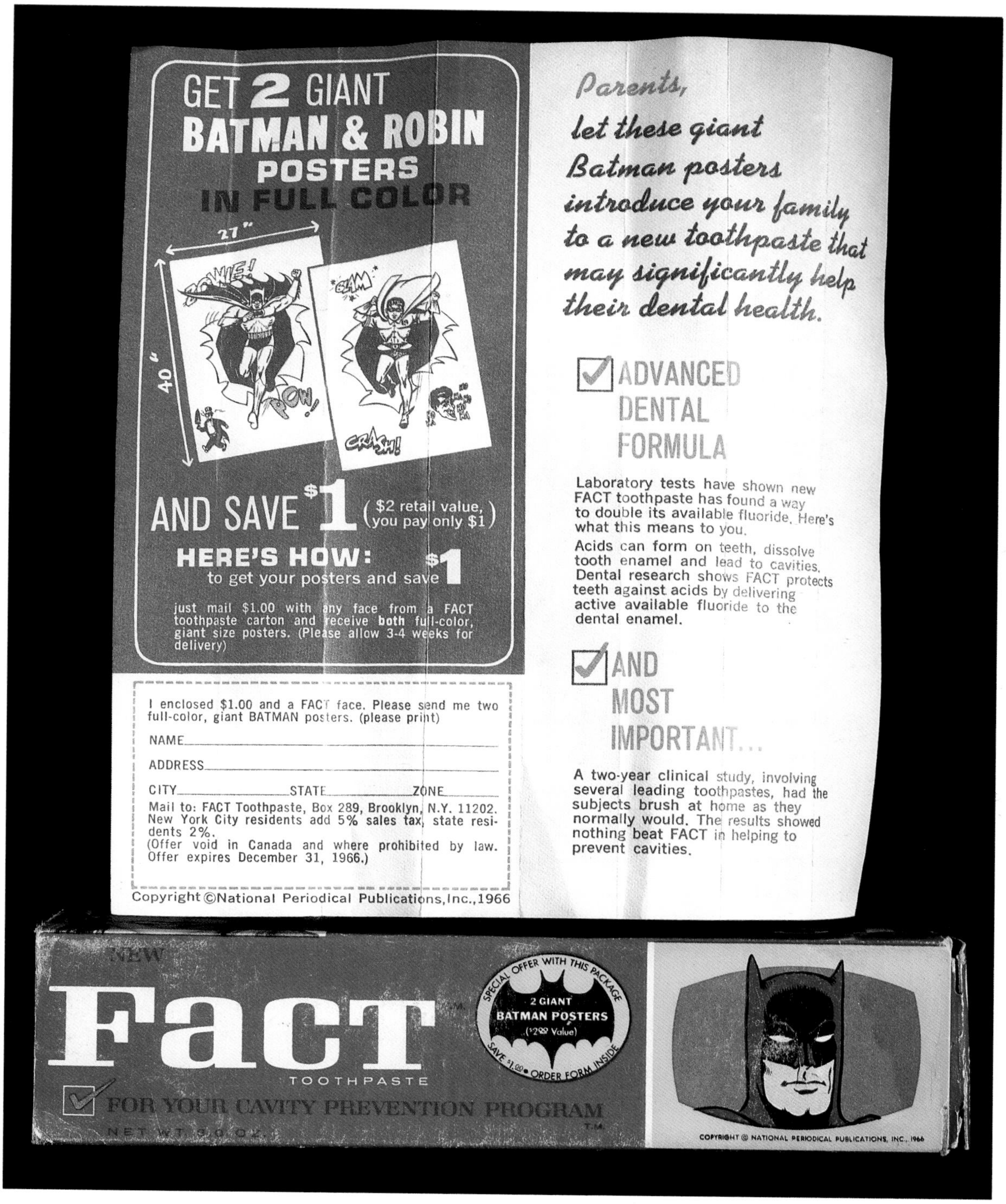

Opposite Left,
BUBBLE BATH BOTTLE
(painted molded plastic)
10″ tall
1966

Opposite Right,
TOOTHBRUSH
(plastic)
5.25″ long
1966

Above and Right,
POSTERS
Mail-in premiums from Fact toothpaste
27″ x 40″
1966

BLAM
HO HA HO HO HA
HO HA
CRASH!

Left and Far Right,
BLANKET 48″ x 55″, 1966

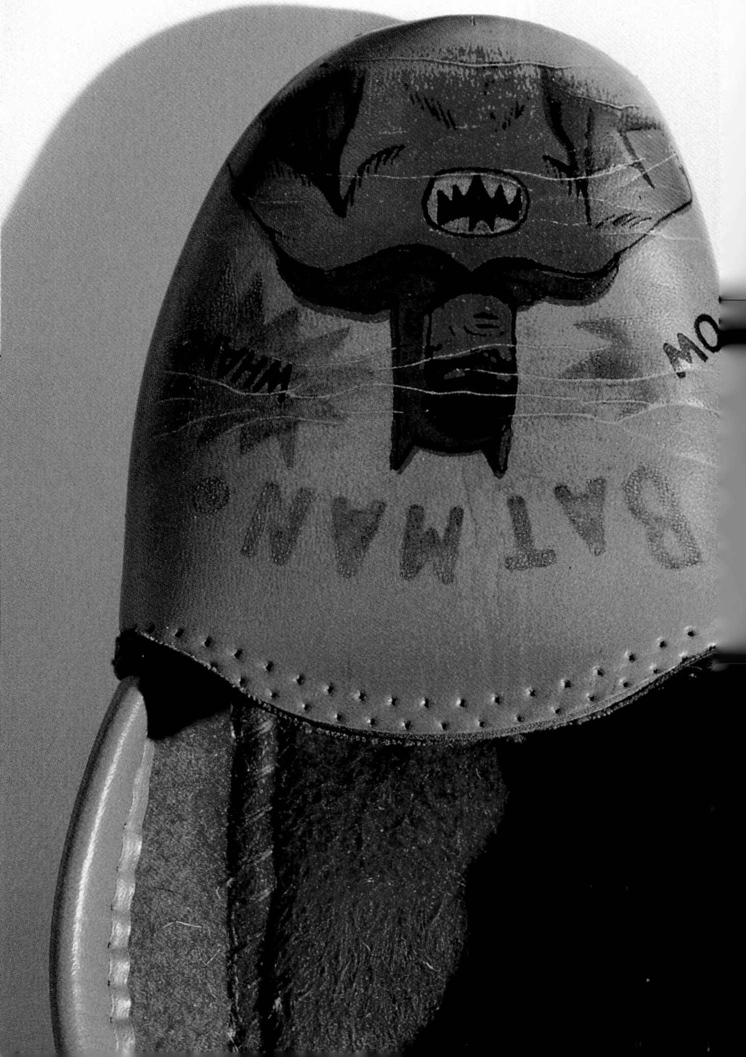

Above and Below,
SLIPPERS (vinyl), 1966

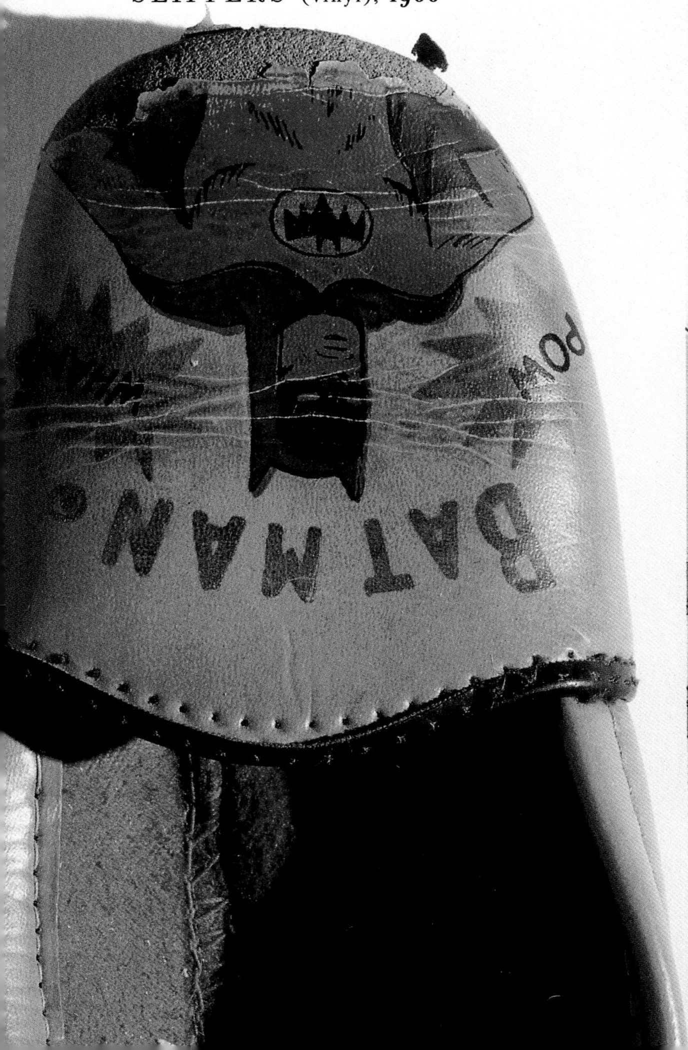

Above,
PAJAMA BAG
(felt)
20.5" tall
1966

RAG DOLL
(plastic. cloth. stuffing)
14.75" tall
1966

Right,
PILLOW
(cloth. stuffing)
11" x 10"
1966

1966

BATMAN
with ROBIN The Boy Wonder
POW!
Design "BATMAN" © National-Periodical-Publications, Inc. 1966.

the PENGUIN V/S
WHAMM!

ft,
ANGING
oth)
x 26″
66

d Bottom,
GUIN
SE KIT
″ tall
66

ow,
Y BOX
3.75″
66

the RiDDLER

ve,
N
al)
diameter
6

ft,
ANGING
th)
26″
6

d Below,
LER
SE KIT
″ tall
6

BATMAN ®
©NATIONAL PERIODICAL PUBLICATIONS, INC., 1966
the JOKER v/s

ft,
NG BAG
69"
66

d Bottom,
KER
SE KIT
tall
66

ow,
N
tal)
diameter
66

Above,
POSTER
28″ x 44″
1966

Right,
COIN BANK
(glazed ceramic)
7″ tall
1966

R

DOLL

unauthorized

(painted plastic)

10" tall

1966

Opposite Above,
PIN
(metal)
.875″ in diameter
1966

Left,
HAND PUPPET
(cloth, molded plastic)
8″ x 6″ x 3″
1966

Below Left,
FRICTION
BATMOBILE
(tin, molded plastic)
4.125″ wide
England
1966

Below,
BEACH TOWEL
(terry cloth)
36″ x 66″
1966

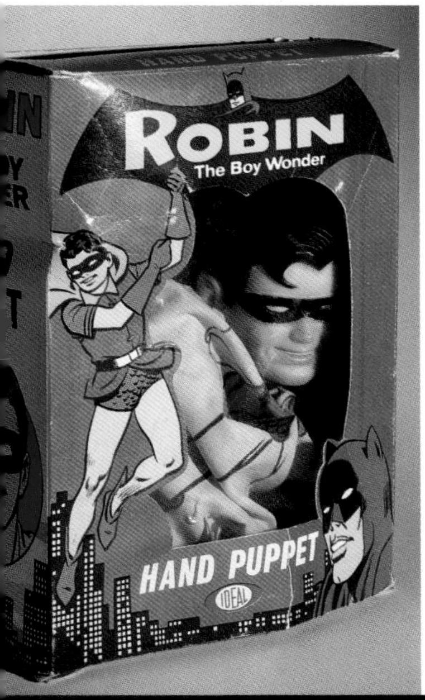

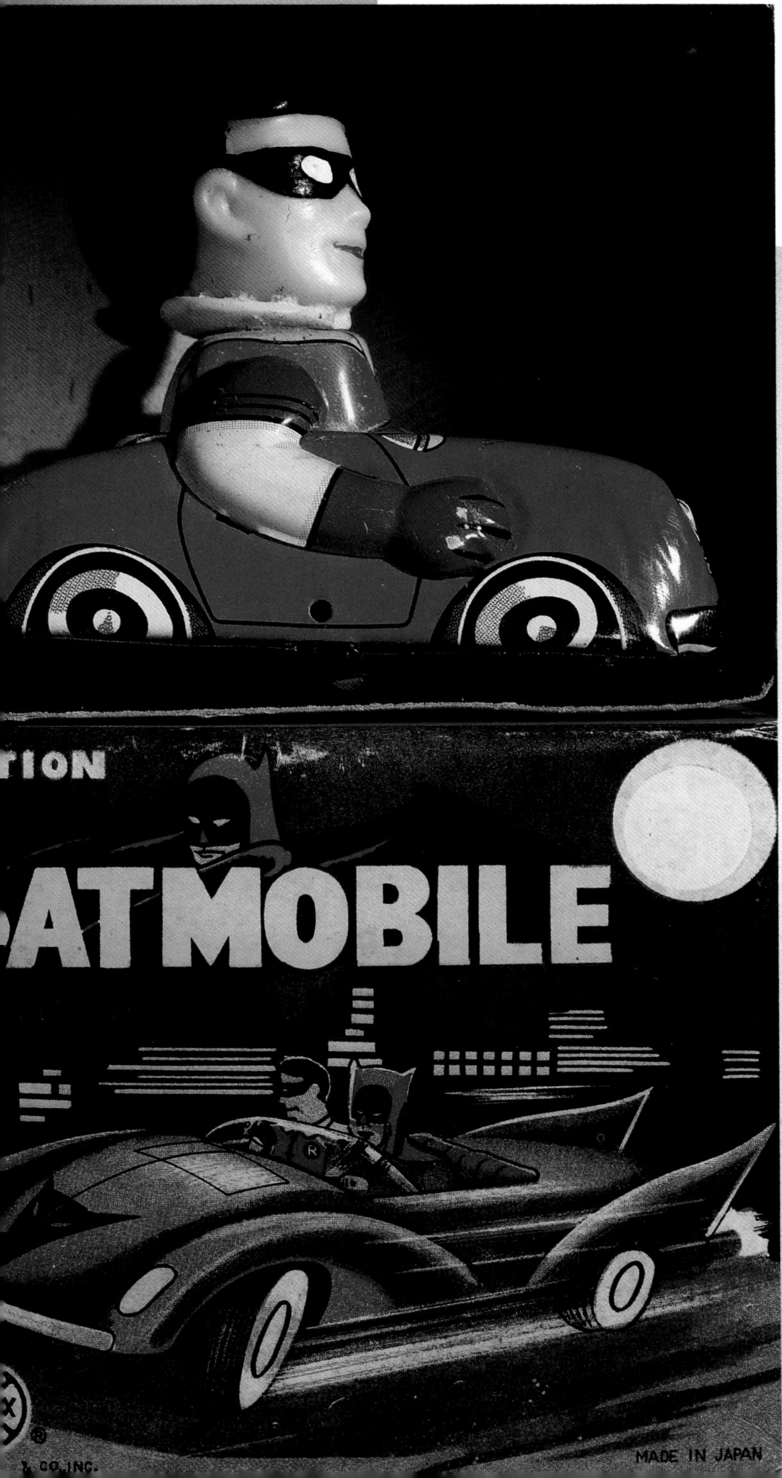

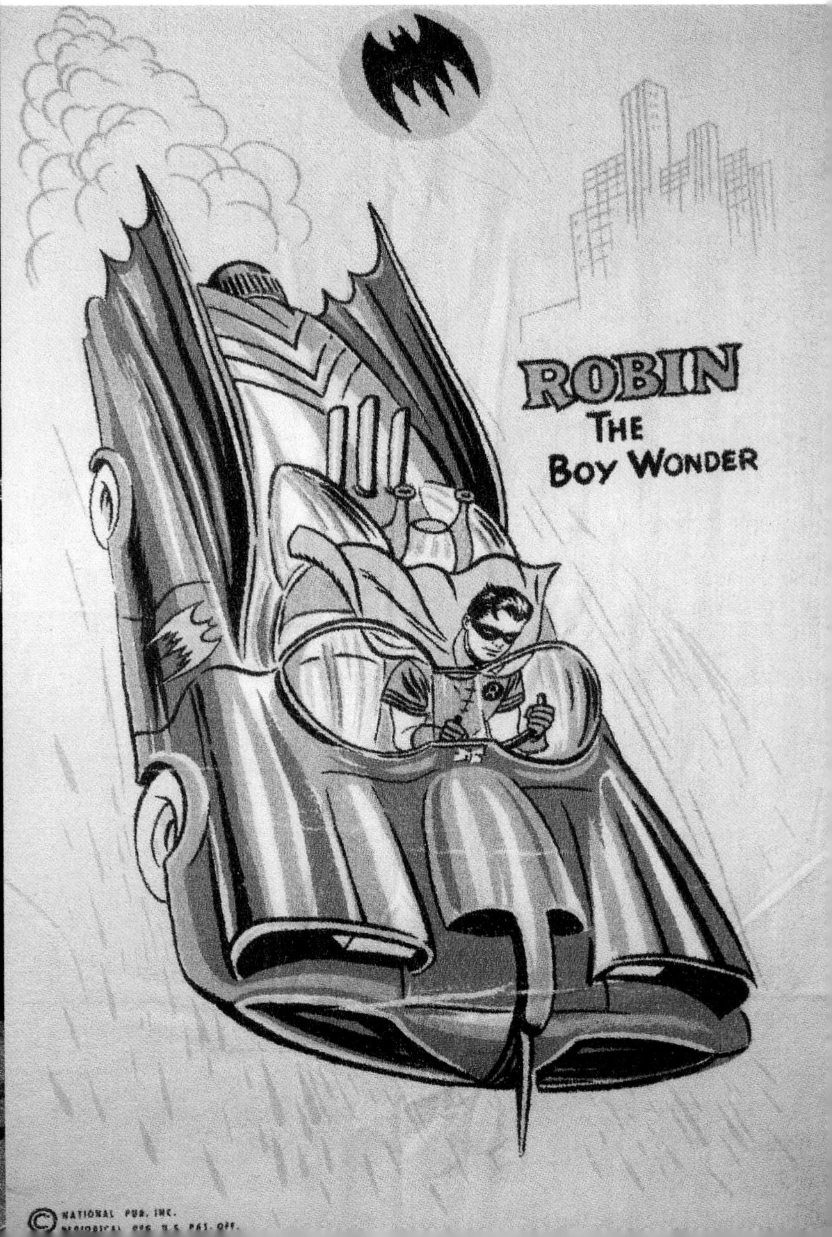

Clockwise, from Top Left:

ALL STAR DAIRY PRODUCTS POSTER
MILK CARTON
CHOCOLATE MILK CARTON
ORANGE DRINK CARTON
JUICE BAR CARTON
ICE CREAM POSTER
FUDGE BAR WRAPPER
MILK POSTER
DRINKING GLASSES
1966

DairyPak
BATMAN®
Y OF CHARACTERS
CUT ON LINE
PENGUIN
CUT ON LINE
CUT OUT & WATCH FOR OTHER CHARACTERS
B-6

BATMAN
HOMOGENIZED VITAMIN D
ONE HALF GALLON LIQUID
COW POW
COPYRIGHT © NATIONAL PERIODICAL PUBLICATIONS, INC., 1966
GRADE A SOFT CURD VITAMIN D
HOMOGENIZED
STANDARDIZED PASTEURIZED
MILK
3.5% BUTTER FAT
ALL STAR DAIRIES
HEADQUARTERS FOR BATMAN DAIRY PRODUCTS
HARMONY FARMS
COLUMBUS OHIO

Reiter and Harter
OPEN
BATMAN
CHOCOLATE FLAVORED MILK
POW
BATMAN MASK
CUT OUT
CUT OUT
GRADE A
PASTEURIZED STANDARDIZED
CHOCOLATE FLAVORED MILK
3.5% BUTTER FAT
CUT OUT & SAVE
B-2
ONE QUART LIQUID

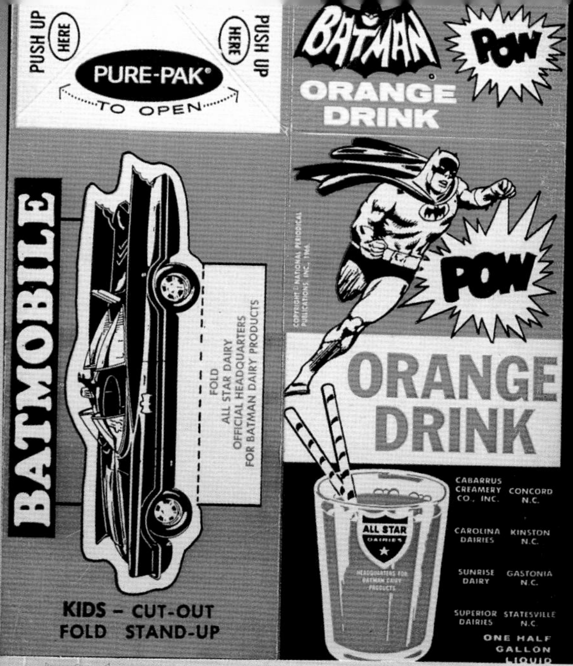
PUSH UP HERE
PURE-PAK®
TO OPEN
PUSH UP HERE
BATMAN
POW
ORANGE DRINK
BATMOBILE
FOLD
ALL STAR DAIRY
OFFICIAL HEADQUARTERS
FOR BATMAN DAIRY PRODUCTS
KIDS – CUT-OUT
FOLD STAND-UP
POW
ORANGE DRINK
ALL STAR DAIRIES
CABARRUS CREAMERY CO., INC. CONCORD N.C.
CAROLINA DAIRIES KINSTON N.C.
SUNRISE DAIRY GASTONIA N.C.
SUPERIOR DAIRIES STATESVILLE N.C.
ONE HALF GALLON LIQUID

Hendrie's ALL STAR
12 ASSORTED FLORIDA JUICE BARS
NET CONTENTS 12 CONFECTIONS
SCREEE

BATMAN
12 FLORIDA
JUICE BARS
ORANGE LEMON LIME
VITAMIN C ENRICHED
Hendrie's ALL STAR
ZAP!
MFD. BY HENDRIE'S, INC., MILTON, MASS.

12 ASSORTED FLORIDA JUICE BARS

BATMOBILE
KIDS – CUT-OUT
FOLD STAND-UP

SLAM BANG
VANILLA
ICE CREAM
WITH BANANA MARSHMALLOW
by
ALL STAR
ICE CREAM

BATMAN
and ROBIN
TAR

W. H. MARVIN CO. URBANA, OHIO, U.S.A.
BATMAN
NET WT.
16 OZ.
Everbest® BAT
PURE Apple Jelly
©1966 NATIONAL PERIODICAL PUBLICATIONS, INC.
W. H. MARVIN CO., URBANA, OHIO, U.S.A.
POW
GET 5 BATMAN
PENNANTS
BATMAN
ROBIN
JOKER
RIDDLER
PENGUIN
4"x 9"
BATMAN
SEND 50¢ AND ANY PART OF THE LABEL TO:
BATMAN (Pennant) BOX 48
PT. WASHINGTON, N. Y. 11050
NET WT. 16 OZ.
BATMAN
SOK!
PURE
ORANGE
MARMALADE
SUGAR, ORANGE PEEL, WATER,
ORANGE JUICE, FRUIT ACID, CITRUS PECTIN
INC., GARDEN CITY PARK, NEW YORK, U.S.A.
NET WT.
1 LB. 4 OZ.

Opposite Above,
LUNCH BOX AND THERMOS
(lithographed tin)
8″ x 7.5″ x 3.75″
1966

Below,
SOFT DRINK BOTTLE
12″ tall
1966

CONTENTS
ONE QUART
Cott®
QUALITY
BATMAN®
Sparkling
COLA
AUTHORITY OF COTT CORPORATION MANCHESTER, N. H.

Opposite Below,
JELLY and MARMALADE JARS
5.5″ tall
1966

Left,
SPOON AND FORK
(stainless steel)
4.5″ x 10″
1966

Below,
BREAD BAG
(ink on sheet plastic)
8.5″ x 14.5″
1966

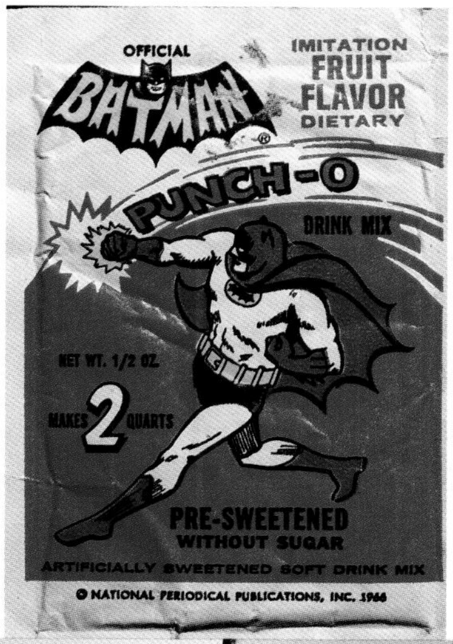

Right,
DRINK MIX
1966

Below,
BREAKFAST CEREAL
(boxes)
1966

Above and Below,
CANDY BOXES
(with retail display box)
2.5″ x 3.75″
1966

Left,
PEZ DISPENSER
(molded plastic)
Approx. 4.25″ tall
1966

Below,
CANDY BOX
2.5″ x 3.75″
1966

THE MEGO DECADE

Batman toys in the 1970s were largely the domain of the Mego company, which produced its first Batman doll in 1972, seen at left and below. It was part of "The World's Greatest Superheroes" collection, which included Robin, Superman, Aquaman, Captain America and Tarzan. The company's idea was to make the figures eight inches tall, four inches shorter than GI Joe. While this might not seem like an innovation on the order of the electric toaster, in terms of sales it had an equally dramatic effect. To this day, toy collectors refer to any doll that is eight inches high as "Mego-sized."

The dolls were inexpensive and didn't need extra clothes. The first editions of Batman and Robin had removable masks, which were immediately lost by most young consumers. New dolls with the masks permanently attached soon followed. Visually, there was little to distinguish this version of the Caped Crusader from the way he looked in 1966. He still seemed to be relentlessly upbeat.

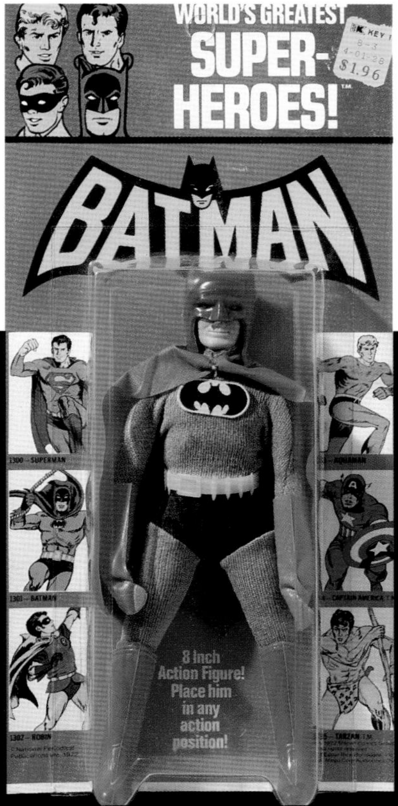

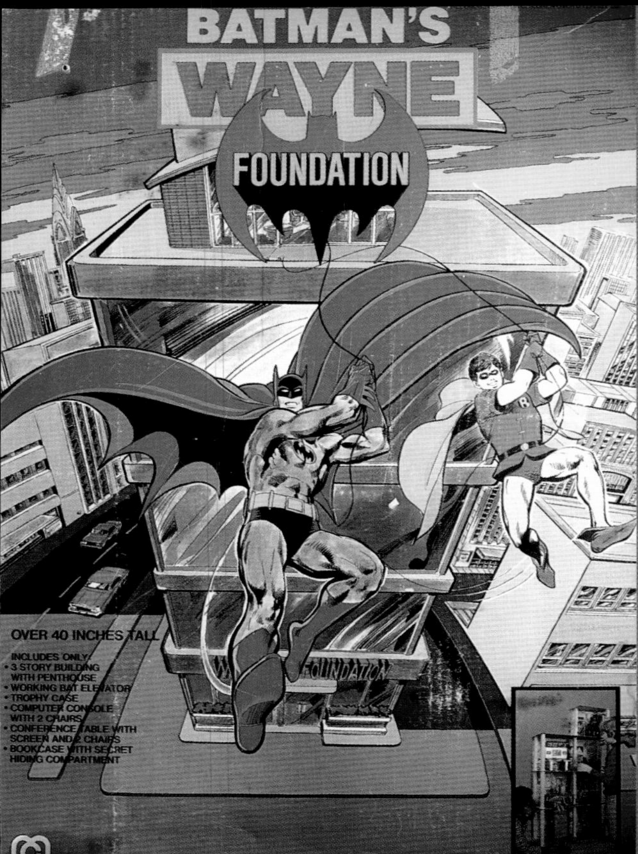

Above,
WAYNE FOUNDATION
(packaging,
front and back)
17.25″ x 25.25″ x 4.75″
1977

Left,
BRUCE WAYNE DOLL
Montgomery Ward exclusive
8″ tall, 1974

Left,
BATCOPTER
(plastic)
7.5″ tall
1974

Left,
JOKER MOBILE and
MOBILE BAT LAB
(packaging)
15.25″ x 7.75″ x 8.75″
1975

Below,
BATCAVE
(packaging)
15.6″ x 11.5″ x 5.7″
1974

Opposite,
BATMAN SUPER SOFTIE
(detail)
(plastic, polyester)
18″ tall
1978

Right,
BATMAN TALKING SUPER SOFTIE
(prototype)
(plastic, polyester)
24″ tall
1978

Above,
DOLL
(packaging)
3″ x 9″
1973

Above,
DOLL
(plastic, polyester)
8″ tall
Japan
1979

Above,
DOLL
(plastic, polyester)
8″ tall
1973

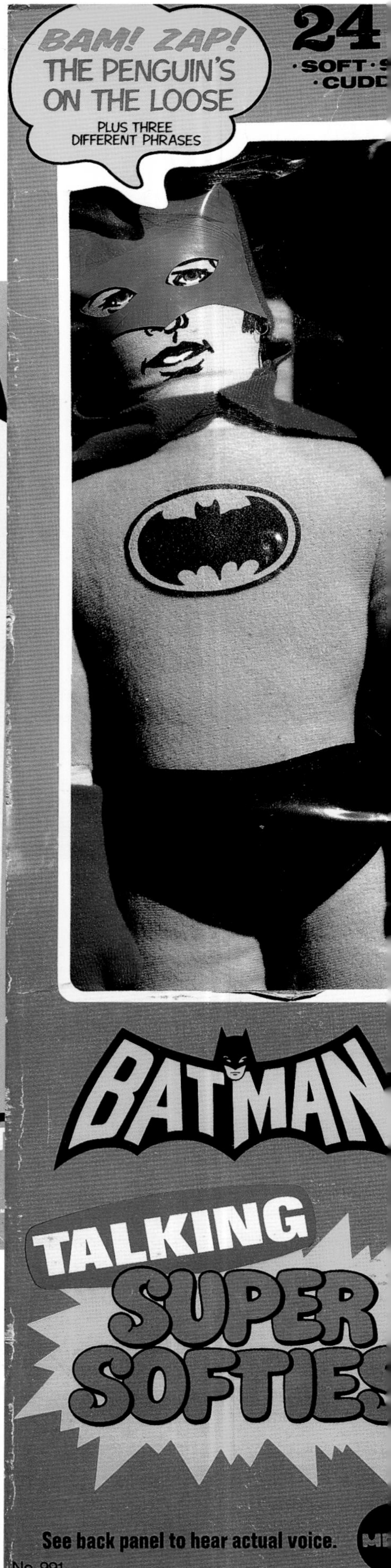

Above,
PENGUIN COIN BANK
(molded plastic)
Approx. 8″ tall
1974

Right,
BATMAN DOLL WITH
MAGNETIC HANDS AND FEET
(detail)
12″ tall
1979

Far Right,
JOKER COIN BANK
(molded plastic)
Approx. 8″ tall
1974

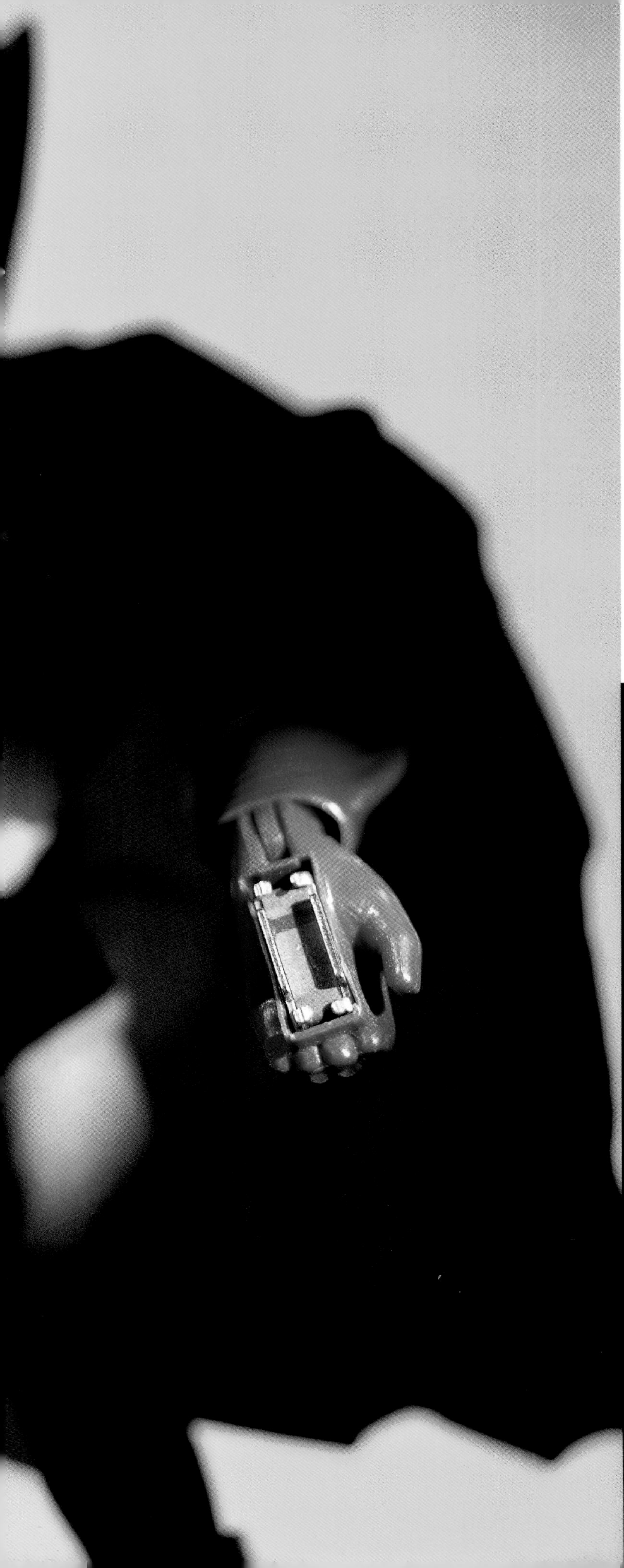

The Mego toys were extremely popular, and the company expanded its product line to meet the demand. One of the odder ideas was for a Batman doll with magnetic hands and feet that could stick to refrigerators or to its accompanying Robin doll. The usual array of Bat-vehicles soon appeared too, as well as the Batcave and an unusually large structure called the Wayne Foundation, the name of Bruce Wayne's corporation in the comics. In 1974, the Montgomery Ward catalogue featured exclusive "alter ego" outfits for Batman, Robin, Superman and Spider-Man, so that they could change into (respectively) Bruce Wayne (p. 180), Dick Grayson, Clark Kent and Peter Parker. The low distribution of this catalogue and the ensuing widespread lack of interest in the offer has today lent these dolls a value akin to that of a bottle of Chateau d'Yquem of the same year. This is even more amusing when you consider their appearance.

Equally scarce are the "Talking Super Softies" (p. 182), 24-inch-stuffed dolls with voice boxes that are activated by pulling a string. Their existence seemed just a rumor until I plundered the DC Comics archives; the one I found said, "I love you!" and "I'm your little huggie bear!" when the string was yanked. These two extremely un-Batmanlike sentiments would seem to indicate that this was a prototype with another toy's voice-box inside.

Top,
UTILITY BELT
(plastic)
Approx. 14″ wide
1978

Above,
COIN BANK
(plastic)
7.625″x 7.5″
England
1970s

Opposite Bottom,
AIR FRESHENERS
(scented cardboard, string)
Approx. 5″ tall
1974

Right,
BRASS MOLD
FOR A PUPPET HEAD
Approx. 4″ tall
1978

Below,
BATMAN
EXECUTIVE SET
(packaging)
12″ x 8″ x 5″
1978

Above,
GREETING CARDS
4″ x 9.25″
1978

Right,
MARIONETTE
In retail store display
(plastic, polyester, cord)
Approx. 11″ tall
1978

Left,
PATCHES
(embroidered cloth)
3.25″ x 3.75″
1974

Right,
POGO STICK
(plastic, metal, spring
Approx. 48″ tall
1978

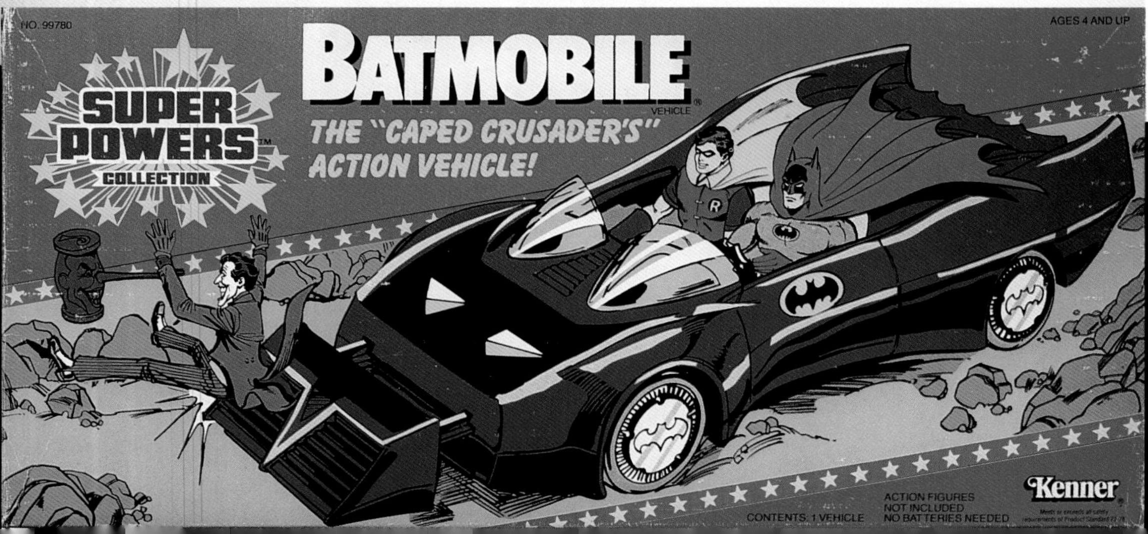

Left,
SUPER POWERS BATMAN AND ROBIN IN SUPER POWERS BATMOBILE
(plastic)
Figures 5″ tall; car 12″ long
1985

Opposite Right,
PUBLIC SERVICE ADVERTISEMENT
1980

Left,
NIGHT LIGHT
(ceramic)
Approx. 7″ tall
Japan
1989

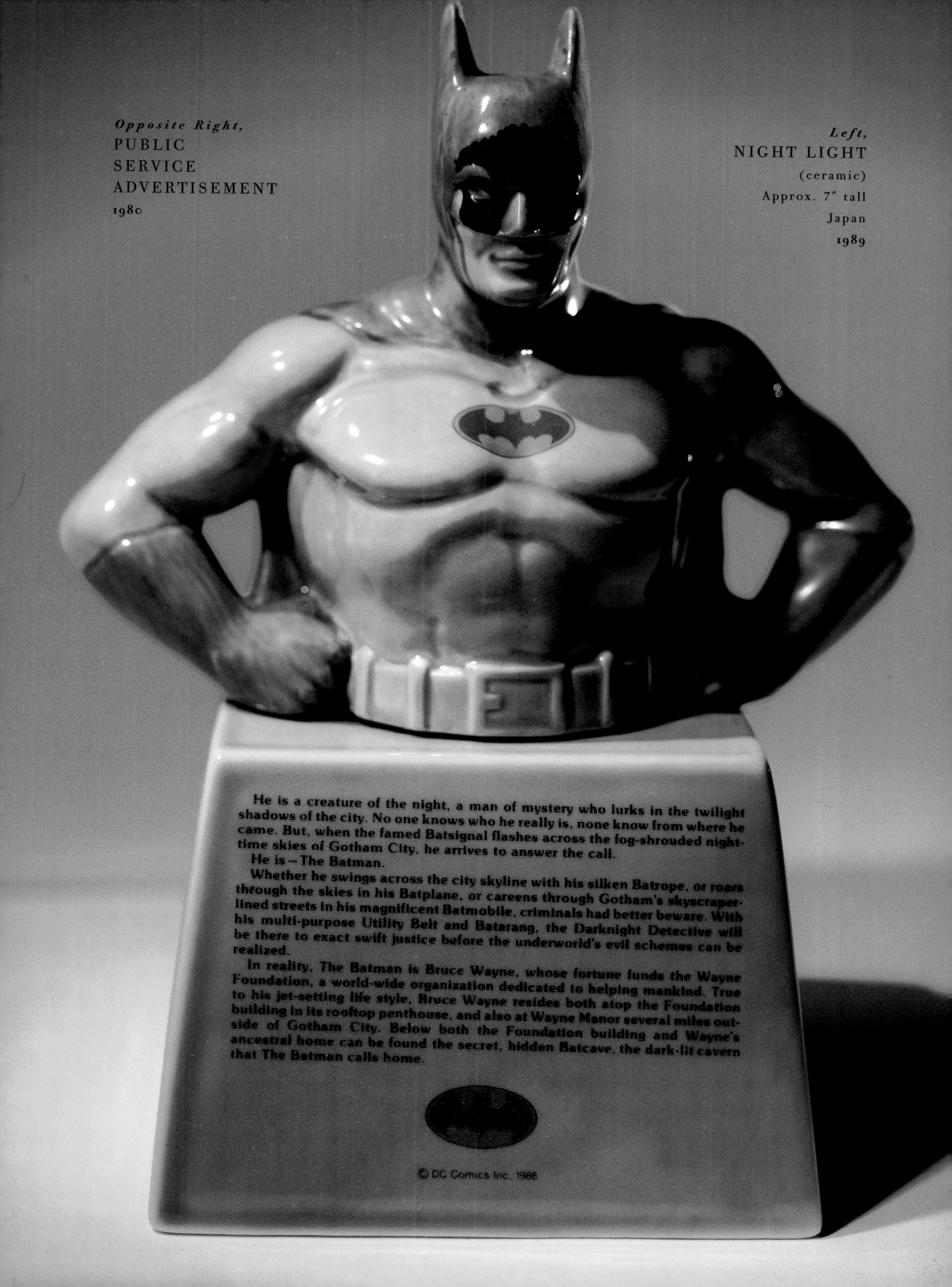

He is a creature of the night, a man of mystery who lurks in the twilight shadows of the city. No one knows who he really is, none know from where he came. But, when the famed Batsignal flashes across the fog-shrouded night-time skies of Gotham City, he arrives to answer the call.
He is—The Batman.
Whether he swings across the city skyline with his silken Batrope, or roars through the skies in his Batplane, or careens through Gotham's skyscraper-lined streets in his magnificent Batmobile, criminals had better beware. With his multi-purpose Utility Belt and Batarang, the Darknight Detective will be there to exact swift justice before the underworld's evil schemes can be realized.
In reality, The Batman is Bruce Wayne, whose fortune funds the Wayne Foundation, a world-wide organization dedicated to helping mankind. True to his jet-setting life style, Bruce Wayne resides both atop the Foundation building in its rooftop penthouse, and also at Wayne Manor several miles outside of Gotham City. Below both the Foundation building and Wayne's ancestral home can be found the secret, hidden Batcave, the dark-lit cavern that The Batman calls home.
© DC Comics Inc. 1986

Left,
PIÑATA
(papier-mâché)
Approx. 18″ tall
Mexico
LATE 1980S

Above,
UNDEROOS
BATMAN
UNDERWEAR
Packaging
1983

Above,
SNORKEL SET
(black rubber, glass)
11″ x 18″
1991

Above,
SNOW GLOBE
Unauthorized
(glass, liquid,
glitter and wood)
6″ tall
1994

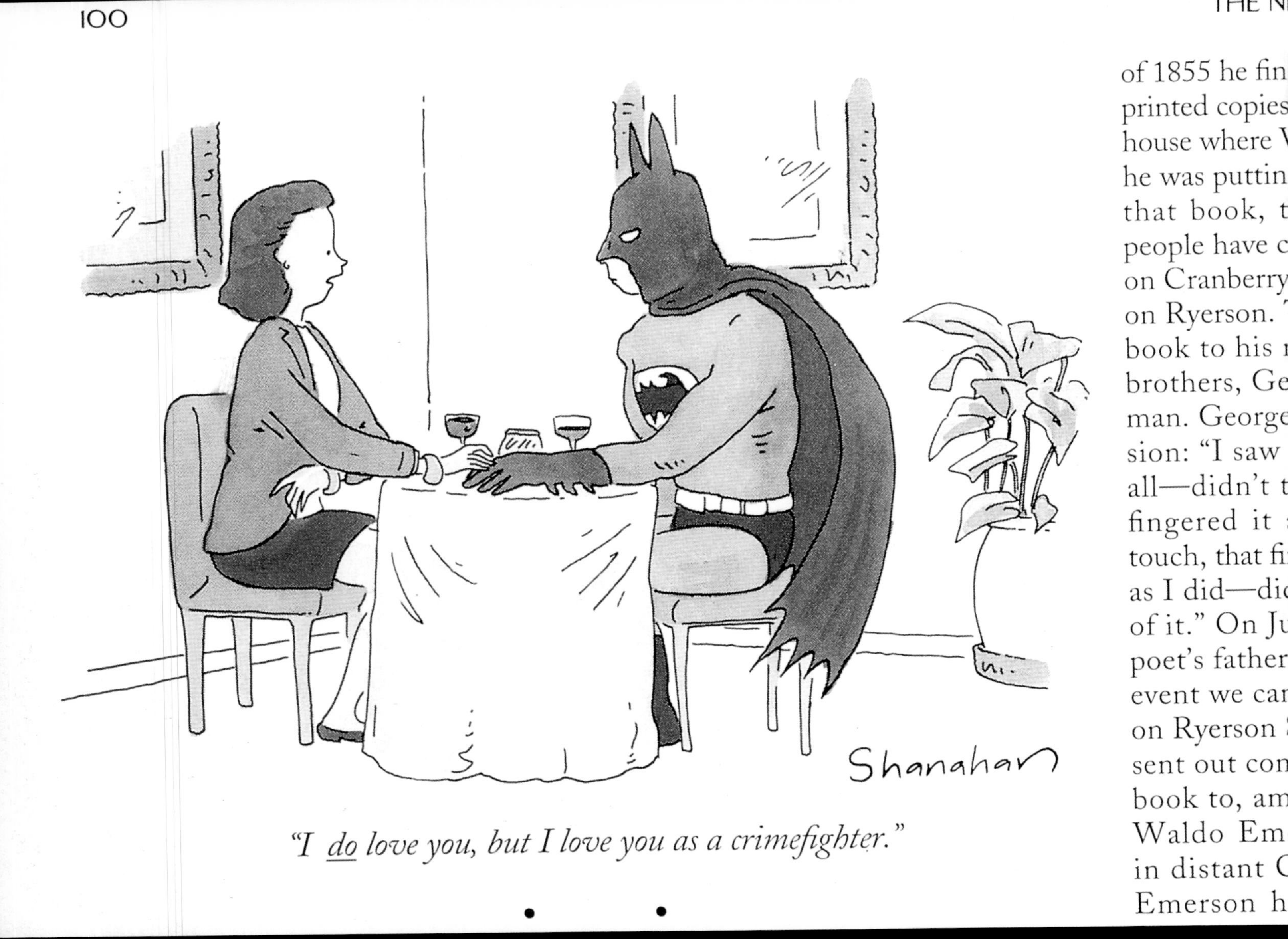
100 THE N

of 1855 he fin
printed copies
house where W
he was puttin
that book, t
people have c
on Cranberry
on Ryerson.
book to his r
brothers, Ge
man. George
sion: "I saw
all—didn't t
fingered it
touch, that fi
as I did—dic
of it." On Ju
poet's father
event we car
on Ryerson S
sent out con
book to, am
Waldo Em
in distant C
Emerson h

"I do love you, but I love you as a crimefighter."

Above,
CARTOON
From THE NEW YORKER
Drawing by Danny Shanahan

Opposite Top Right,
CLOCK
(ceramic, glass)
5.5″ wide
Japan
1989

Opposite Top Left,
CROSSWORD PUZZLE
From THE NEW YORK TIMES
Will Shortz, editor
1996

Opposite Bottom,
UNAUTHORIZED FIGURE
(plastic)
Approx. 5″ tall
Mexico
1995

d | Edited by Will

43 Not much
45 Bills
47 1915 Gallipoli fighter
51 By the —— (what's more)
53 Some canines
54 Actress Lords of "A Time to Die"
55 Some Arab kings
57 "Vissi d'——" (Puccini aria)
58 Outward, in anatomy
59 Carried away
61 View from Basel
62 Therapy
63 Part of PBS: Abbr.
64 Phone book info

DOWN

1 Masked savior
2 Constellation south of Cygnus

Puzzle b

11 Au
"Th

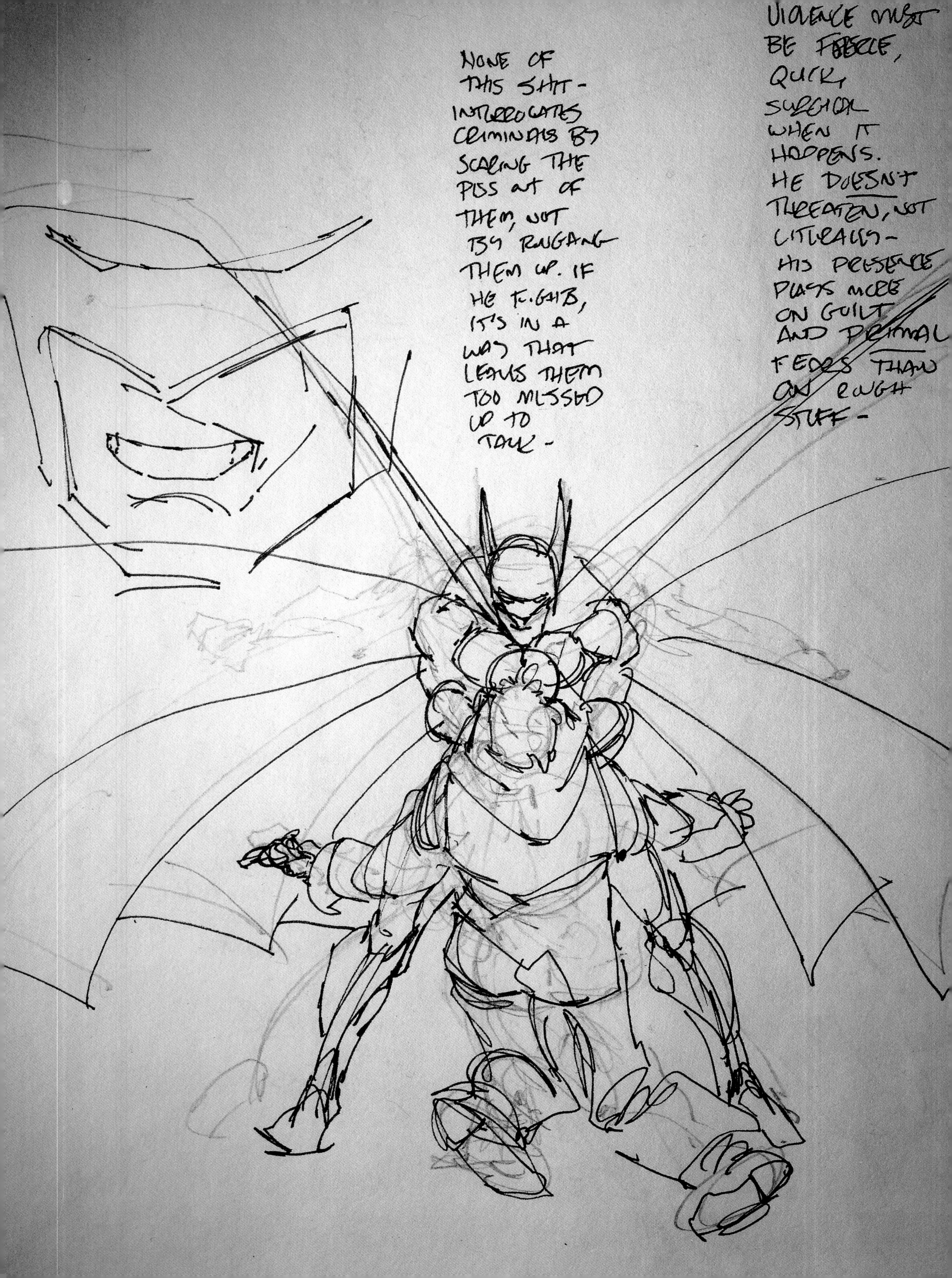
NONE OF THIS SHIT - INTERROGATES CRIMINALS BY SCARING THE PISS OUT OF THEM, NOT BY ROUGHING THEM UP. IF HE FIGHTS, IT'S IN A WAY THAT LEAVES THEM TOO MESSED UP TO TALK -
VIOLENCE MUST BE FIERCE, QUICK, SURGICAL WHEN IT HAPPENS. HE DOESN'T THREATEN, NOT LITERALLY - HIS PRESENCE PLAYS MORE ON GUILT AND PRIMAL FEARS THAN ON ROUGH STUFF -

1986:

THE NEW ERA BEGINS

The Dark Knight Returns is artist and writer Frank Miller's gift to Batman, and to comic book history. In just four 32-page issues, released in the summer of 1986, the books single-handedly revived worldwide interest in Batman and enticed people who normally wouldn't be caught dead reading a comic book to do just that. It could be convincingly argued that its success made Hollywood realize that a new Batman movie (in "development hell" for seven years already) could have a mass audience. How did it—or rather, he—do this?

First of all, by telling a great story. Remember, Batman is a fictional character. He is only as effective as whoever is writing or drawing his exploits. Miller proved to be brilliant at both, and he had an inspired idea. He asked himself this question: What would be the last Batman story? The answer was a saga that takes place in the near future. Batman, pushing sixty, has been in retirement for ten years, having called it quits after Jason Todd (Robin number two, Dick Grayson's successor) is murdered by the Joker. Crime in Gotham City has reached crisis proportions, but an increasingly alcoholic Bruce Wayne no longer cares. Batman, however, still does. He is a memory and a voice inside of Wayne, taunting him to be freed. "You try to drown me out . . . but your voice is weak," he says. "You cannot escape me . . . for I am your soul." Of course, he is right.

Soon, Gotham City police phone lines are jammed with reports of "battered, wounded criminals" and sightings of "a large, bat-like creature. . . ."

Left,
NOTEBOOK PAGE
Featuring preparatory sketches and notes for
THE DARK KNIGHT RETURNS
Frank Miller, artist
(pencil, pen and ink on paper)
1985

Right,
THE DARK KNIGHT RETURNS #1
(cover)
Frank Miller and Lynn Varley, artists
6.5″ x 10″
1986

Below,
RETAIL STORE DISPLAY (detail)
For THE DARK KNIGHT RETURNS
(cardboard)
7″ x 12″
1986

"This should be *agony*. But... I'm born *again*."

from THE DARK KNIGHT RETURNS #1, by Frank Miller, 1986

Left,
UNAUTHORIZED "GARAGE KIT" FIGURE
Based on THE DARK KNIGHT RETURNS, by Frank Miller
(polychrome on cold-cast plaster)
Approx. 8″ tall
1993

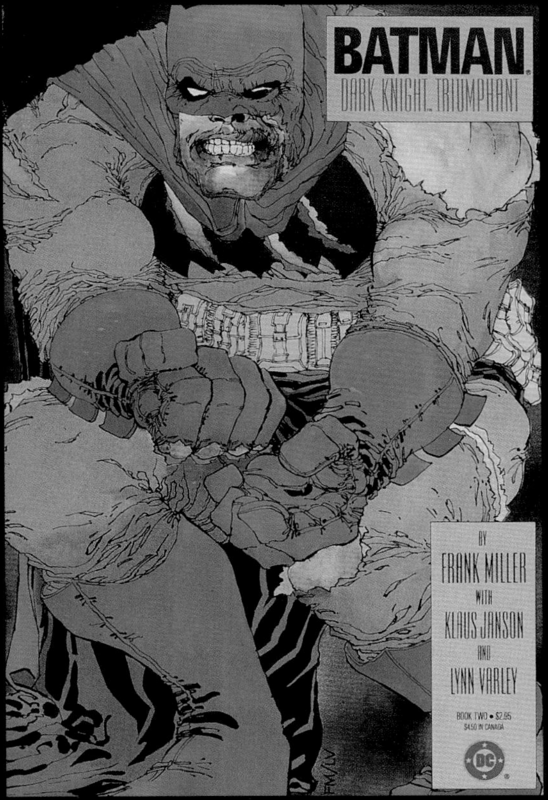

Above,
THE DARK KNIGHT RETURNS #2
"The Dark Knight Triumphant"
(cover)
Frank Miller and Lynn Varley, artists
6.5″ x 10″
1986

FRANK MILLER – DAREDEVIL'S NEW WRITER! SEE "NEWSWATCH"!
The Comics Journal
No. 101 ■ $2.95
$3.95 in Canada
The Magazine of News & Criticism
FRANK MILLER INTERVIEW
Jan Strnad on "Shatter"
Summer Reading
"Executive's Forum" with Mike Gold

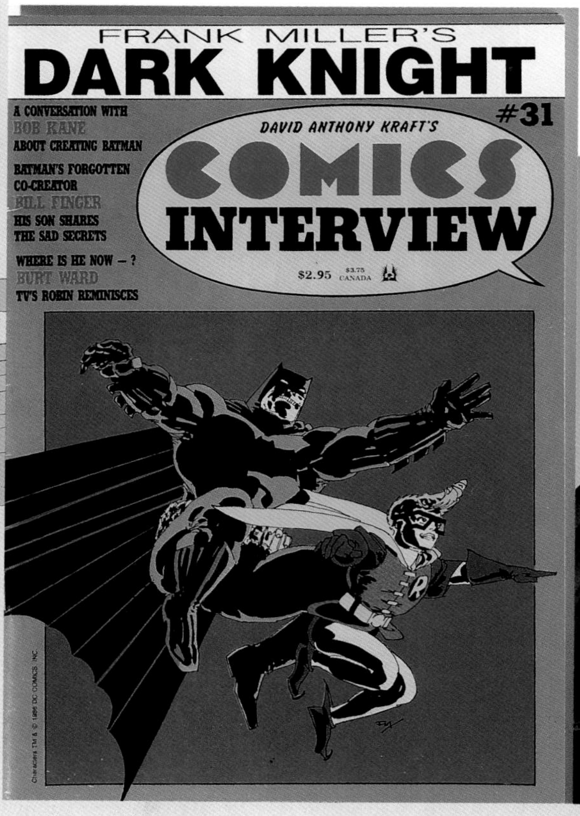
FRANK MILLER'S
DARK KNIGHT
#31
A CONVERSATION WITH
BOB KANE
ABOUT CREATING BATMAN
BATMAN'S FORGOTTEN CO-CREATOR
BILL FINGER
HIS SON SHARES THE SAD SECRETS
WHERE IS HE NOW – ?
BURT WARD
TV'S ROBIN REMINISCES
DAVID ANTHONY KRAFT'S
COMICS INTERVIEW
$2.95
$3.75 CANADA

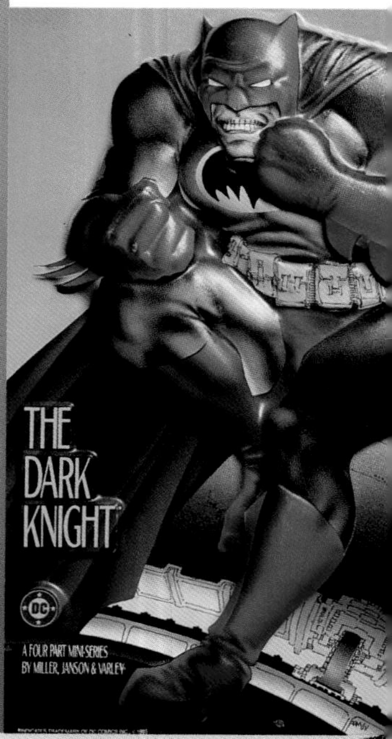
THE DARK KNIGHT
A FOUR PART MINI-SERIES
BY MILLER, JANSON & VARLEY

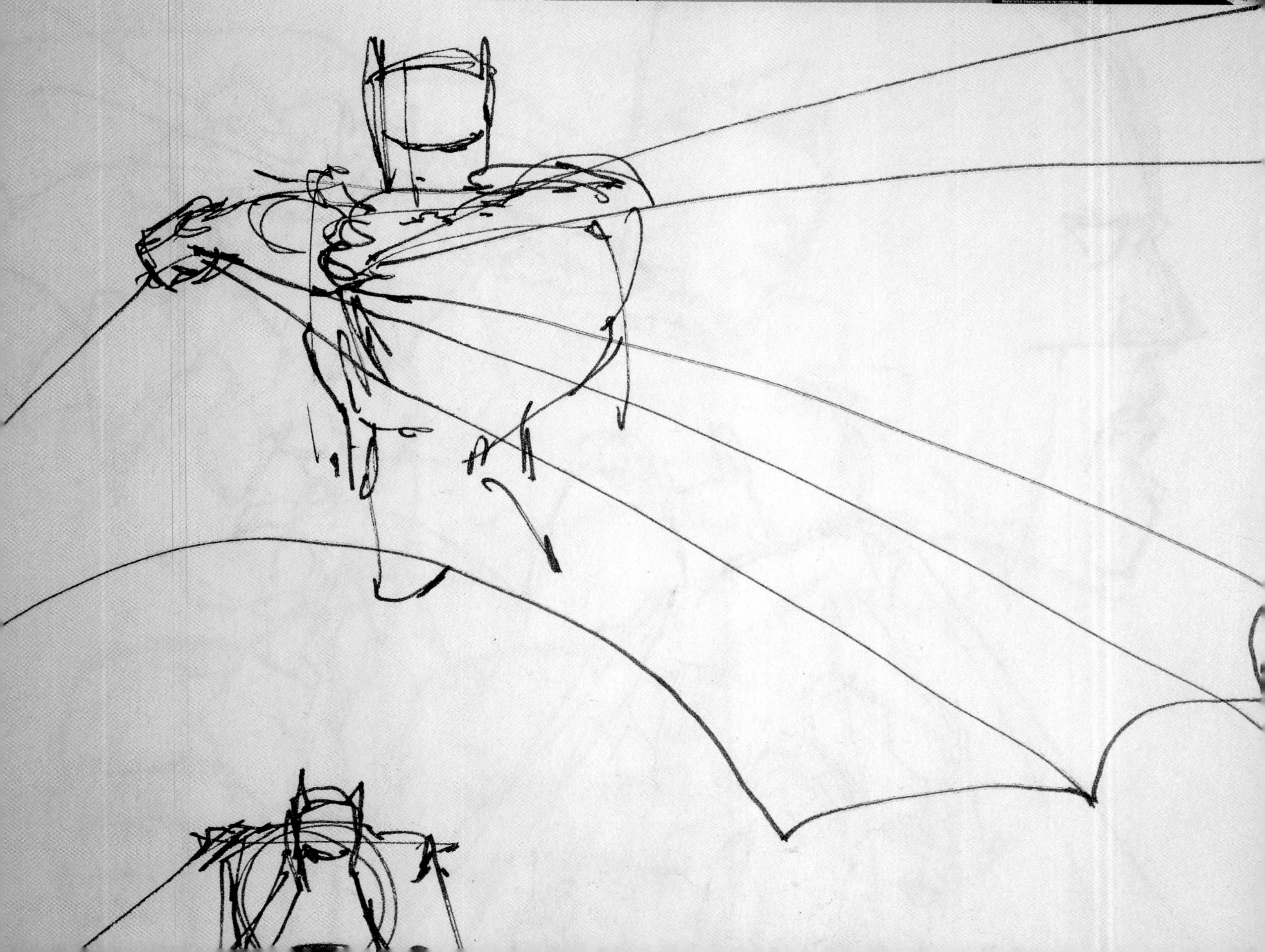

Opposite Left,
THE COMICS JOURNAL #101
(cover)
Frank Miller, artist
1986

Opposite Center,
COMICS INTERVIEW #31
Frank Miller, artist
1986

Opposite Right,
RETAIL STORE DISPLAY
(Vacuform plastic over cardboard)
Frank Miller and Lynn Varley, artists,
8″ x 11″
1986

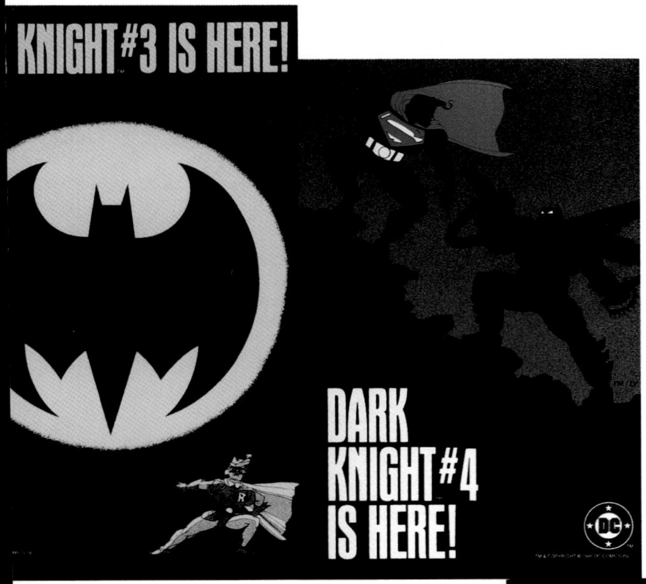

The Dark Knight Returns achieves a genuine sense of satire with Miller's canny depiction of mass media and how they would logically react to Batman's reemergence. Furious debates about vigilantism erupt all over Gotham's TV talk shows, and the Joker (who revives from a comalike state the instant Batman resurfaces) is released from a home for the criminally insane by earnest pop psychologists who claim that he is merely "a victim of Batman's psychosis." He then goes on a television talk show and kills everyone in the studio with poison gas. An adolescent girl whom Batman saves from the clutches of a youth gang called the Mutants takes it upon herself to become the new Robin, and her ex-hippie parents are too stoned to even realize that she's gone. Superman has become a covert tool of the government, and his orders from the president (a cadaverous Reagan) to put a stop to Batman's activities provide the tale's operatic conclusion: Superman (representing omnipotent conformity) fights Batman (symbolizing the rebel spirit of individuality) to the death.

Above Left,
ADVERTISEMENT
Announcing the arrival
of THE DARK KNIGHT #3
4.5″ x 6″
1986

Above Right,
ADVERTISEMENT
Announcing the arrival
of THE DARK KNIGHT #4
4.5″ x 6″
1986

Left,
PREPARATORY SKETCH
Frank Miller, artist
(pen and ink on paper)
7″ x 4″
1985

Above,
THE DARK KNIGHT RETURNS #3
"Hunt the Dark Knight"
(cover), Frank Miller
and Lynn Varley, artists
6.5″ x 10″, 1986

Above,
THE DARK KNIGHT RETURNS #4
"The Dark Knight Falls"
(cover), Frank Miller
and Lynn Varley, artists
6.5″ x 10″, 1986

Left,
THE DARK KNIGHT RETURNS #3
(page 47)
"Hunt the Dark Knight"
Frank Miller, Klaus Janson and Lynn Varley, artists
6.5″ x 10″
1986

Right,
PREPARATORY SKETCH
For THE DARK KNIGHT RETURNS (detail)
(pencil and ink on paper)
Frank Miller, artist
1985

Vith the death of the Joker in *The Dark Knight Returns* #3, Miller's work assumed sense of finality that had never been een before in mainstream comics. Every ction had a series of dire consequences. 'he usual understanding that the charac-ers would live to fight again another day vas eliminated, forcing the reader to ccept an unforeseen, even unwanted urn of events. Though still rooted in the amiliar exaggeration of the comics (gar-h costumes, mind-controlling lipstick, eings from other planets, poison cotton andy and the like), Miller's work dis-layed a sense of realism that made the takes seem much higher. Batman's bat-es became desperate struggles and took tremendous toll, with no guarantee of ictory. At the end of the story, Bruce Vayne survives, but Batman, for all ntents and purposes, is dead.

This approach was applied even more ntensely on Miller's next Batman project. Iaving so successfully chronicled the nale of Batman's career in *The Dark Knight Returns,* Miller received permis-on to retell the character's origin, in an xtraordinary four-part story entitled *Batman: Year One.* For this project, Miller nlisted the talents of artist David Iazzucchelli, with whom Miller had pre-iously worked to marvelous effect on the *Daredevil* comic book series.

Year One made its debut in 1987, a year fter *Dark Knight,* not as a special edition, ut as part of the ongoing *Batman* comics. 'his gave readers the impression that the tory was taking place within the series' egular continuity (an issue of paramount nportance to fans), and thereby made it eem all the more "real."

Above,
ORIGINAL ART
For trade paperback cover of BATMAN: YEAR ONE
(ink on paper) David Mazzucchelli, artist
Approx 3.25″ x 5.0625″, 1987

Opposite,
ORIGINAL ART
For trade paperback cover of BATMAN: YEAR ONE
(colored paper on illustration board)
David Mazzucchelli, artist
Approx 11″ x 14″, 1987

Opposite Inset,
TRADE PAPERBACK COVER
For BATMAN: YEAR ONE
David Mazzucchelli, artist
6.5″ x 10″, 1987

BATMAN
YEAR · ONE
BY FRANK MILLER
AND DAVID MAZZUCCHELLI
WITH RICHMOND LEWIS

ıstration below reveals Mazzucchelli's childhood enthusiasm for Batman, and exemplifies an important phe
ıat has gradually taken hold of the comic book industry, starting in the early 1970s. By the time Batma
red in 1939, the comic book industry was generally seen as the domain of people who really wanted to be
else: painters, novelists, editorial illustrators, journalists, and so on. By the '70s, a generation of people who g
comics saw creating them as something actually to which to aspire, a vocation in itself. Today it is assumed
ork in comics it's because you are devoted to them, which indicates that the fans are now literally running the
azzucchelli's image of Batman is even more naturalistic than Miller's and, while still fearsome, actually looks
a costume. This perfectly serves the requirements of *Year One*, which is one of the most believable Batman
ritten. The rough sketches shown to the right indicate that Mazzucchelli toyed with the idea of "casting" a
ry Peck as Bruce Wayne.

atman: Year One draws its dramatic strength from several elements. One is James Gordon, who at the outset
om Chicago to be a lieutenant on the Gotham City police force. Through him we discover the way things w
m, and in the process learn the answer to a question about Batman that had festered for decades: If Bruce
ıted to fight crime, why didn't he become a policeman? Because, Miller tells us, the police in Gotham, from t
beat up to the commissioner and the mayor, were gladly, madly, wildly corrupt. This idea makes so much
s logic seems shocking. It also explains why Gordon—who we know will eventually become police commissi
ever want to work with a vigilante. Essentially a moral person, Gordon is faced with the trial of his life, a
is with him every step of the way. Gordon is really the star of *Year One*, a fully three-dimensional, symp
ter.

significance is the absence of any of the familiar Batman villains. None is needed, because in Gotham the *po*
iminals. We see instead the emergence of the Catwoman, a disaffected dominatrix. Though traditionally view
Batman's foes, hers is a parallel story in *Year One*, and they encounter each other only briefly. Batman's true
hown to us in the third installment when, cornered by a trigger-happy SWAT team in an abandoned building,
of light hits his face and he thinks, "The enemy is closing in, relentless, unstoppable . . . through a crack in th
at him." He is referring to the sun, slowly rising, gradually removing his cover of darkness and his chances of e

Below,

"BATMAN COMICS"

David Mazzucchelli, age six, artist

(crayon on newsprint)

11″ x 8.5″, 1966

Above, PREPARATORY SKETCH
For BATMAN: YEAR ONE (ink on paper)
David Mazzucchelli, artist, 15″ x 5″, 1986

Below, CHARACTER STUDIES
For BATMAN: YEAR ONE (ink on paper)
David Mazzucchelli, artist, 13″ x 11″, 1986

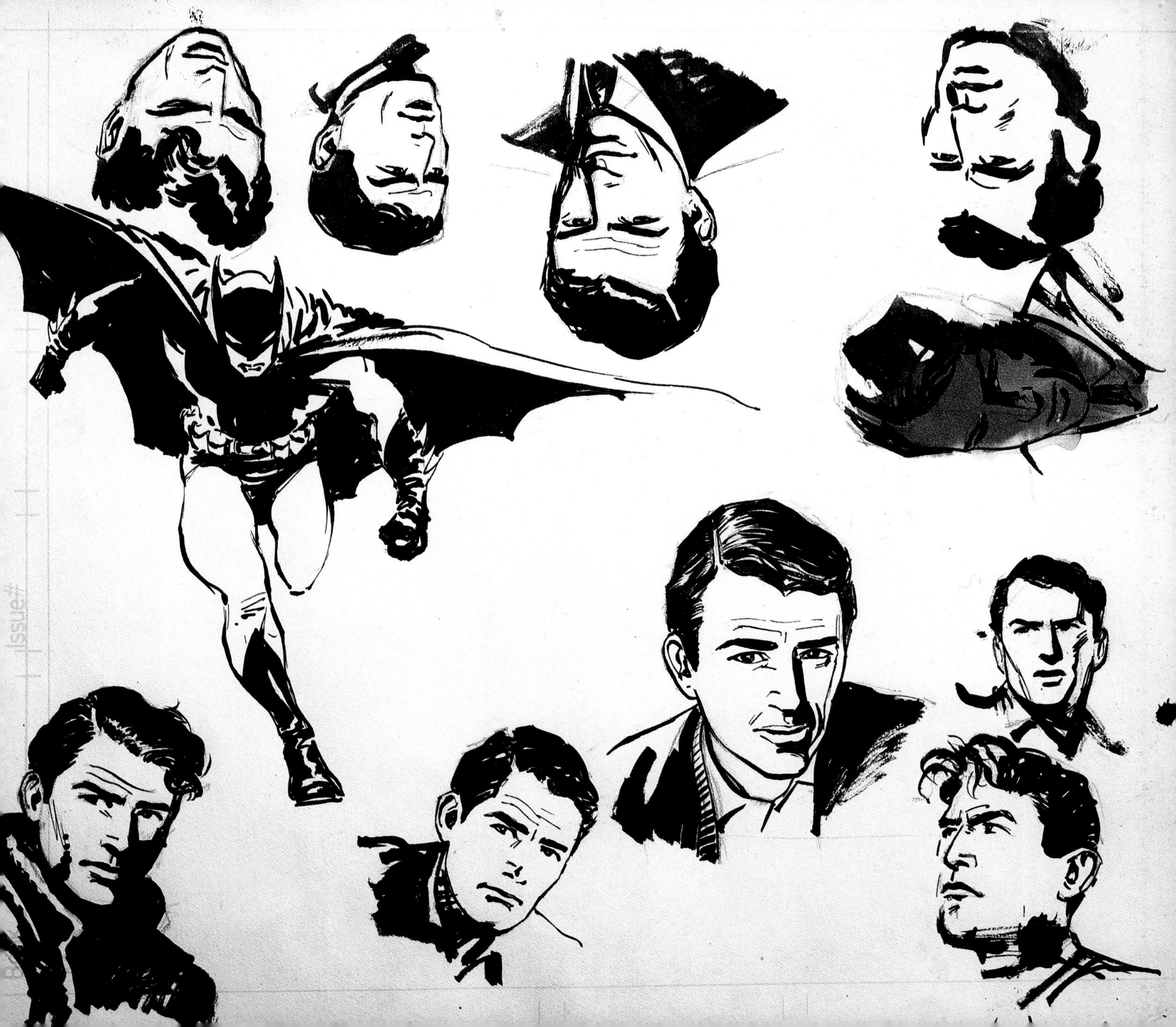

"Father…
I'm afraid I may
have to die tonight."

"You've eaten Gotham's wealth.
Its spirit.
Your feast is nearly over.
From this moment on…
none of you are safe."

"I'd rather die…than wait.
I have waited eighteen years,
since that night…
since all sense left my life."

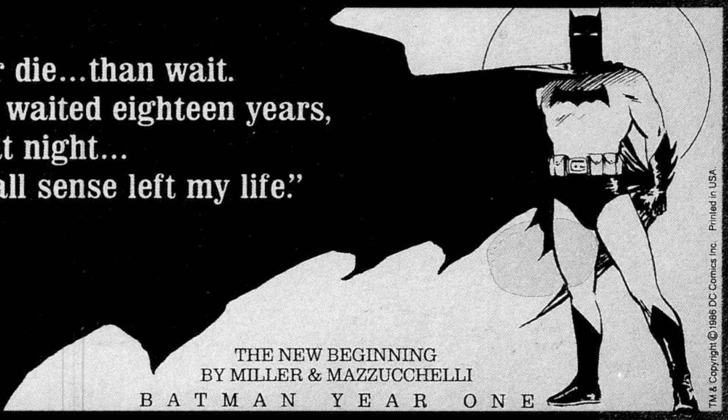

"How, father?
How do I do it?
What do I use…
to make them afraid?"

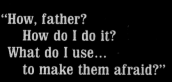

Above,
PROMOTIONAL
STICKERS
For BATMAN: YEAR ONE
David Mazzucchelli, artist
6″ x 2.875″
1987

Below,
ADVERTISEMENT
For BATMAN: YEAR ONE
David Mazzucchelli, artist
6.5″ x 10″
1986

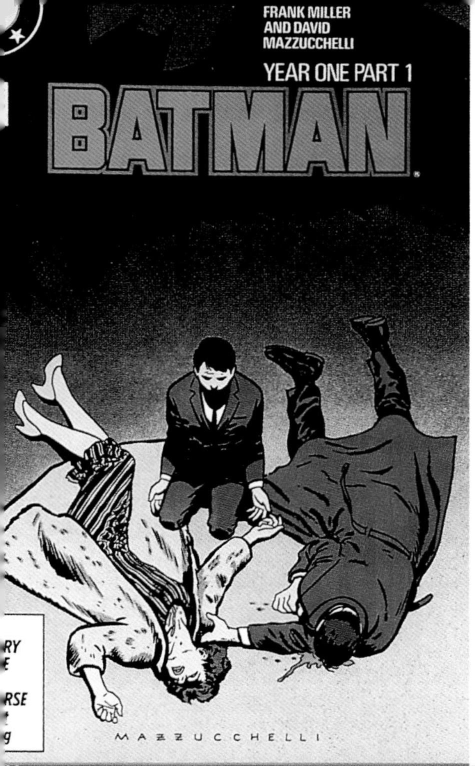

Dark Knight and *Year One* restored the Batman myth to its original form—fierce, frightening, complex, engaging and, in its own way, logical. At one point in *Year One* Alfred the butler asks Bruce Wayne if he shall be requiring his Batman uniform for the afternoon. The reply, "Never during the ***day***, Alfred," was what fans had waited so many years to hear. Batman hasn't been the same since. These two books changed everything. Their narrative power, depth of characterization and seamless fusion of words and pictures brought Batman into a realm rarely associated with comic strip characters: that of literature.

Left and Below,
COVERS
For BATMAN: YEAR ONE #1-4
David Mazzucchelli and Richmond Lewis, artists
6.5″ x 10″
1987

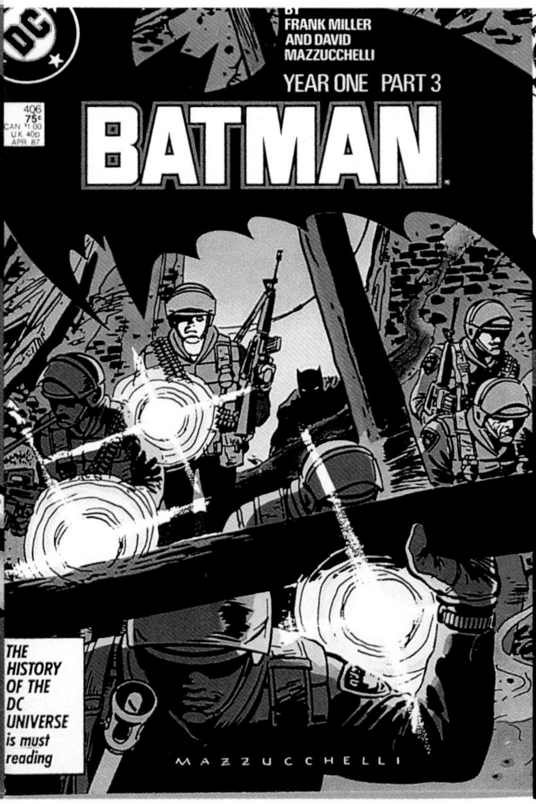

OVERLEAF
BATMAN: YEAR ONE #2
"War is Declared" (page 14)
David Mazzucchelli and Richmond Lewis, artists
6.5″ x 10″
1987

PAGE 213
ORIGINAL ART (detail)
For BATMAN: YEAR ONE advertisement
(ink on paper) David Mazzucchelli artist
14″ x 20″
1986

LADIES. GENTLEMEN.
YOU HAVE EATEN WELL.
YOU'VE EATEN GOTHAM'S WEALTH. ITS SPIRIT.
YOUR FEAST IS NEARLY OVER.
FROM THIS MOMENT ON--
--NONE OF YOU ARE SAFE.

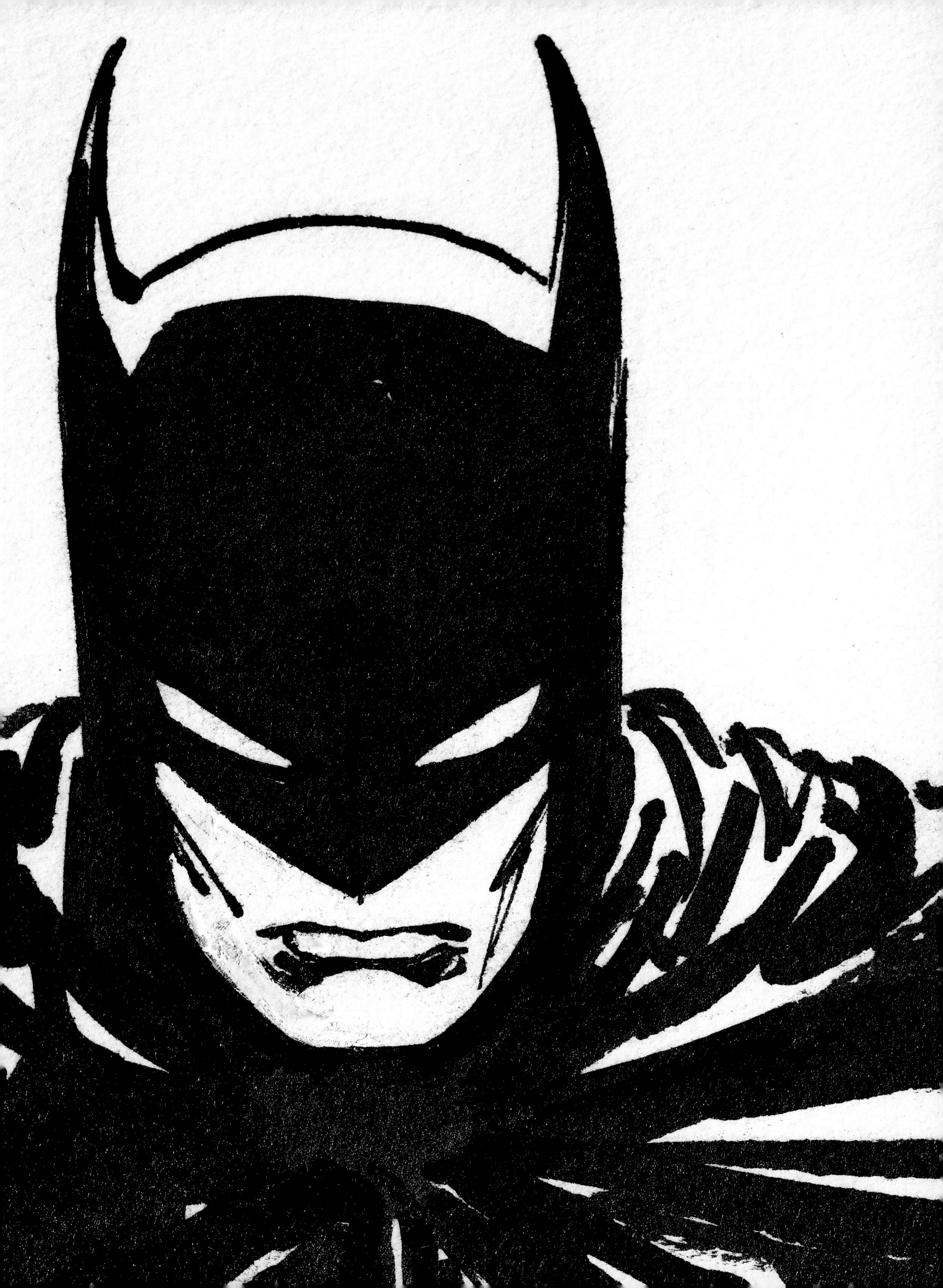

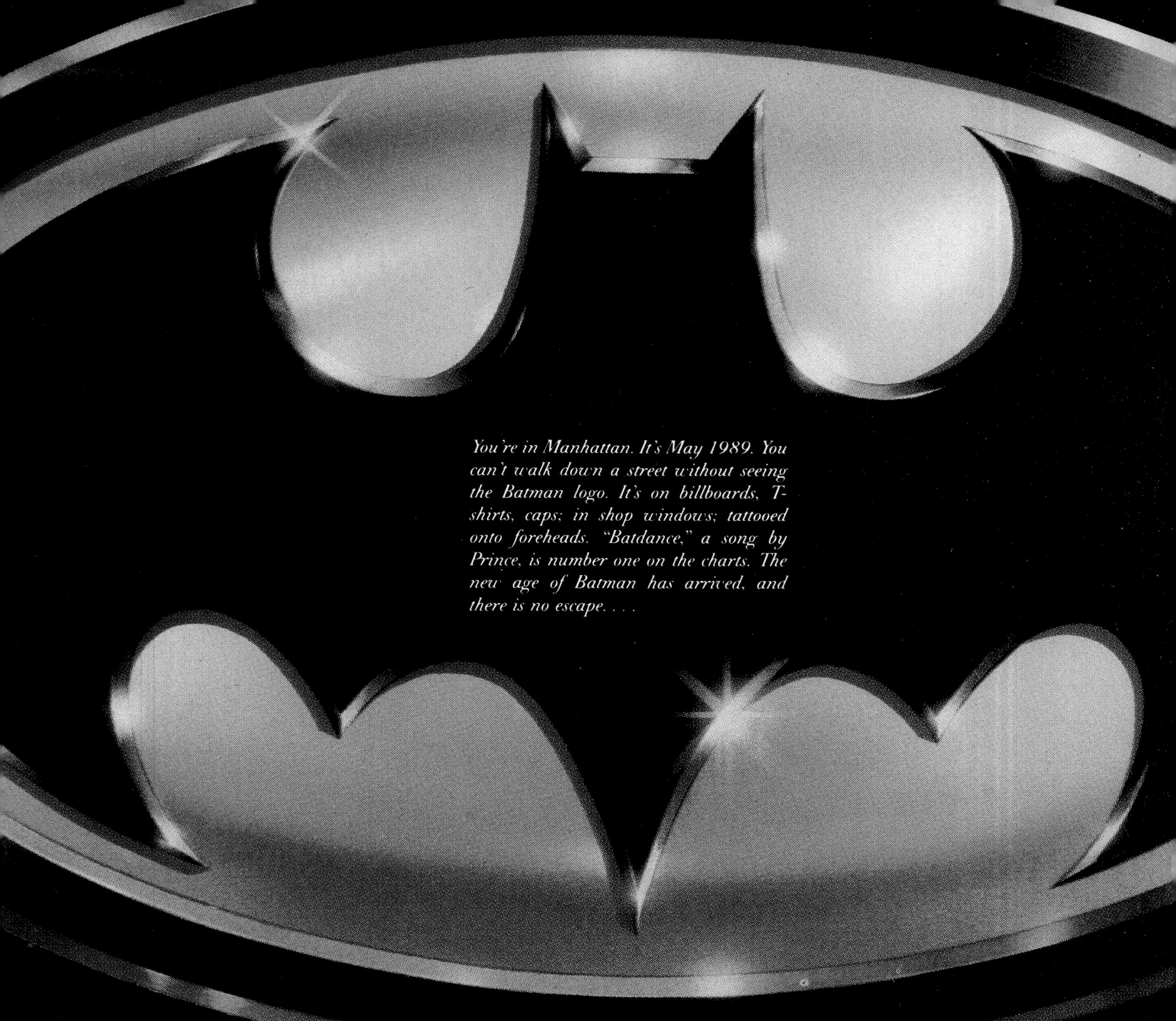

You're in Manhattan. It's May 1989. You can't walk down a street without seeing the Batman logo. It's on billboards, T-shirts, caps; in shop windows; tattooed onto foreheads. "Batdance," a song by Prince, is number one on the charts. The new age of Batman has arrived, and there is no escape. . . .

1989

Above,
LOGO FOR THE FIRST BATMAN MOVIE
Anton Furst, artist
1989

Opposite,
MODEL KIT
Assembled and painted by Michael Stutelberg
(molded vinyl, glue, paint)
Approx. 11″ tall
Japan, 1989

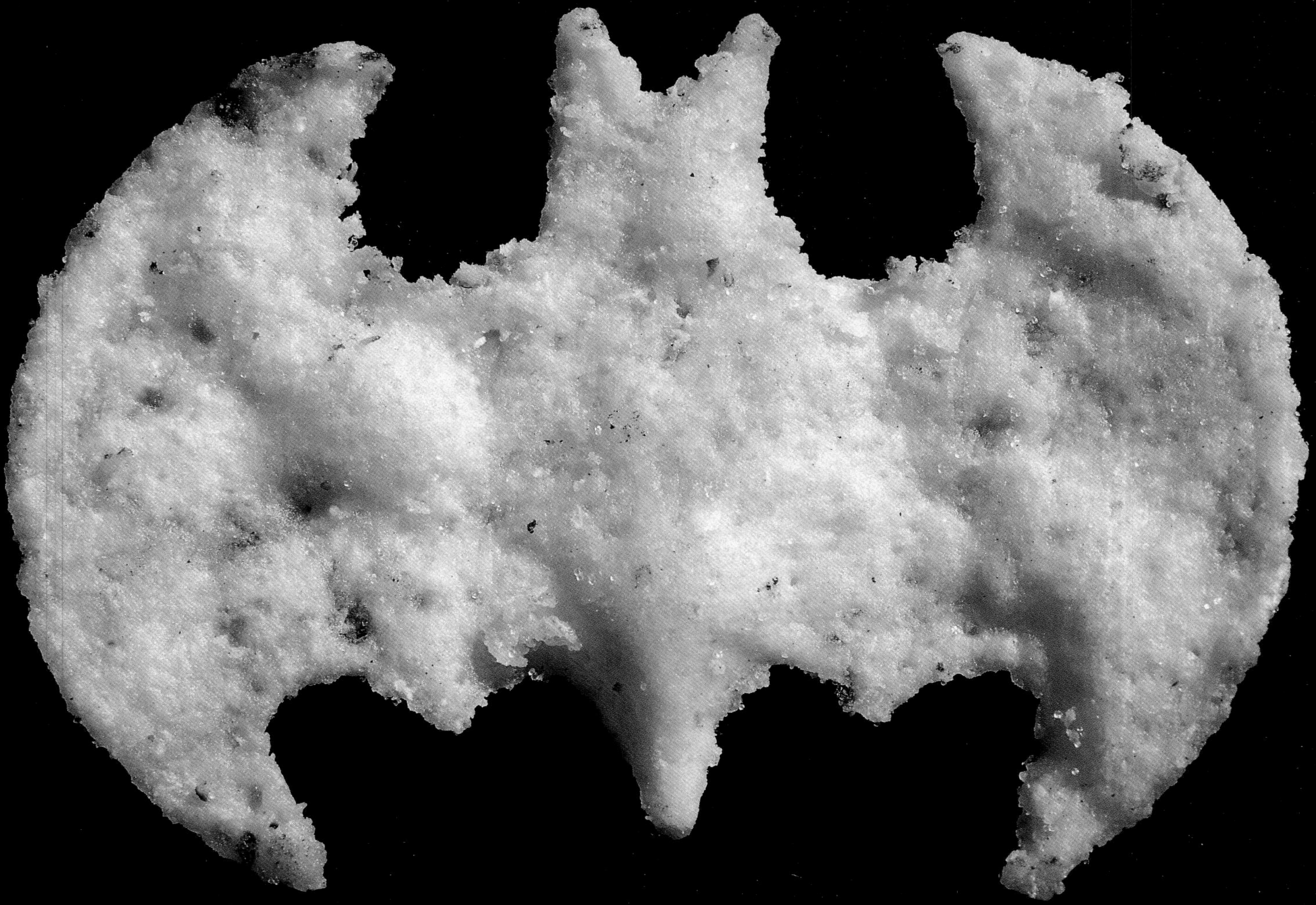

TORTILLA CHIP
Approx. 1.5″ wide
1989

Two things helped free the Batman movie from its "development" prison. The first was the flurry of interest in the character generated by *Dark Knight.* The second was the success of a movie called *Beetlejuice,* by an eccentric young director named Tim Burton. *Batman*'s producers, Jon Peters and Peter Guber, were impressed enough to place their baby in the hands of this still relatively unknown quantity.

Burton wanted Michael Keaton, the star of *Beetlejuice,* to play the title role because he felt they had worked well together. He also thought it would be a funny idea. Keaton is the physical antitype of Batman. The director felt it would make more sense that, as Bruce Wayne, Keaton would need the enhancement of the costume to fight crime. This logic escaped a nation of angry Batman fans, who shuddered at the thought of seeing the TV show all over again, especially since Keaton's character in *Beetlejuice* had a manic, goofy, obnoxious manner. The protest was loud and long. I should know. I was part of it.

What we *didn't* know, however, was the ingenuity of execution that was planned for the look of the film. The Batman costume was designed so that *anyone* wearing it would embody menace and power, with its devillike horns, built-in muscles and cape that doubled as enormous bat wings. Anton Furst's designs for Gotham City alluded to the nightmarish aspects of Fritz Lang's *Metropolis,* Ridley Scott's *Blade Runner* and Terry Gilliam's *Brazil,* while appearing specific to the Batman story itself. His version of the Batmobile was a more elegant take on Frank Miller's, who sensibly envisioned it as an armored tank. Gone was the whimsy of the '60s convertible. In its place was a sleek, black, fully enclosed bulletproof module complete with shields, weapons and a voice-activated remote control.

And then there was Jack Nicholson as the Joker.

"If only we could show people ahead of time what we're doing, they'd understand," thought the producers. So that's just what they did.

Left,
STATUES
Warner Bros. catalog exclusive; limited edition of 50 (hand-painted cold-cast plaster)
Approx. 8″ tall
1989

Left,
DAILY NEWS MAGAZINE
JUNE 4, 1989

Below,
NEWSWEEK
JUNE 26, 1989

Batman was being filmed in the fall of 1988 under a veil of secrecy. The premiere was to be the following June. Unwittingly creating one of movie marketing's true strokes of genius, the producers decided to piece together a trailer for theatrical release a full six months early, in January 1989. This may have seemed quite a gamble at the time. If the trailer flopped, everyone involved with the film would be in for a long, cold spring. They needn't have worried.

I remember attending a comic book convention in New York a week before the trailer was shown. A bootleg video dealer I knew took my arm and asked if I wanted to see what the new Batman movie was going to look like. He pulled out a videotape and played it on one of his monitors, in full view of anyone in proximity. I couldn't believe it. "Play it again," I managed to say. He replied, "All right, just once. But then I gotta put it away. I could get in *big* trouble." Word had spread quickly, so by now a large crowd had formed. After the second viewing, a collective voice screamed, "I want it! How much? Did you see that? Oh my GOD!" He wasn't selling.

This was the reaction, a week later, across the country.

LIFESTYLE

3atmania

ımmer struggle for the dark soul of a mythic erican hero—and a boom in Bat-products

3ILL BAROL

started so simply in the spring of 939, when comics cost a dime and ıe bad guys only came out at night. ational Comics wanted a new uperhero. An 18-year-old cartoonist l Bob Kane had an idea: "a vigilante ı the law." The Bat-Man, as he was known, made his first appearance in tive Comics #27. How could Kane known that 50 years later almost to ıonth, as anticipation built for the 23 première of director Tim Burton's ıillion "Batman," a Bat-fever would he land?

s descend on multiplexes, ask which er is showing the "Batman" trailer, uy tickets regardless of what is playıere, even if it is "Pink Cadillac." A ington theater chain sells thousands ance seats two weeks before the pre-. Arguments break out among fans: hat kind of Batman is this? Where's ı? Who does this Michael Keaton guy he is? And everywhere you turn this , there is the bat logo. It comes walkoward you on Wabash in Chicago, s around a corner on Melrose in Los les, looms high on a billboard over s Square. "It's the biggest thing I've had in 19 years," says Stuart Taylor of rica, Mass., a distributor of movie-lid merchandise. "It's . . ." And here or pauses, groping for precisely the analogy so that we may fully grasp normity of the thing: ". . . *bigger than California Raisins.*"

e story of Batmania is a story about truggle for the soul of a great Amerihero. It is also a story about canny ıotion, the tectonic movements of poptaste and the nostalgia of a self-obd generation for its own fading youth. ecause of a guy in a cape and mask.

ke all mythic heroes, Batman has a ry. It stretches from Detective Comics to Batman #1 in April 1940, through s movie serials and finally to the 1966-68 TV series starring Adam West. The series is fondly remembered by aging baby boomers for a *Zap! Pow!* visual style that, in retrospect, seems to have captured perfectly the pop climate of those à-go-go years. A lot of Bat-fans, however, hated the show's exaggerated campiness and bright palette. "All those pinks," shudders Jon Peters, producer of this summer's "Batman." "I didn't like it. I wanted the guy to be New York, to be street." A dozen years would pass before Peters got the chance to do anything about that. In 1979 executive producers Benjamin Melniker and Michael Uslan secured the movie rights from DC Comics and took them to Peters and his partner, Peter Guber. Peters and Guber brought the project to Warner Bros. Warners, it seems fair to say, saw some interesting cross-promotional possibilities in a movie character licensed from its own DC subsidiary. After some fits and starts, the producers connected with Tim Burton, the young director who had shown a quirkily original eye in "Pee-wee's Big Adventure" and "Beetlejuice." Production was slated to start in September 1988.

In England, meanwhile—and here's one of those breathtaking narrative leaps that comics fans love—labor troubles knocked the morning show "TV-am" off the air for several months last winter and spring. Management replaced it with reruns of the 1960s Batman series. "Things went a bit Bat-crazy," a spokesman for the show says now. One of the immediate effects of Britain's Bat-craziness was a sharp rise in Bat-fashions, and as street fashions will, they drifted east to west across the Atlantic. "That's really what started the merchandising," an industry insider says. "It was very big last summer with skateboarders in L.A., and in the East Village in New York." The street popularity of Batman perked up what Warners worldwide merchandising president Dan Romanelli calls "a classic license, going back at least 25 years."

Comic-book Gothic: Back in England, the filmmakers knew from the start what kind of picture they wanted to make. "When we got into this I thought, what a great opportunity to have this guy kick some ass," producer Peters says. This "Batman" would be a comic-book Gothic, a dark fable that would restore Bob Kane's original gloomy luster to the story of millionaire playboy Bruce Wayne—*who, unbeknownst to the good people of crime-ridden Gotham, leads a secret life as the dark avenger of the*

MURRAY CLOSE—TMS & © 1989 DC COMICS

This is the dark avenger of the night, and these are his toys: *The Batmobile (left), Bat-merchandise at the Golden Apple comic store in Los Angeles*

HERB RITTS—VISAGES

DOUGLAS C. PIZAC—AP

NEWSWEEK : JUNE 26, 1989

Opposite,
MOVIE POSTER PROPOSAL
Unused
(pastels on black paper)
20″ x 30″
1988

Left,
BATMOBILE MODEL KIT
Assembled and painted by Calvin Chu
(plastic, glue, paint)
Approx. 7″ long
1989

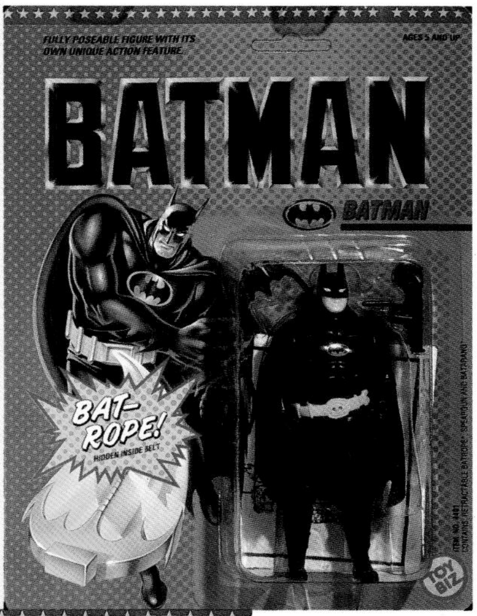

Left,
ACTION FIGURE
(plastic, cord)
3″ tall
1989

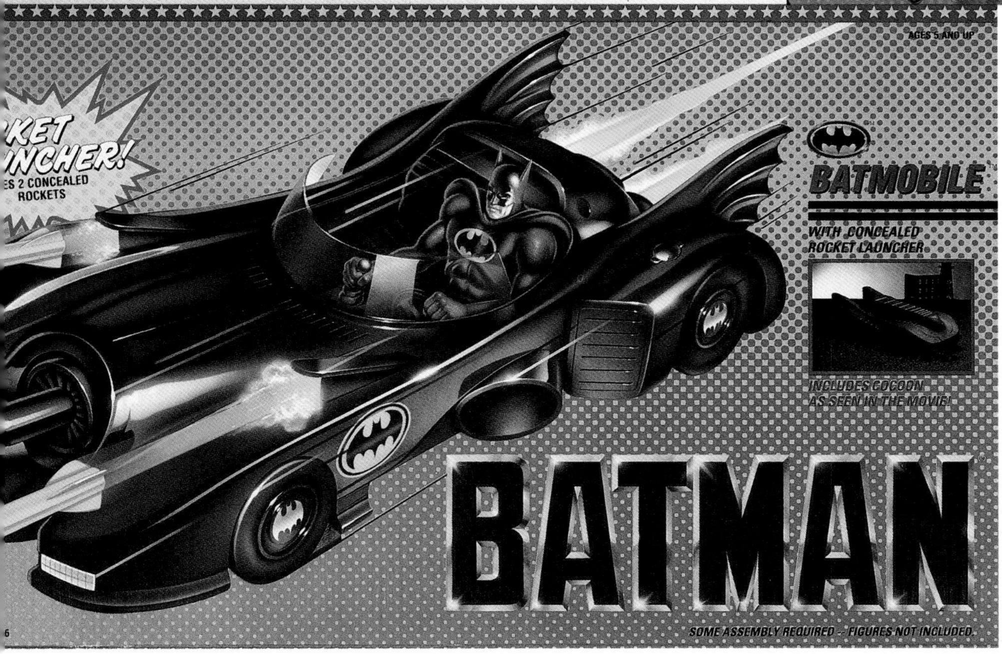

Left,
BATMOBILE
(packaging)
14″ x 8″ x 7″
1989

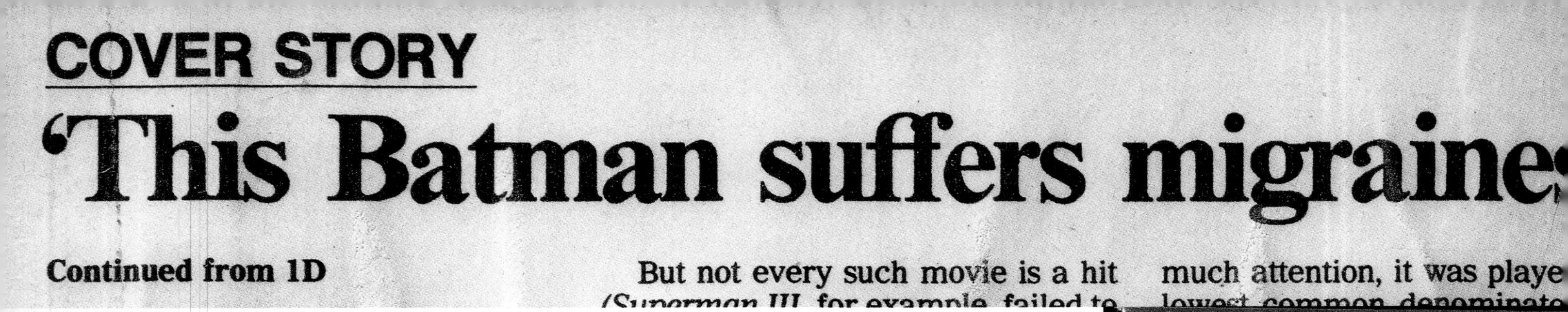
COVER STORY

‘This Batman suffers migraine

Continued from 1D

But not every such movie is a hit

much attention, it was playe

Batman became the fifth-highest-grossing film of all time, earning over $400 million worldwide. It won Oscars for art direction and costume design, and set a standard for production that has rarely been matched.

Not that it was perfect. The script took unnecessary liberties with Batman's origin and depicted the Joker as the murderer of Bruce Wayne's parents, a circumstance that would have made the villain a generation too old. Worse, a cardinal rule of the game was broken: at the end of the story, the Joker plummets to the street—and to his death. This is pure anathema. According to tradition, the Joker falls; but *always* into water, and his body is never recovered. Burton & Co. probably got the idea from *The Dark Knight Returns*, but the effect was different because the movie chronicled the beginning of Batman's career, not the end. That sequel-mad movie moguls would want to rule out the possibility of the Joker's return, especially after Nicholson's virtuoso performance, seems to go against everything Hollywood stands for.

The pros, however, far outweighed the cons. The first scenes are absolutely right. "Why wouldn't someone just shoot Batman and kill him?" we asked each other as kids. We are given the answer immediately, as we watch a petty thief do exactly that, or so he thinks. The crook looks at the dark form lying on the ground. Believing it dead, he turns away. We see it slowly rise behind him, unstoppable. Whatever Batman is wearing, we realize, is obviously bullet-proof.

As for merchandising, it was 1966 all over again, but with a difference. Batman was now shadowy, elegant and no-nonsense. The new rendering of the logo was indicative of the approach. It was no longer flat, but fleshed out and three-dimensional. It had weight, strength, power. And so did Batman. *This* time, he was here to stay.

Top,
USA TODAY
June 22, 1989

Above,
MECHANICAL BATMAN
(packaging)
Japan
1989

Left,
MECHANICAL
BATMAN
(tin)
Approx. 7″ tall
Japan
1989

Below,
NEW YORK POST
JULY 10, 1989

NEW YORK POST, MONDAY, JULY 10, 1989

Batmania takes Hollywood by storm

Page Six

High roller

DONALD Trump has already
gun efforts to hype his Taj Ma-
l hotel in Atlantic City — al-
ough it's not scheduled to open
til next spring. Trump's people
ve started spreading the word

LIKE the beating of little bat wings, rumors about a sequel to the blockbuster "Batman" — and the actors who might star in it — are flying fast and furious around Hollywood.

But Warner, the studio that produced the movie with **Peter Guber** and **Jon Peters**, is keeping the status of the next bat saga as secret as the location of the bat cave.

Charlotte Gee, a spokeswoman for the studio, told PAGE SIX that it has always been Warner's intention to do a trilogy of bat films, but she refused to discuss the sequels' contents: "Until a concept and a script are developed there is nothing to talk about."

That hasn't stopped the bat gossip, which is about as plentiful as black and yellow logos on Gotham streets. The latest bat droppings concern birds of a different feather: **Danny DeVito** is allegedly being eyed for the role of the plucky Penguin in the next film. **River Phoenix's** name has also been batted about, as a potential Robin.

DeVito's publicist **Stan Rosenfield** said he'd heard the Penguin rumors, but that the idea had not been officially proposed to the diminutive actor. "Danny would be interested in doing a 'Batman' type of movie," said Rosenfield, "but there's not been any script sent over and nothing's been formally presented to his agent."

In other bat dish, the oppressive Gotham City sets designed by **Anton Furst** have reportedly been mothballed for the next film. **Kim Basinger** has dropped hints of an expanded role for Vicki Vale in that flick. And even star **Michael Keaton** — who had expressed serious doubts in interviews before the release of "Batman" about doing a sequel — is now open to the idea of winging it one more time, said his spokesman.

In the midst of all the talk about "Batman II," "Batman" continues to break box office records.

Its first two weeks in release have been, respectively, the first and second highest grossing weeks for a single film ever — with receipts totalling $122,410,000.

When you figure in the success of the "Ghostbusters" and Indiana Jones sequels, and the money that the Warner-owned Licensing Corporation of America will make on bat merchandise (estimated now at $200 million) — it becomes apparent that *not* to do a sequel would be flying in the face of conventional Hollywood wisdom.

One Hollywood-based bat wag doesn't expect to see a Batman film for three or four years, but added: "With this kind of box office, nothing short of a 'batastrophe' would stop Warner from doing a sequel."

キートン
デヴィート
ファイファー
バットマン™
リターンズ
ワーナー・ブラザース映画提供
ティム・バートン作品／マイケル・キートン
ダニー・デヴィート／ミシェル・ファイファー／“バットマン リターンズ”／クリストファー・ウォーケン
マイケル・ガフ／パット・ヒングル／マイケル・マーフィー／音楽 ダニー・エルフマン／共同製作 ラリー・フランコ
製作総指揮 ジョン・ピータース, ピーター・グーバー, ベンジャミン・メルニカー&マイケル・ウスラン
バットマン・キャラクター創作 ボブ・ケイン&版権DC・コミックス／原作 ダニエル・ウォーターズ&サム・ハーム
脚本 ダニエル・ウォーターズ／製作 デニーズ・ディ・ノヴィ&ティム・バートン／監督 ティム・バートン
オリジナル・サントラ盤／ワーナーミュージック・ジャパン
原作／竹書房文庫刊
BATMAN
RETURNS

Left,
MOVIE POSTER
For
BATMAN RETURNS
20″ x 30″
Japan
1992

Right,
ONE OF THE PENGUIN'S HENCHMEN
Movie prop from
BATMAN RETURNS
(painted latex)
18″ tall
1992

With the Joker gone, Burton had to find other villains for his sequel, *Batman Returns.* It was decided that three bad guys were better than one–the Penguin (Danny DeVito) and Catwoman (Michelle Pfeiffer) were joined by a new character named Max Shreck (Christopher Walken), an out-of-control business magnate intent on ruling Gotham. The pressure to top the first film must have been intense, and it shows. An effort to make everything bigger, better and bolder creates a cacophonous frenzy that challenges the viewer to keep track of what's going on. DeVito's Dickensian Penguin is off-putting and unrecognizable as a human being, but Pfeiffer saves the movie almost singlehandedly as a Catwoman who widens the eye and quickens the pulse. The film's licensing program was even more massive than that of its predecessor. The market's potential had been firmly established, and Warner Bros. was better able to plan ahead.

RETURNS

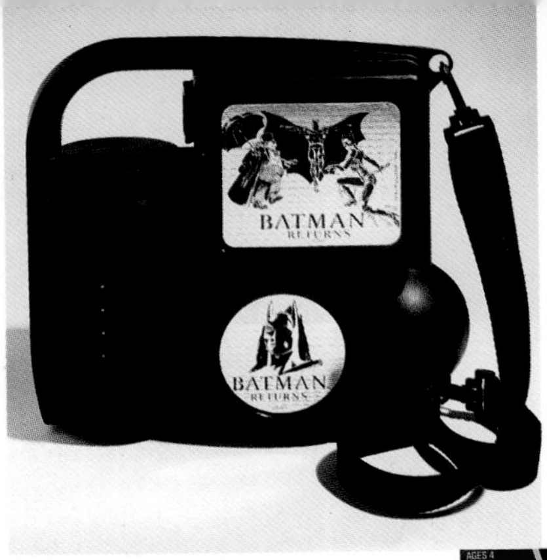

Left,
LUNCH BOX
(molded plastic, decals)
Approx. 10″ tall
1992

Opposite,
PENGUIN STATUE
(clay prototype)
Approx. 11″ tall
1992

PAGE 224
BATMAN MODEL KIT
From BATMAN RETURNS
Approx. 11″ tall

PAGE 225
PENGUIN MODEL KIT
From BATMAN RETURNS
Approx. 8″ tall

PAGE 226
CATWOMAN MODEL KIT
From BATMAN RETURNS
Approx. 10″ tall

(molded vinyl, paint)
All assembled and painted
by Michael Stutelberg
1992

Left,
AIR ATTACK BATMAN
(molded plastic)
5″ tall
1992

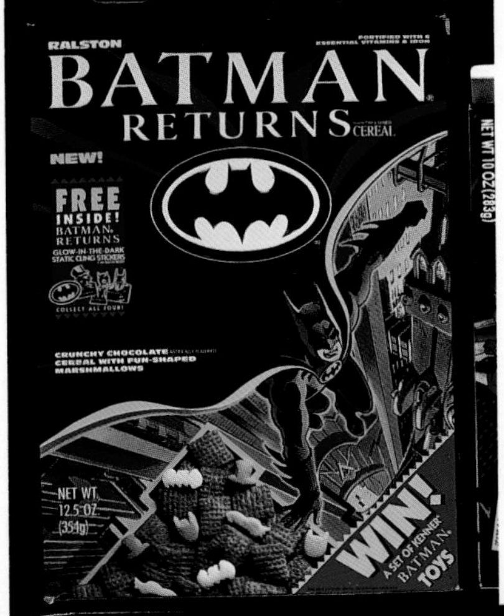

Left,
BREAKFAST CEREAL
(packaging)
7″ x 10″ x 2.5″
1992

Below,
SNACK TRAY
(metal)
18″ x 10″
1992

With *Batman Forever*, the third film, everything changed: The director, the stars, the characters, the designers. Burton wanted to pursue other projects, Keaton dropped out, and Anton Furst fell to his death, an apparent suicide.

Director Joel Schumacher, fresh from his work on *The Client*, was hired to introduce us to the screen's next Batman. Schumacher changed the palette from Burton's blacks and blues to reds, yellows, indigos and, most important, bright shades of green. One of the new villains was the Riddler, and emerald has always been his signature. Brought to nerve-shattering life by the tremendously popular Jim Carrey, the fiendish puzzler came off as even more maniacally crazy than Nicholson's Joker.

The other evildoer was Two-Face, played by Tommy Lee Jones, whose considerable talents went largely unused in a role that required him to do almost nothing. How could he, with Carrey practically vacuuming up the scenery?

And what scenery! Production designer Barbara Ling, new to the Batman milieu, achieved the impossible by taking Furst's already weird design theories even further. Gotham City became so far removed from reality it seemed to be the world's most elaborate, ongoing urban carnival.

Above,
BATMAN AND ROBIN ACTION FIGURES
From BATMAN FOREVER
(molded plastic)
5″ tall
1995

This approach was hardly inappropriate, considering that *Batman Forever* featured the introduction of Robin. A spectacular scene (actually not too different from the original in the comics) showed the Flying Graysons in the middle of their trapeze act at the Gotham Circus. Two-Face had hijacked the act, so young Dick Grayson (Chris O'Donnell) was forced to watch his family fall to their deaths. In the audience was Bruce Wayne (Val Kilmer), who offered to take the lad under his (bat) wing.

Kilmer and O'Donnell are interesting choices. Both are intense young actors with excellent reputations, and not hard to look at either (their new outfits, by Bat-veteran Bob Ringwood, were more sexual than ever). What makes this Batman and Robin different from their predecessors is a dynamic that suggests they are contemporaries—partners of equal stature rather than mentor and protégé. It worked. *Batman Forever* set a record for the most lucrative opening weekend in box-office history, and went on to become the highest grossing movie of 1995. It was Batmania yet again, with the character popping up everywhere from a *New Yorker* cartoon (p. 196) to a *New York Times* crossword puzzle answer (p. 197). The movie secured Batman's position as a big-budget film franchise with an ongoing life in the tradition of *Star Trek* and James Bond. *Batman Forever* is aptly named.

OVERLEAF
STUFFED ROBIN DOLL
From BATMAN FOREVER
(molded plastic, cloth)
12″ tall, 1995

PAGE 233
THE ULTIMATE BATMAN
From BATMAN FOREVER
(molded plastic, cloth)
12″ tall, 1995

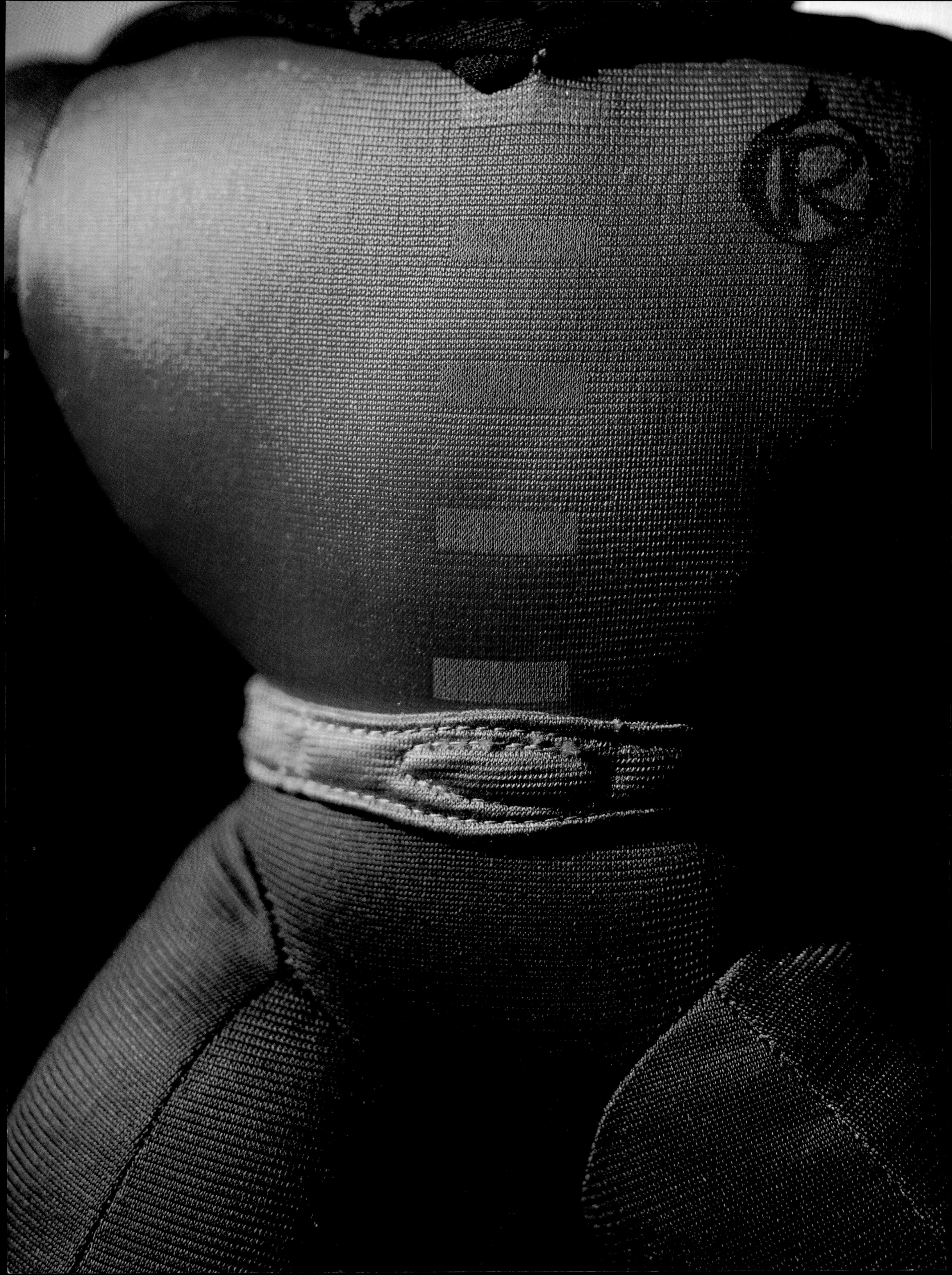

Left,
BATMAN MODEL KIT
From BATMAN FOREVER
Assembled and painted by Michael Stutelberg
(molded plastic, paint)
Approx. 12″ tall, 1995

Below,
BATARANG
Accessory to The Ultimate Batman
Approx. 2″ wide, 1995

Bottom,
COIN-OPERATED BATMOBILE
From BATMAN FOREVER
(fiberglass, motor)
Approx. 84″ long, 1995

The image on the opposite page illustrates a relatively new concept in character licensing. It is not merely a statue of Batman. It is a statue of Val Kilmer dressed as Batman. When Christopher Reeve played Superman in 1976, the dolls that were produced to cash in on the film's popularity looked like Superman, but they did not look specifically like Christopher Reeve. That situation has changed.

Toy manufacturers have discovered that kids don't just want any Batman figure, they want one that looks like the guy they saw in the movie. It's no longer the character, it's the impersonator. Now actors in films that have licensing potential have a decision to make. Will they sign contracts allowing their specific likenesses to be made into three-dimensional objects, to which we instinctively assign a permanence that is far greater than that of print? This cannot be an easy choice to make, especially considering the enormous amount of attention given to a Batman project. It's one thing to be a magazine cover. It's another to become a cookie jar.

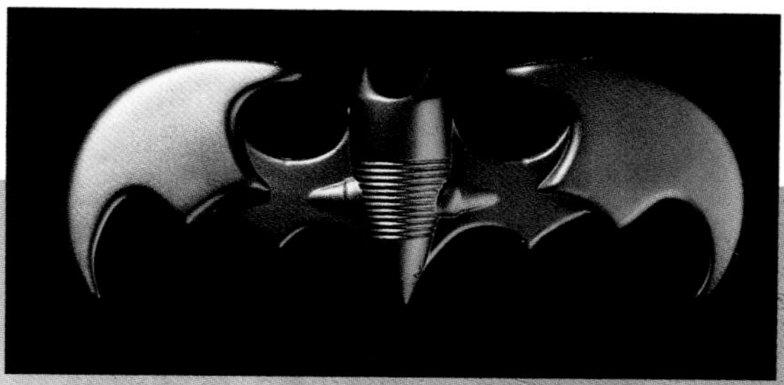

Left,
COOKIE JAR
Warner Bros. Studio
Store exclusive
(painted ceramic)
Approx. 14″ tall
1995

Opposite,
McDONALD'S
RETAIL DISPLAY
(cardboard)
Approx. 48″ tall
1995

Below Left and Right,
KELLOGG'S
CORN POPS
(packaging)
1995

Below,
MUGS
(molded plastic)
Approx. 3″ tall
1995

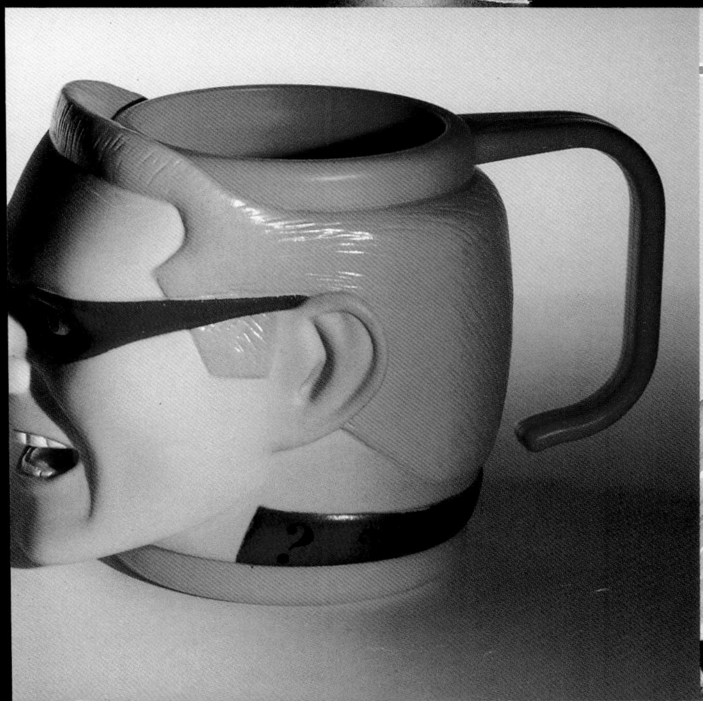

GOOD SOURCE OF 10 ESSENTIAL VITAMINS & MINERALS • SEE SIDE PANEL FOR NUTRITION FACTS
Kellogg's
FAT FREE
CHOLESTEROL FREE FOOD
CORN POPS
CRUNCHY SWEETENED POPPED-UP CORN CEREAL
"The Riddler"
FOREVER
BATMAN FOREVER
NET WT. 15 OZ. (425 GRAMS)

RETAIL STORE DISPLAY
From Sears
(paint, plaster, glaze)
Approx. 20″ tall
1995

Inset,
ROBIN STATUE
Warner Bros. Studio Store exclusive
Kent Melton, sculptor
(hand-painted prototype)
Approx. 11″ tall
1995

RETAIL STORE DISPLAY
From Sears
(paint, plaster, glaze)
Approx. 20″ tall
1995

Inset,
TWO-FACE STATUE
Warner Bros. Studio Store exclusive
Kent Melton, sculptor
(hand-painted prototype)
Approx. 11″ tall
1995

RETAIL STORE DISPLAY
From Sears
(paint, plaster, glaze)
Approx. 20″ tall
1995

Inset,
BATMAN STATUE
Warner Bros. Studio Store exclusive
Kent Melton, sculptor
(hand-painted prototype)
Approx. 11″ tall
1995

RETAIL STORE DISPLAY
From Sears
(paint, plaster, glaze)
Approx. 20″ tall
1995

Inset,
RIDDLER STATUE
Warner Bros. Studio Store exclusive
Kent Melton, sculptor
(hand-painted prototype)
Approx. 11″ tall
1995

Left,
BATMAN STATUE
Limited edition of 5,555 pieces
Randy Bowen, sculptor
(cold-cast plaster, paint)
11″ tall
1994

Right,
JOKER STATUE
Limited edition of 4,650 pieces
Randy Bowen, sculptor
(cold-cast plaster, paint)
12″ tall
1995

usurper and decided on capital punishment."—*Time*

"But the real murderers are the BATMAN readers."
—*Newsweek*

"A group of comic book artists and writers has succeeded in doing what the most fiendish minds of the century . . . have failed to accomplish."—*Reuters*

"Holy Ayatollah, Batman, Robin is dead!"—*Wall Street Journal*

"The Boy Wonder is dead, and the readers of DC Comics' BATMAN want it that way."
—*USA Today*

"Coming this month is a whole new way of doing a book, and you'll see it first from DC with the BATMAN series."
—*The Boston Rock*

The death of Robin in 1988 is a prime example of a directive that is gospel in the comic book industry: Give the fans what they want. And they wanted Robin, but not breathing. What later stirred up the media was the misconception that the Robin who died was Dick Grayson, the original Boy Wonder. Not so. He had long since grown up to become an adult super hero called Nightwing. In 1983, the baton had been passed to Jason Todd (whose last name echoes *Tod*, the German word for "death"), a juvenile delinquent who was caught trying to steal the hubcaps off the Batmobile. The readers found him insufferable, and DC decided to use this situation to perform an experiment. In *Batman* #427, Jason would get himself into an awful scrape with the Joker, and for two days fans could vote via phone to decide if he'd survive in the next issue. Two endings were prepared for #428. One showed Robin alive but injured; in the other he was killed.

The vote was close, with 5,271 voting for, and 5,343 against, but the decision was made. Jason's fate was sealed. At DC, phone lines jammed, hate mail rained and editors hid. "They reacted as if we killed a real person," recalled DC editor Denny O'Neil. Eventually things got back to normal, and readers needn't have feared. Batman wouldn't be alone for long.

Lef
BATMAN #427 (detai
Jim Aparo, Mike DeCarl
and Adrienne Roy, artist
198

Below
ADVERTISEMENT
Jim Aparo and Mike DeCarlo, artist
198

Left,
JOKER MODEL KIT (detail)
(molded vinyl, glue, paint)
Approx. 11″ tall
1993

428

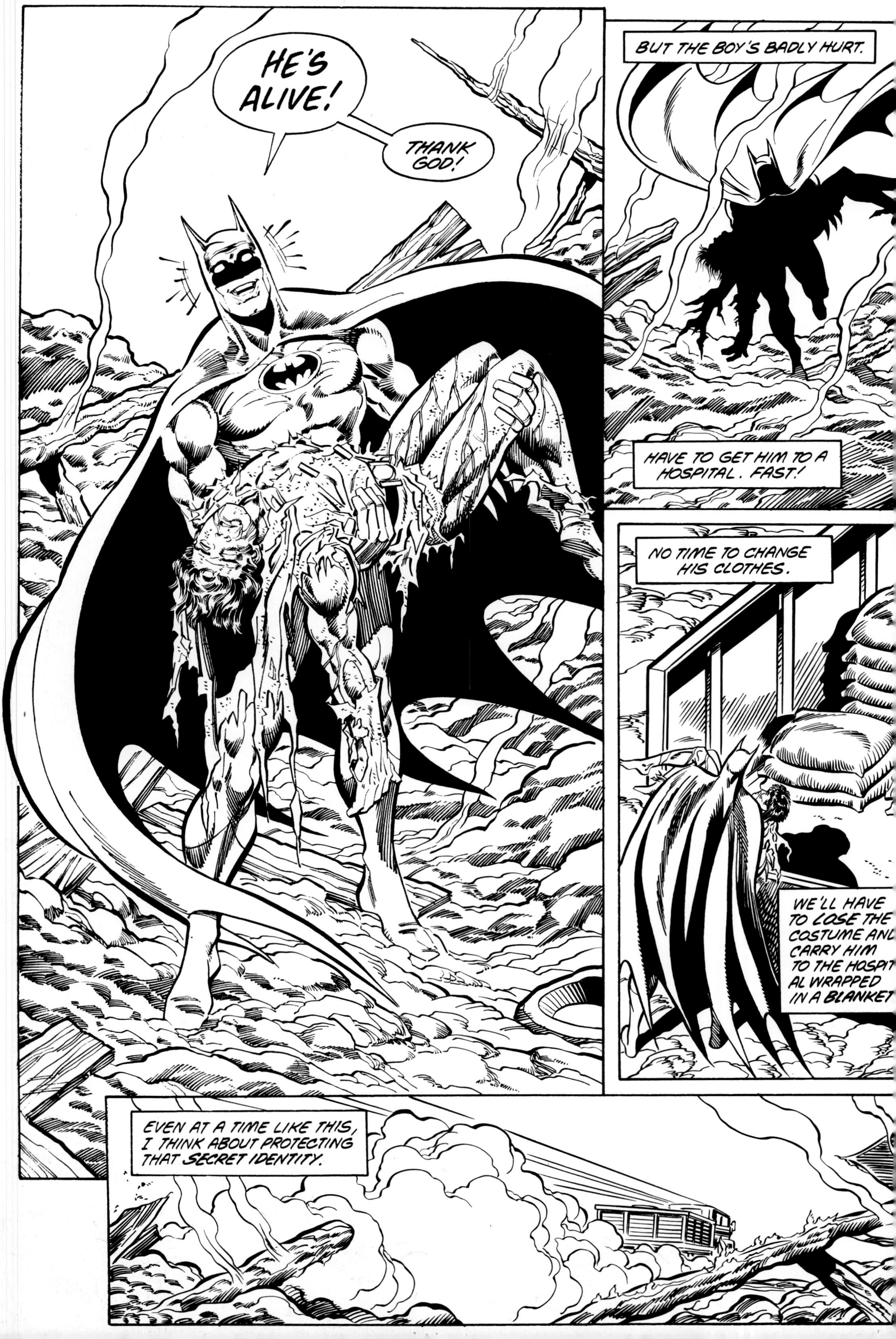
HE'S ALIVE!
THANK GOD!
BUT THE BOY'S BADLY HURT.
HAVE TO GET HIM TO A HOSPITAL. FAST!
NO TIME TO CHANGE HIS CLOTHES.
WE'LL HAVE TO LOSE THE COSTUME AND CARRY HIM TO THE HOSPITAL WRAPPED IN A BLANKET
EVEN AT A TIME LIKE THIS, I THINK ABOUT PROTECTING THAT SECRET IDENTITY.

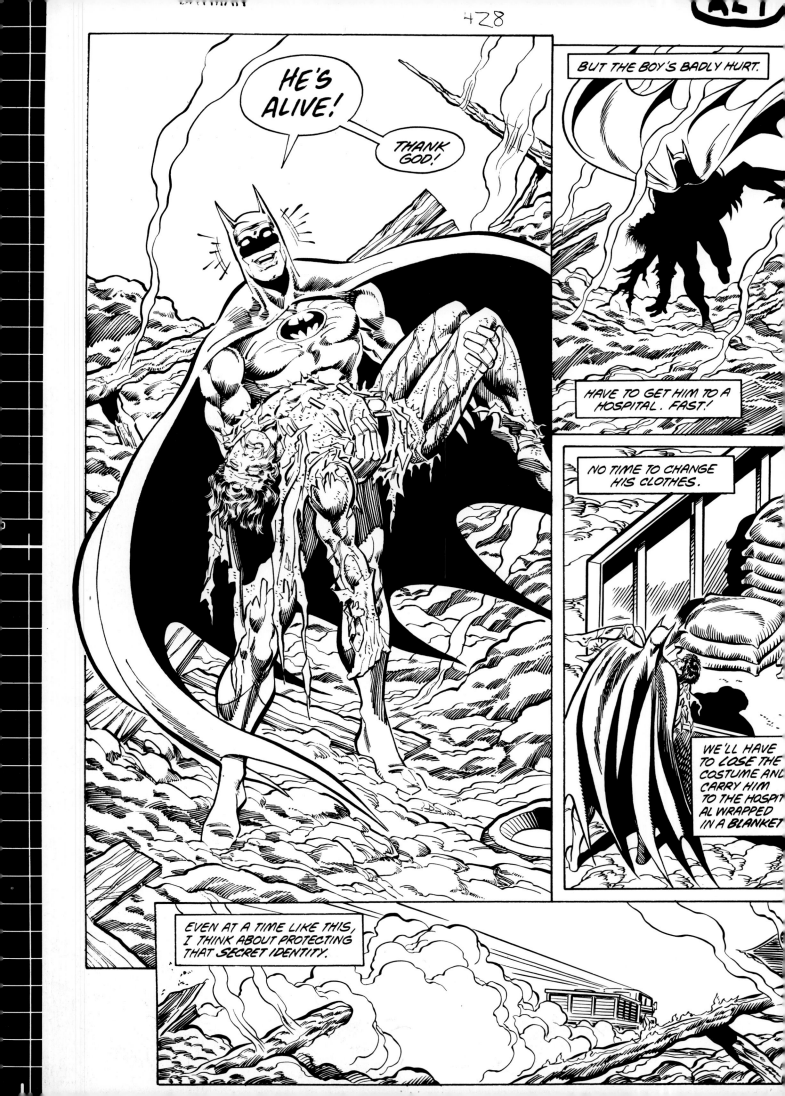

actly Who
led the
y Wonder?

said the JOKER, even
n that pestilent perpe-
r of practical perfidy
up ROBIN in the latest is-
Batman. Not I, said the
book's editor, Dennis
, who blames his readers
e deadly deed. When
decided to let them vote
ether Robin should stay
book, 10,000 Batfans
up their phones and
thumbs down to the

d Crusader's sidekick.
)'Neil: "Robin has been a
f the BATMAN mythos
years, and I was hoping
aders would have pity on
But after the vote, the
was given the joyous job
ing out Robin.
ll, friends of Dick Gray-
the original Robin and
vard of Bruce Wayne
. Batman) need not
. In 1984, Grayson's
shed his green-and-yel-
ostume and abandoned
n to become a super-
n another comic book.
ce at Batman's side was
by a chap named Jason
whom Wayne adopted
ward that year. Readers
regarded the new Rob-
whining usurper and de-
on capital punishment.
)'Neil: "Now Batman is
much reduced to Alfred
tler for companionship."
atcave had better be
for an unholy quiet.

Opposite,
UNPUBLISHED ALTERNATIVE ENDING
For BATMAN #428
Jim Aparo and Mike DeCarlo,

Left,
TIME MAGAZINE
1988

Above,
PUBLISHED ENDING
For BATMAN #428
Jim Aparo, Mike DeCarlo and Adrienne Roy, artists, 1988

Jason Todd died, but Robin lived on. Jason's replacement was Tim Drake, whose knowledge of computers, skill with a bo staff, punkoid hair-do and comatose father more than qualified him for the job. He was rewarded with a new costume that, while lacking the kicky charm of the original, is certainly more functional. It features long tights (finally!), and a cape that's not only bullet-proof but black on the outside, making Robin less of a moving target. Fans were pleased. As O'Neil puts it, "This time we got it right."

ROBIN STATUE
Limited edition of 3,900 pieces
Randy Bowen, sculptor
(cold-cast plaster, paint)
9″ tall
1995

The ears on Batman's cowl are to comics what hemlines are to fashion. In the beginning they were enormous, and then they gradually shrank. By the time the TV show aired in 1966 they were practically an afterthought. In the 1970s cartoonists like Neal Adams and Marshall Rogers helped bring them back to their demonic glory. Nowadays anything goes, and the size is left up to the artist. For example, Kelley Jones, who regularly draws for *Batman* comics, depicts them as long, thin knife blades; occasional Batman illustrator Matt Wagner keeps them stubby. Those on the "garage kit" bust at right are at the baroque extreme, and are most likely based on the work of artist Simon Bisley.

"GARAGE KIT" BUST

(Unauthorized)

(Resin, paint)

7″ tall

1995

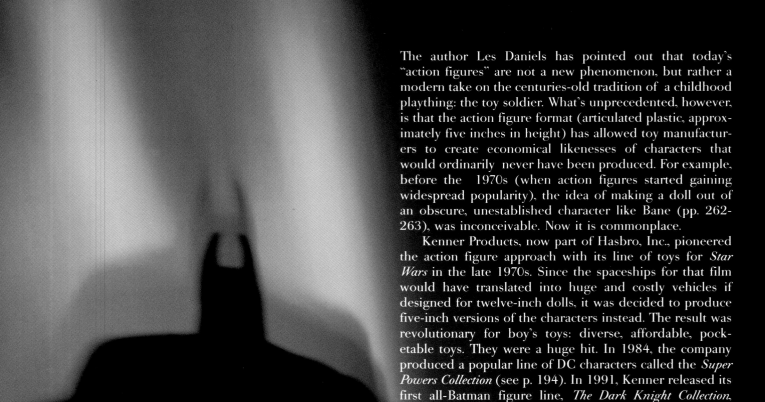

The author Les Daniels has pointed out that today's "action figures" are not a new phenomenon, but rather a modern take on the centuries-old tradition of a childhood plaything: the toy soldier. What's unprecedented, however, is that the action figure format (articulated plastic, approximately five inches in height) has allowed toy manufacturers to create economical likenesses of characters that would ordinarily never have been produced. For example, before the 1970s (when action figures started gaining widespread popularity), the idea of making a doll out of an obscure, unestablished character like Bane (pp. 262-263), was inconceivable. Now it is commonplace.

Kenner Products, now part of Hasbro, Inc., pioneered the action figure approach with its line of toys for *Star Wars* in the late 1970s. Since the spaceships for that film would have translated into huge and costly vehicles if designed for twelve-inch dolls, it was decided to produce five-inch versions of the characters instead. The result was revolutionary for boy's toys: diverse, affordable, pocketable toys. They were a huge hit. In 1984, the company produced a popular line of DC characters called the *Super Powers Collection* (see p. 194). In 1991, Kenner released its first all-Batman figure line, *The Dark Knight Collection*, which achieved a degree of success that even the company didn't expect. In 1995, Kenner sold over $163 million worth of Batman toys in the United States alone.

By 1996, there were four separate Batman action figure toy lines available: *Legends of Batman*, which places the character in different time periods and locales (Medieval Batman, Pirate Batman, Future Batman, Ancient Egyptian Batman and so on), two lines based on *Batman: The Animated Series* and a set of figures modeled on the movie *Batman Forever*. An assortment of DC heroes called *Total Justice* followed as sort of a *Super Powers* restyled for the "tougher, take-no-prisoners" attitude of the 1990s. At right, *Total Justice* Batman and Robin prepare to channel their rage.

Right,
ACTION FIGURE
CRUSADER BATMAN
From the LEGENDS OF BATMAN series
(molded plastic)
5″ tall
1995

Opposite,
TOTAL JUSTICE BATMAN AND ROBIN
Prototypes
(molded plastic)
5″ tall
1996

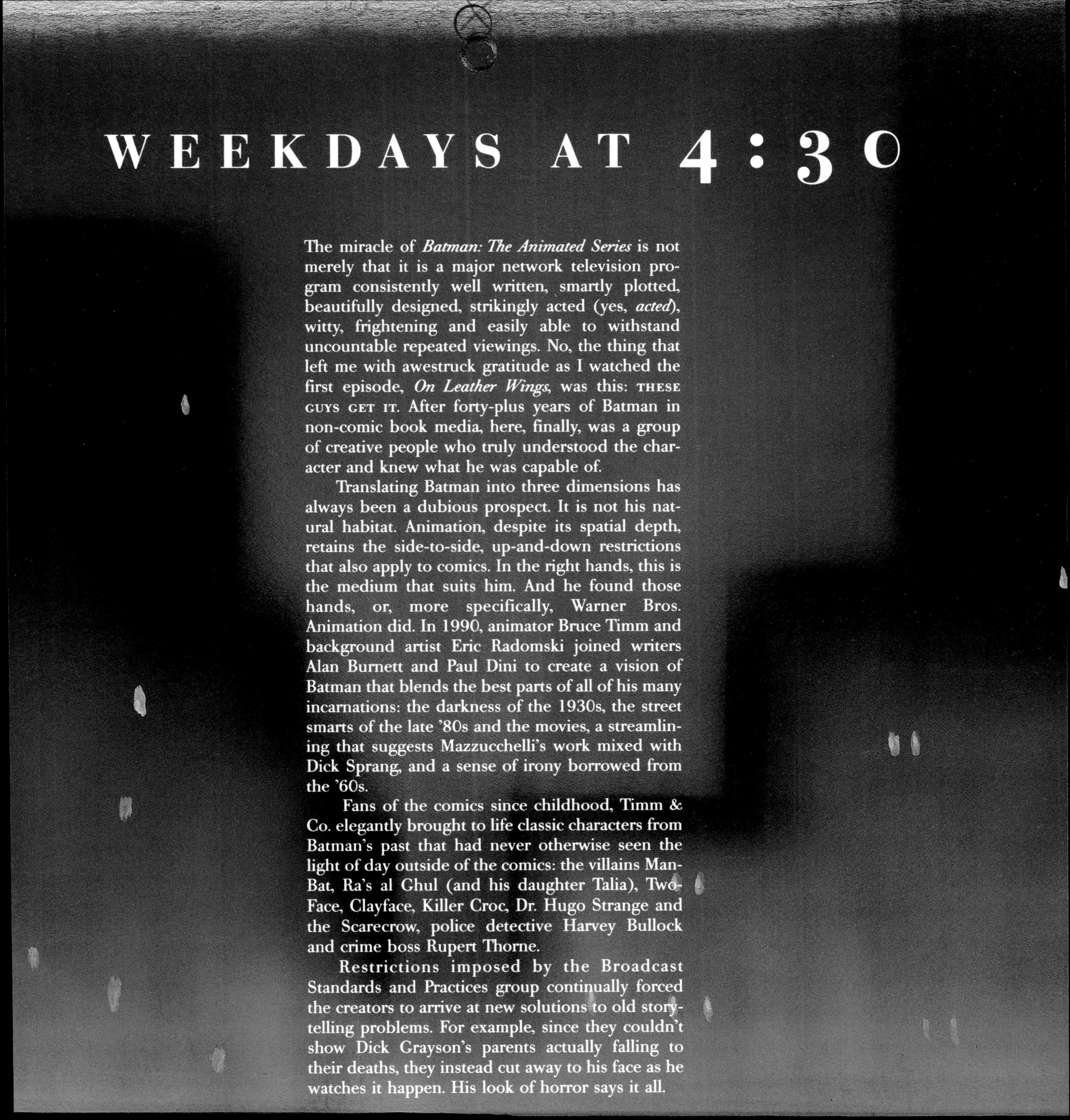

WEEKDAYS AT 4:30

The miracle of *Batman: The Animated Series* is not merely that it is a major network television program consistently well written, smartly plotted, beautifully designed, strikingly acted (yes, *acted*), witty, frightening and easily able to withstand uncountable repeated viewings. No, the thing that left me with awestruck gratitude as I watched the first episode, *On Leather Wings*, was this: THESE GUYS GET IT. After forty-plus years of Batman in non-comic book media, here, finally, was a group of creative people who truly understood the character and knew what he was capable of.

Translating Batman into three dimensions has always been a dubious prospect. It is not his natural habitat. Animation, despite its spatial depth, retains the side-to-side, up-and-down restrictions that also apply to comics. In the right hands, this is the medium that suits him. And he found those hands, or, more specifically, Warner Bros. Animation did. In 1990, animator Bruce Timm and background artist Eric Radomski joined writers Alan Burnett and Paul Dini to create a vision of Batman that blends the best parts of all of his many incarnations: the darkness of the 1930s, the street smarts of the late '80s and the movies, a streamlining that suggests Mazzucchelli's work mixed with Dick Sprang, and a sense of irony borrowed from the '60s.

Fans of the comics since childhood, Timm & Co. elegantly brought to life classic characters from Batman's past that had never otherwise seen the light of day outside of the comics: the villains Man-Bat, Ra's al Ghul (and his daughter Talia), Two-Face, Clayface, Killer Croc, Dr. Hugo Strange and the Scarecrow, police detective Harvey Bullock and crime boss Rupert Thorne.

Restrictions imposed by the Broadcast Standards and Practices group continually forced the creators to arrive at new solutions to old storytelling problems. For example, since they couldn't show Dick Grayson's parents actually falling to their deaths, they instead cut away to his face as he watches it happen. His look of horror says it all.

BACKGROUND STUDY
From BATMAN: THE ANIMATED SERIES
(airbrushed ink on paper)
8″ x 10″, 1991

Opposite,
BUBBLE BATH BOTTLE
(molded plastic, liquid soap) 10.75″ tall
England, 1993

Opposite,
CHARACTER STUDY
(pencil on paper)
2″ x 4″
Dan Haskett, artist
1991

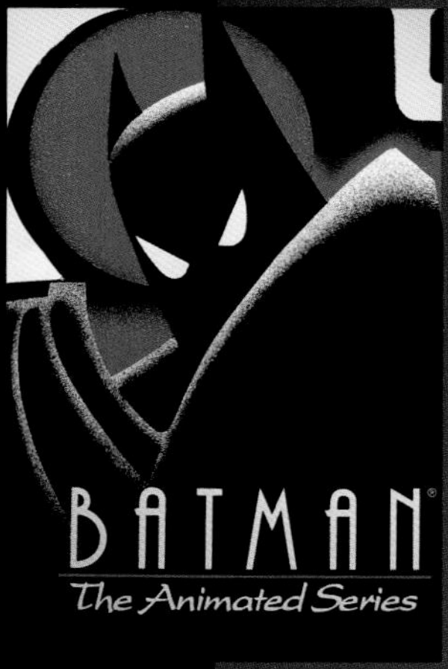

Left,
LOGO
From packaging
1990

Right,
TWO-FACE BOOKENDS
Part one
Warner Bros. Studio Store exclusive
(painted plaster)
8″ tall
1995

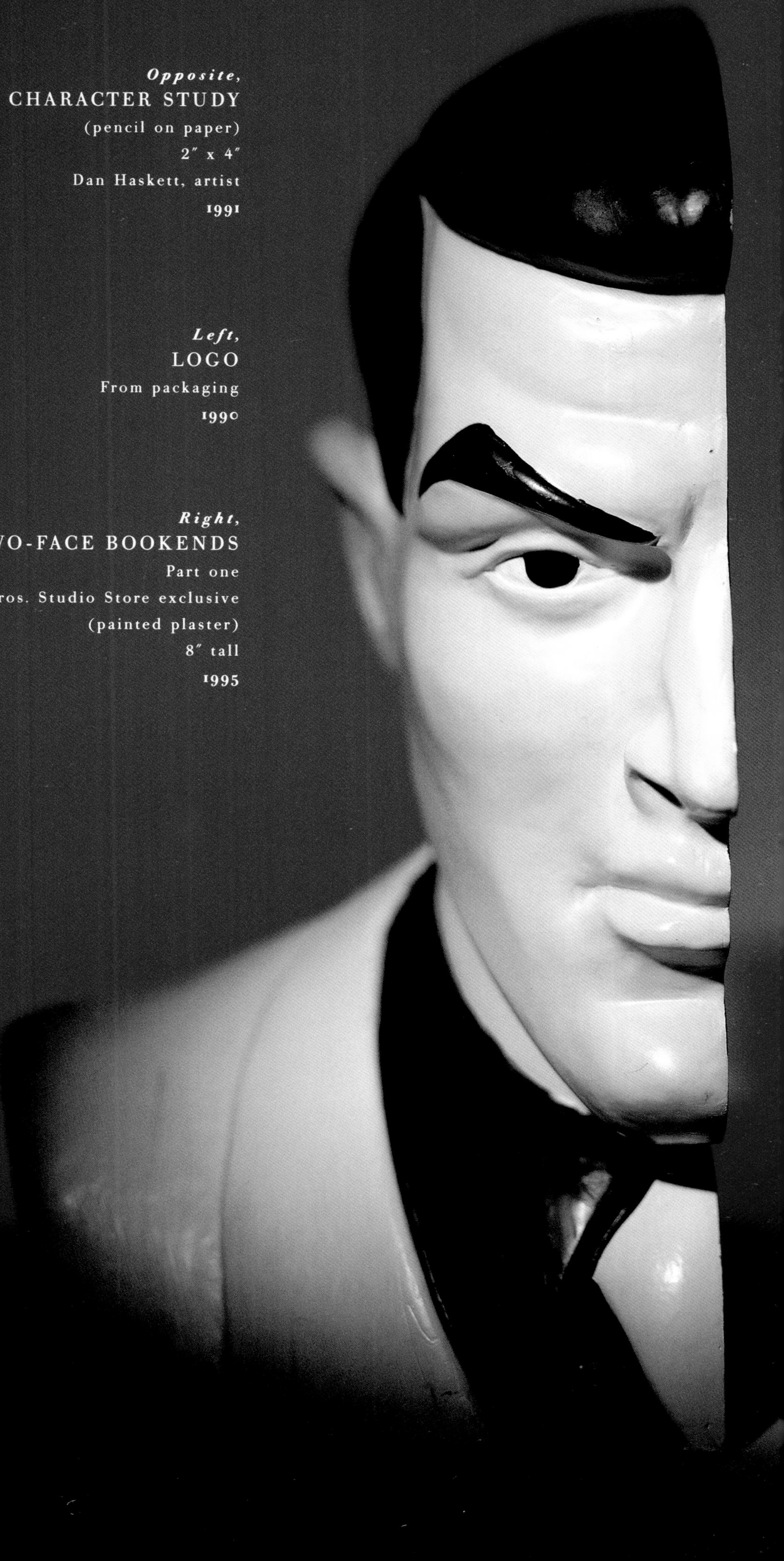

Left,
TWO-FACE BOOKENDS
Part two
Warner Bros. Studio Store exclusive
(painted plaster)
8″ tall
1995

Opposite Above,
CHARACTER STUDY
Dan Haskett, artist
(pencil on paper)
4″ x 3″
1990

Opposite Center,
FRUIT SNACKS
8″ x 6″
1995

Opposite Below,
HEAD THEORIES
Bruce Timm, artist
(ink on paper)
8″ x 10″
1990

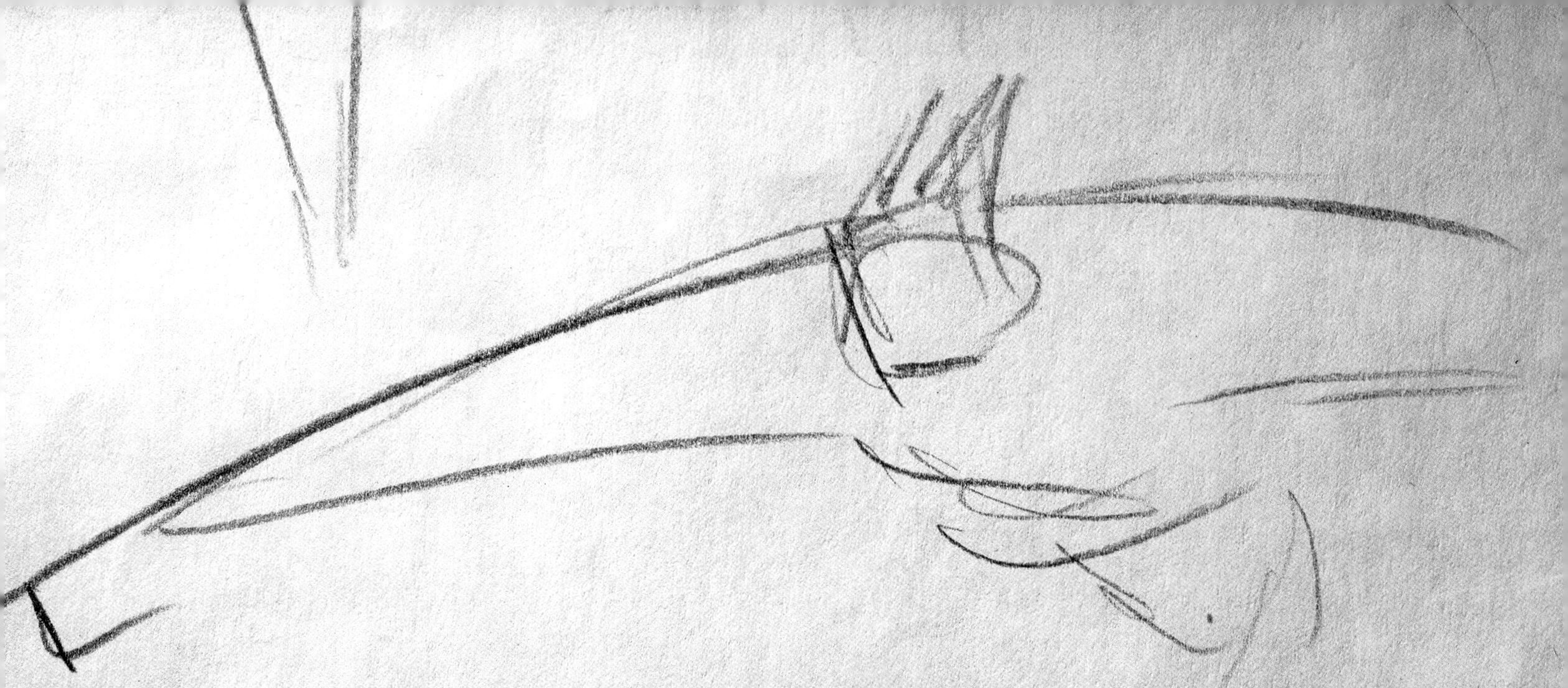

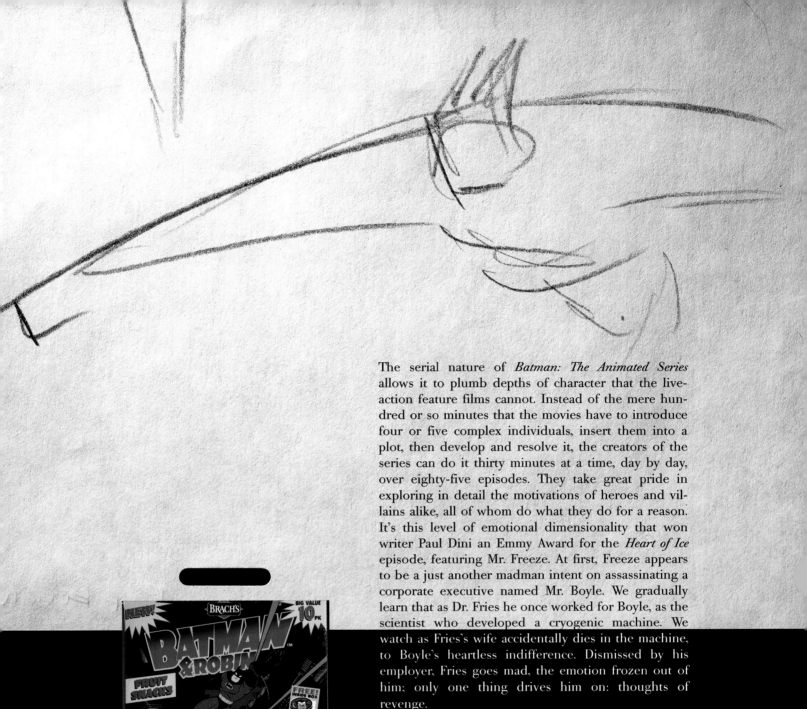

The serial nature of *Batman: The Animated Series* allows it to plumb depths of character that the live-action feature films cannot. Instead of the mere hundred or so minutes that the movies have to introduce four or five complex individuals, insert them into a plot, then develop and resolve it, the creators of the series can do it thirty minutes at a time, day by day, over eighty-five episodes. They take great pride in exploring in detail the motivations of heroes and villains alike, all of whom do what they do for a reason. It's this level of emotional dimensionality that won writer Paul Dini an Emmy Award for the *Heart of Ice* episode, featuring Mr. Freeze. At first, Freeze appears to be a just another madman intent on assassinating a corporate executive named Mr. Boyle. We gradually learn that as Dr. Fries he once worked for Boyle, as the scientist who developed a cryogenic machine. We watch as Fries's wife accidentally dies in the machine, to Boyle's heartless indifference. Dismissed by his employer, Fries goes mad, the emotion frozen out of him; only one thing drives him on: thoughts of revenge.

The show operates on the simple but rarely employed principle that if you hire a group of extremely talented people who take pride in what they do and work very hard, and you STAY OUT of their way (most of the time, anyway), the end result will be extraordinary. *Batman: The Animated Series* took everyone by surprise and was favorably reviewed by sources like the *New York Times* and *Newsweek*, who normally wouldn't give a daily animated children's program serious critical notice, much less on the positive side. It won four Emmy Awards, for writing and for composer Shirley Walker's stunning musical scores. It became a worldwide hit on a par with its 1966 predecessor. It spawned the inevitable licensing blitz, but the design of everything was so handsome it seemed as if we'd never seen it before. And we hadn't, not quite this way. With impeccable craft and style, *Batman: The Animated Series* cares deeply for its subject matter and, in so doing, does the same for its audience.

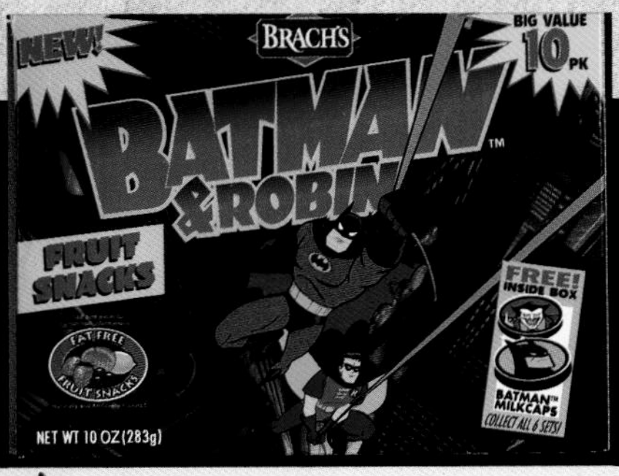

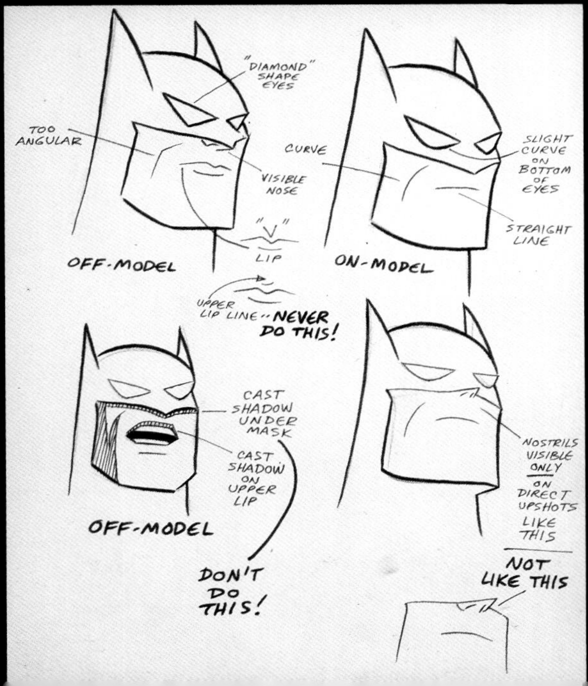

FEET DON'T LIFT
HIGH— IT'S A
GLIDE..A TENSE
GLIDE. HE'S
TENSE BUT NOT
STIFF,—"TINY
LITTLE MOVES"
Exp Roughs #22

Right,
INSTANT NOODLE SOUP
Canada
1992

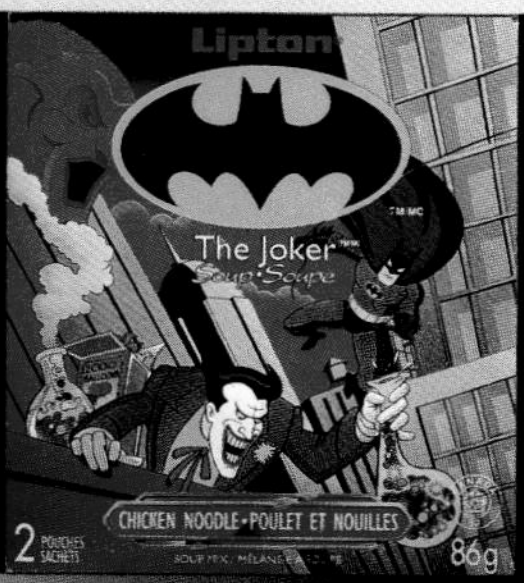

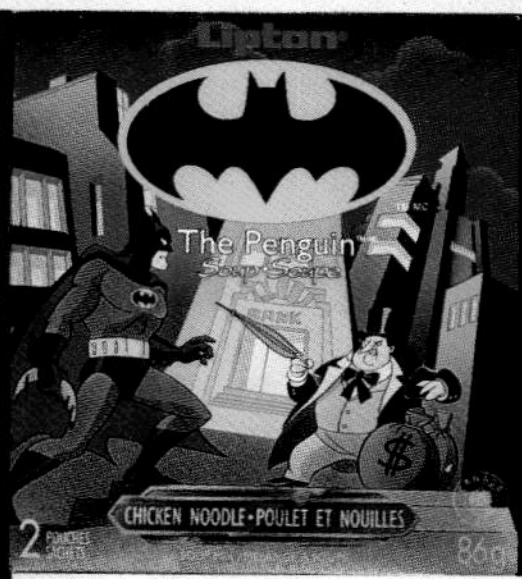

Above,
CUP TOPS
(molded plastic)
Approx. 3″ tall
New Zealand
1994

Below,
THE NEW YORK TIMES
Television supplement
August 30-September 5
1992

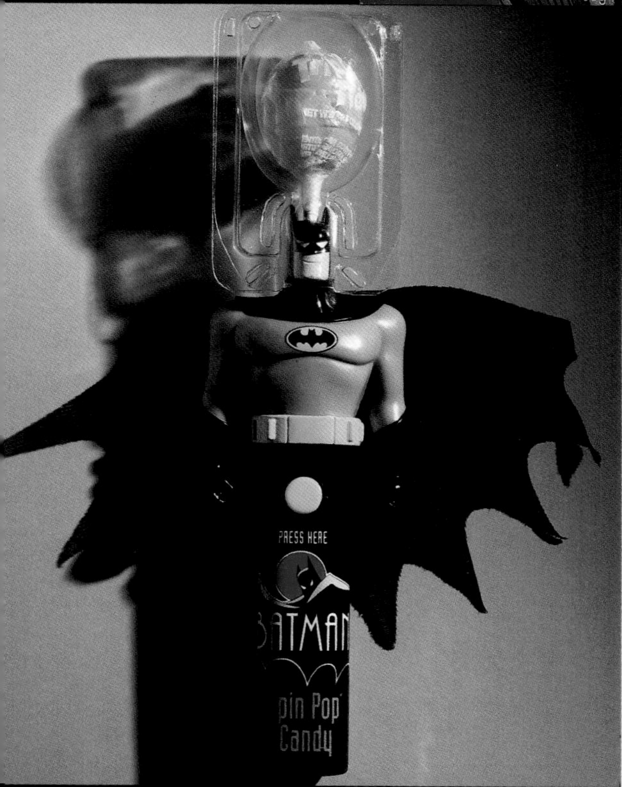

OVERLEAF
JOKER CHARACTER STUDIES
Mike Kim, artist
(pencil on paper), 1990

PAGE 261
ANIMATION CELL WITH BACKGROUND SETUP
From opening title sequence
TMS studio, artists
11″ x 14″, 1991

The New York Times

Section 12
Copyright © 1992 The New York Times

Television

AUGUST 30-SEPTEMBER 5

Fox Broadcasting

Dark Knight "Batman: The Animated Series" follows the adventures

JOKER
ATTITUDES

Right,
BANE
ACTION FIGURE
(molded plastic)
5.25″ tall
1995

PAGE C80
SCENE. (CONT.) BG.
SCENE C94 BG
--GRABS BATMAN!
BATMAN SPINS--
BATMAN'S P.O.V:
BANE IS PISSED!

Above and Opposite Right,
STORYBOARDS
Bruce Timm, artist
11″ x 17″, 1994

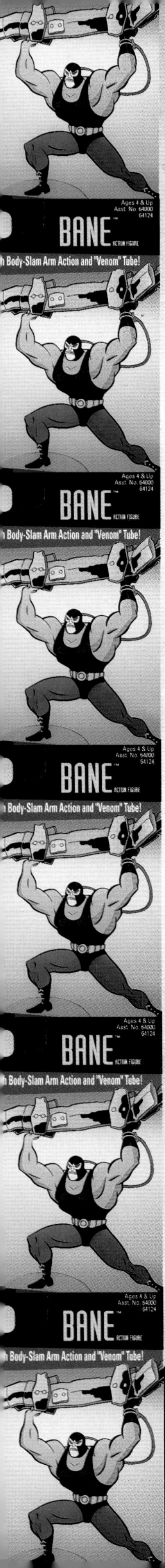

Ages 4 & Up
Asst. No. 64000
64124
BANE
ACTION FIGURE
h Body-Slam Arm Action and "Venom" Tube!

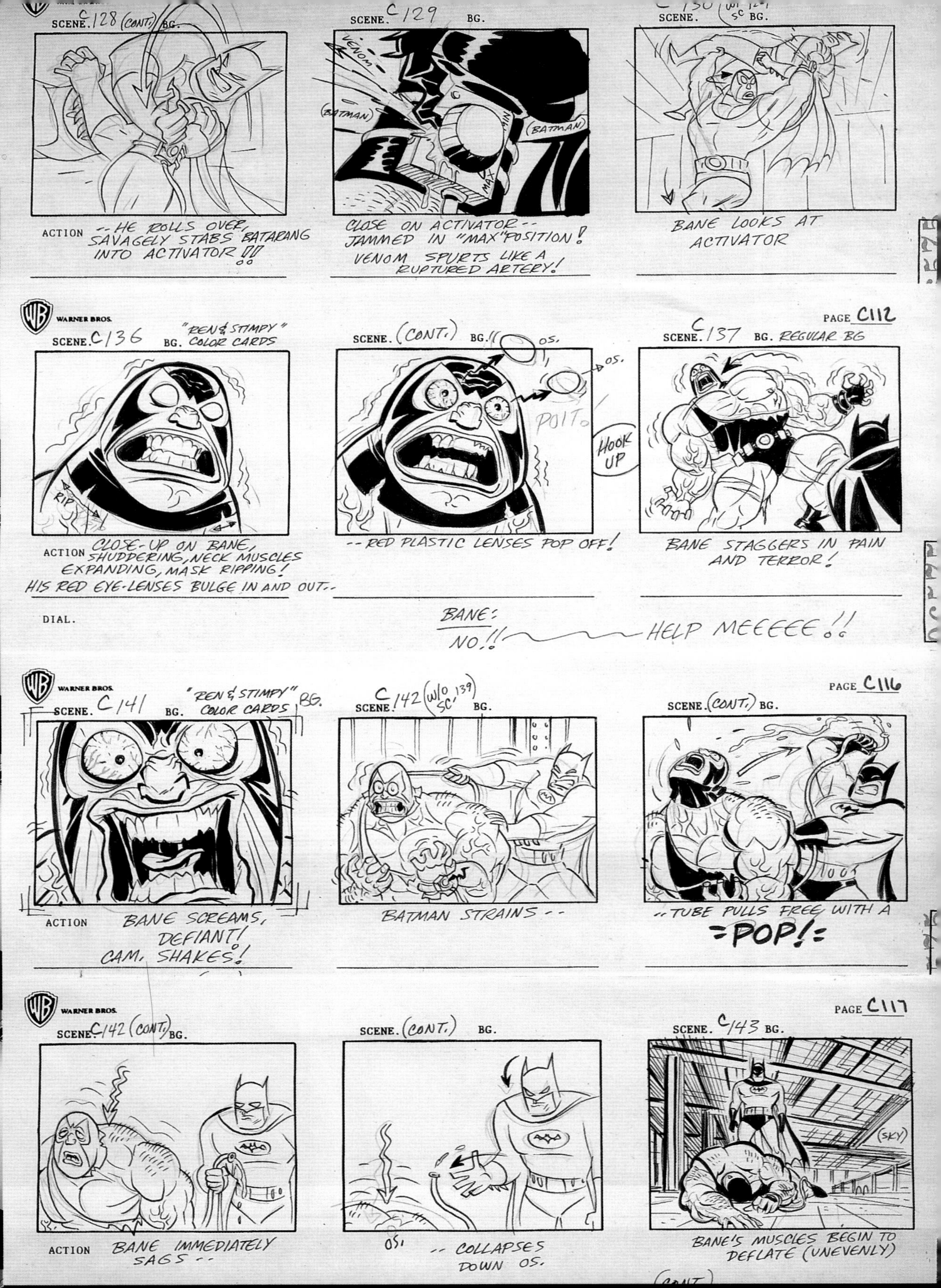

SCENE. C128 (CONT.) BG.
ACTION --HE ROLLS OVER, SAVAGELY STABS BATARANG INTO ACTIVATOR!!
SCENE. C129 BG.
VENOM
(BATMAN)
(BATMAN)
MAX
CLOSE ON ACTIVATOR-- JAMMED IN "MAX" POSITION! VENOM SPURTS LIKE A RUPTURED ARTERY!
BANE LOOKS AT ACTIVATOR
WARNER BROS.
SCENE. C136 BG. "REN & STIMPY" COLOR CARDS
RIP
ACTION CLOSE-UP ON BANE, SHUDDERING, NECK MUSCLES EXPANDING, MASK RIPPING! HIS RED EYE-LENSES BULGE IN AND OUT.-
SCENE. (CONT.) BG.
OS.
POIT.
HOOK UP
--RED PLASTIC LENSES POP OFF!
PAGE C112
SCENE. C137 BG. REGULAR BG
BANE STAGGERS IN PAIN AND TERROR!
DIAL.
BANE: NO!! HELP MEEEEE!!
WARNER BROS.
SCENE. C141 BG. "REN & STIMPY" COLOR CARDS
ACTION BANE SCREAMS, DEFIANT! CAM. SHAKES!
SCENE. C142 (W/O SC 139) BG.
BATMAN STRAINS--
PAGE C116
SCENE. (CONT.) BG.
--TUBE PULLS FREE WITH A =POP!=
WARNER BROS.
SCENE. C142 (CONT.) BG.
ACTION BANE IMMEDIATELY SAGS--
SCENE. (CONT.) BG.
OS.
--COLLAPSES DOWN OS.
PAGE C117
SCENE. C143 BG.
(SKY)
BANE'S MUSCLES BEGIN TO DEFLATE (UNEVENLY)

The Vengeance of Bane is one of the series' most popular episodes, featuring a villain introduced to the comics in 1992. An immediate hit with fans, Bane seems to be a comment on drug abuse. He is addicted to a substance called Venom, which flows from a regulated storage pack on his left wrist through a tube connected to the base of his skull. It makes him savagely strong and mercilessly cruel. An indication of his power is eerily demonstrated early on during a monstrous battle in which he literally wipes the sewers with Killer Croc, another of Batman's foes and no pansy himself. In the pulse-pounding conclusion, Bane finally catches up with Batman, beats the tar out of him and is just about to go in for the kill when the plug

NESTING DOLLS
(prototypes)
(painted wood)
Russia
1995

Above,
ACTION FIGURE
Retro Batman
(molded plastic), 5″ tall, 1994

Right,
NOVELTY FOAM CHAIR
(plush fabric)
18″ tall, 1996

Left,
PILLOW DOLL
(prototype)
(cloth, stuffing) 7″ tall
1995

Left,
SKETCH
For title sequence
TMS studio, artists
9″ x 12″
1991

Below,
BATMOBILE
(molded plastic)
15″ long
1992

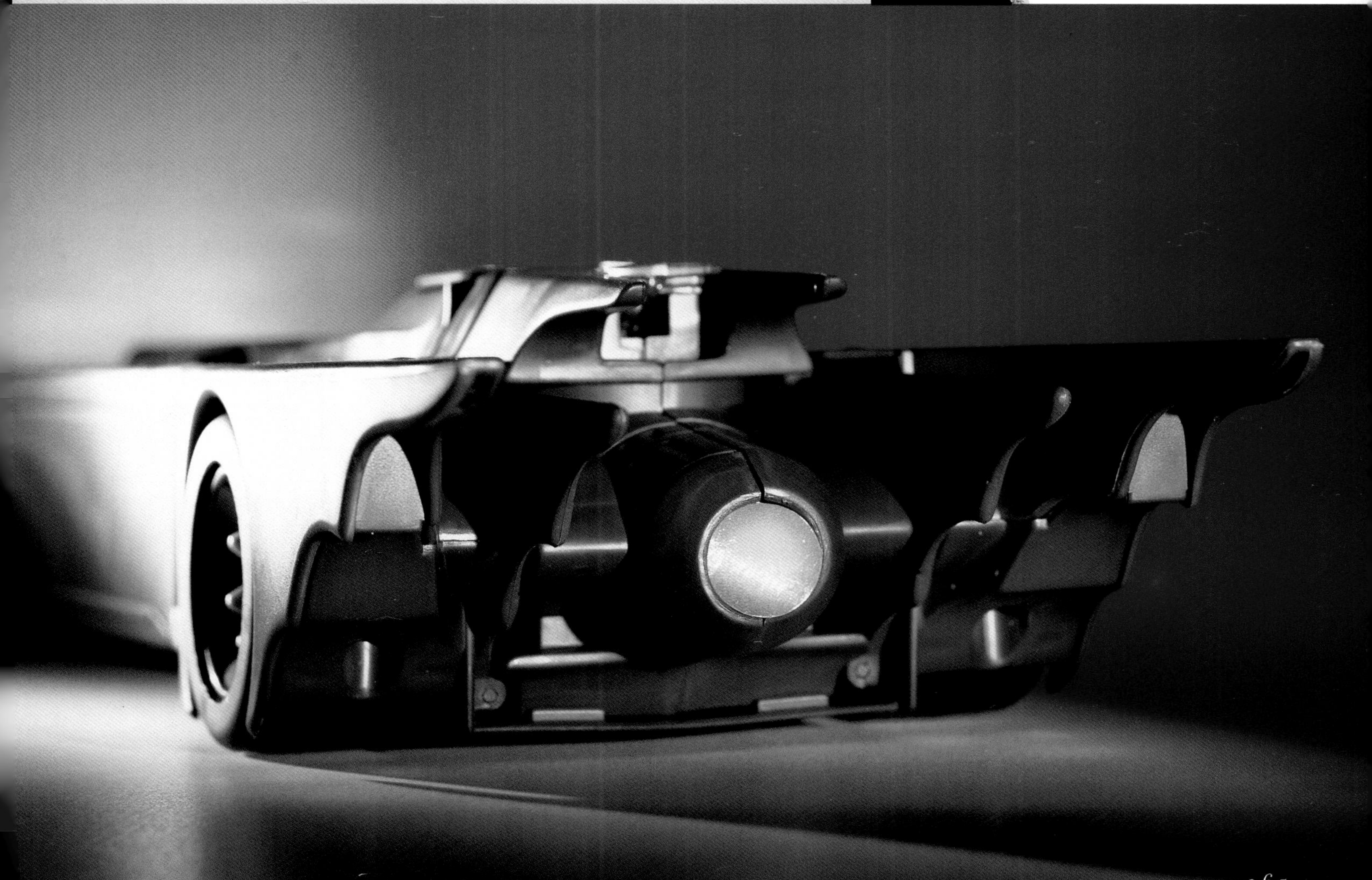

Bottom,
STUDIES
For mouth movement
Christopher Dent, artist
(ink on paper)
8″ x 10″
1991

PAGE 268
THE ULTIMATE BATMAN
(molded plastic, interior lamps)
12″ tall
1994

Opposite,
SKETCH
For title sequence
TMS studio, artists
(pencil on paper)
10″ x 14″
1991

PAGE 269
BACKGROUND PAINTING
For title sequence
TMS studio, artists
10″ x 14″
1991

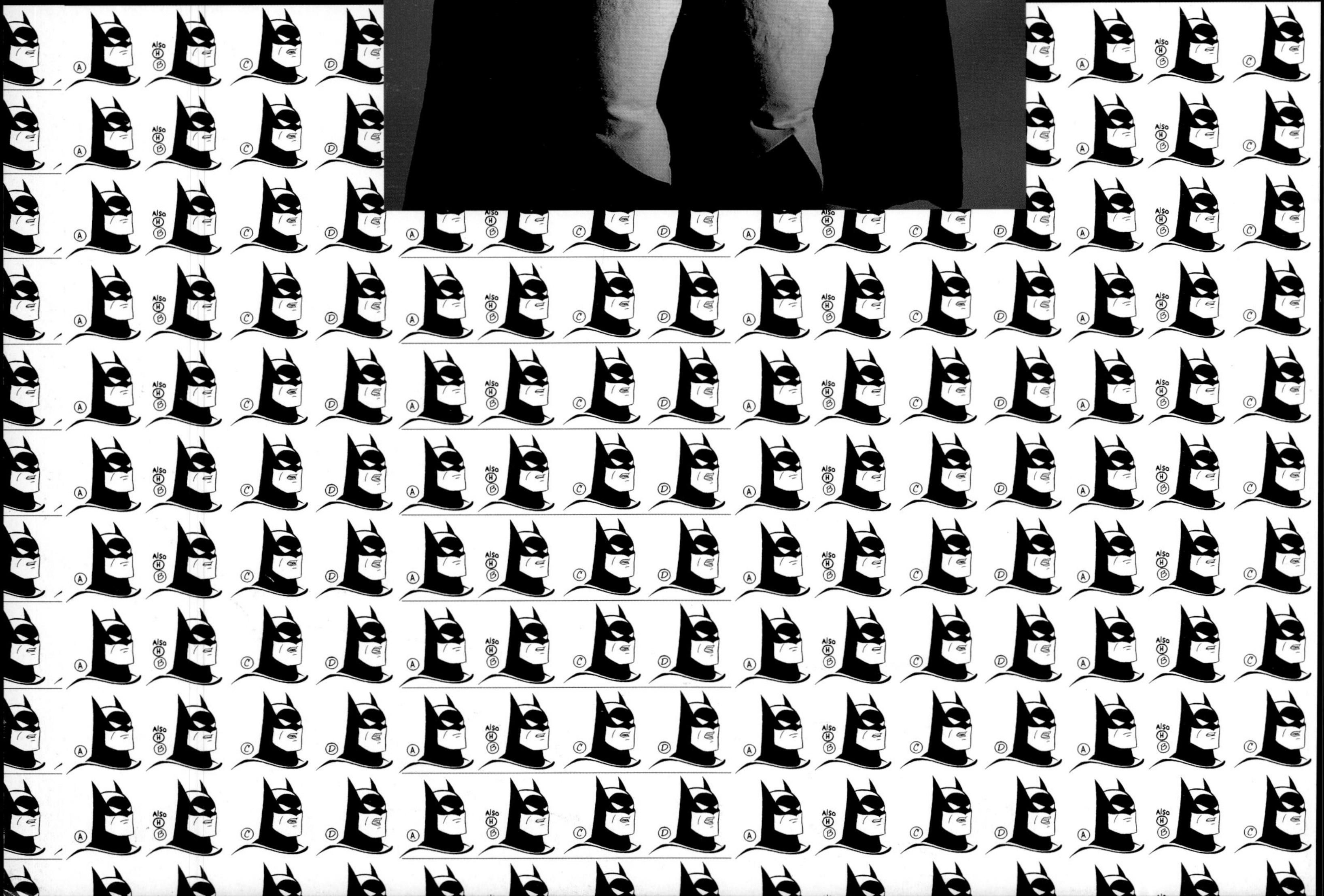

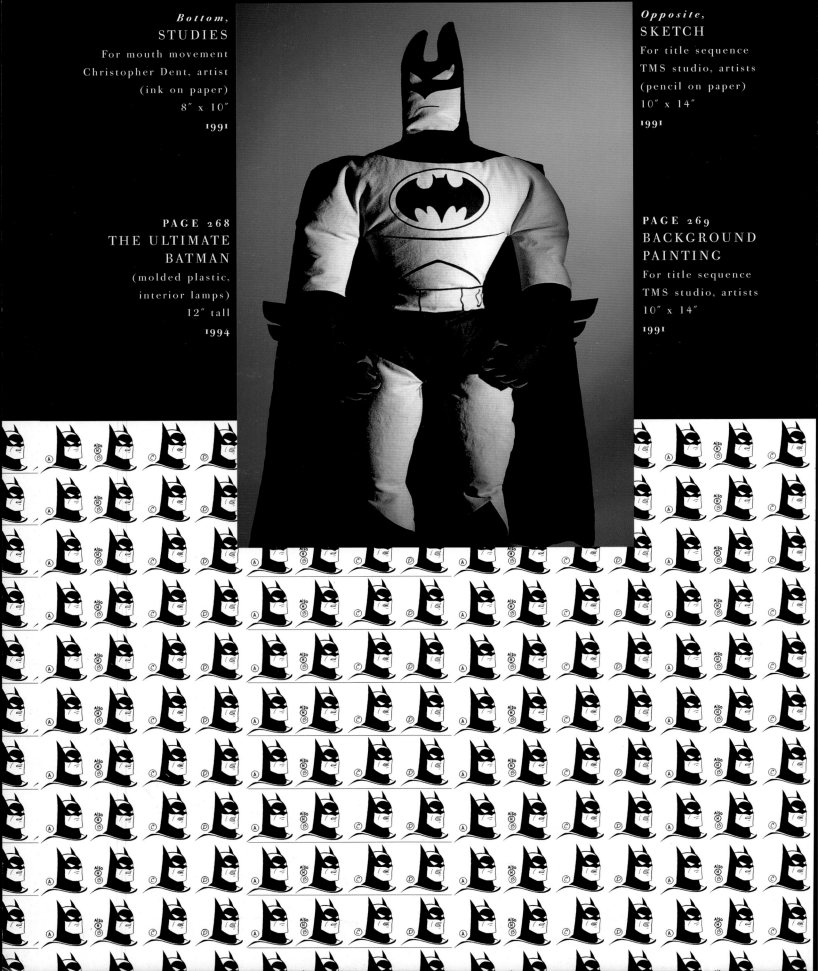

S. C. 22 TIME (

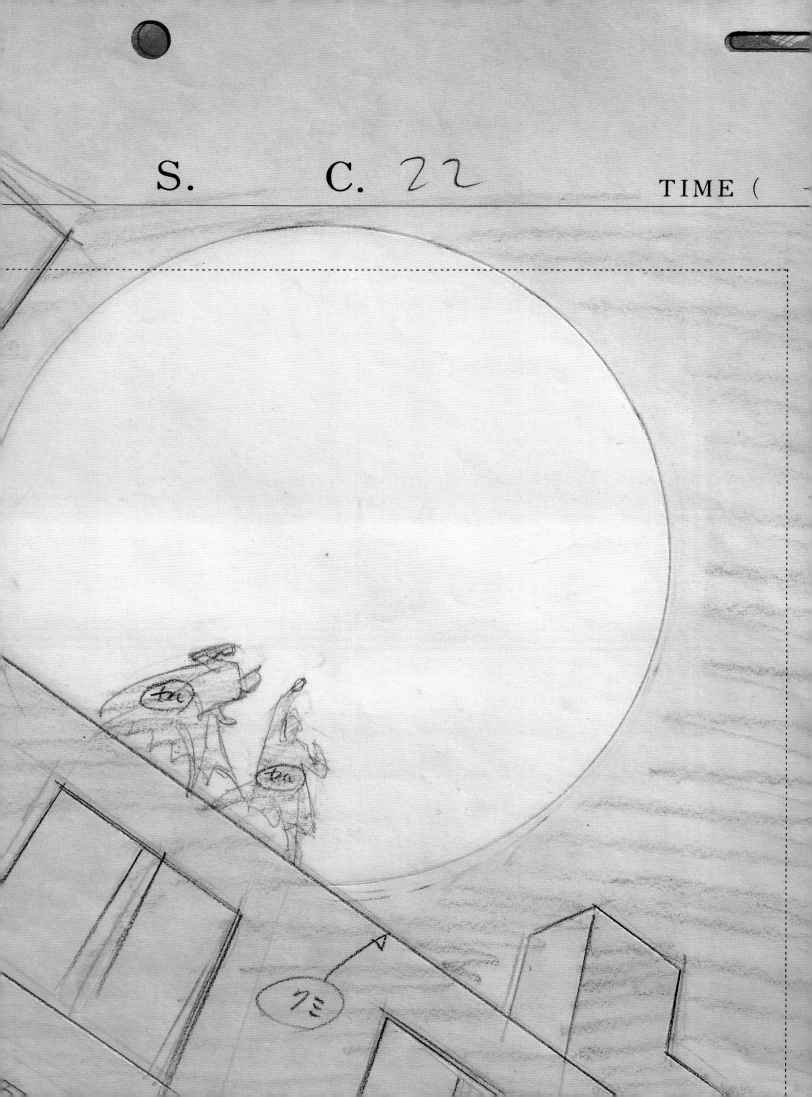

To collect Batman is to gather together a part of the history of the twentieth-century American imagination. From the trials of the Depression and the Second World War to the anxieties of the new millennium and beyond, Batman has been with us in one form or another. This is a collection of those forms, and as they change they show us how we and our mythologies have also changed.

America, which thrives on change, has always needed abiding myths. Ours is the country that invented itself, and we invent our myths as well. They are unique and unintentional. They reenact the primal stories of our national struggle—of our independence, our ambitions, our complexity, our strengths and vulnerabilities. They are voted into favor over time by popular opinion, and they are symbols of what we want, for ourselves and for our nation. *That*, I think, is why Batman endures: because America wants what Batman wants. America wants revenge. America wants to acquire. America wants to look fabulous. America wants to be feared. America wants a good fight. America wants to triumph. America wants to protect, and America wants to be saved.

Opposite Top,
BOB KANE'S WRITING PAPER
8″ x 8″
1940s

Opposite Bottom,
EXTENDING TELESCOPE
Packaging. (offset lithography on paper)
6″ x 2″ x 2″
England
1966

AFTERWORD

Since this book's original publication in 1996, toy-collecting has evolved dramatically. We are now living in the Global Flea Market. I'm referring, of course, to the internet—and, more specifically, to e-mail and eBay. People everywhere from across town to the other side of the Earth e-mail me weekly with Batman toys I didn't even know existed, either to buy or just to share. It is in this spirit that I present these sixteen pages of new material, much of it from the collection of Saul Ferris, who I "met" on-line, and who graciously allowed these items to be collected for this edition.

Overleaf Top,
ORIGINAL ART
From the Batman daily newspaper strip
(pen and ink, Zipatone on illustration board)
6″ x 5″
Bob Kane, artist
1946

Overleaf Bottom,
PRESSBOOKS
For the Columbia Batman serials
(offset lithography on paper)
11″ x 14″
1943, 1946

IN RESPONSE TO THE BAT SIGNAL, BRUCE WAYNE AND DICK GRAYSON SWITCH TO THEIR WORLD-FAMOUS IDENTITIES OF BATMAN AND ROBIN...
531
COME ON, YOUNGSTER— INTO THE BATMOBILE!

BATMAN
BASED ON THE BATMAN COMIC MAGAZINE FEATURE APPEARING IN DETECTIVE COMICS AND BATMAN MAGAZINES
with
Lewis Wilson · Douglas Croft
J. Carrol Naish · Shirley Patterson
Screen Play by Victor McLeod, Leslie Swabacker, Harry Fraser
Produced by RUDOLPH C. FLOTHOW · Directed by LAMBERT HILLYER
A COLUMBIA CHAPTER PLAY
COPYRIGHT, DETECTIVE COMICS, INC., 1942

Another Mighty COLUMBIA Super-Serial Zooms out of the Comics onto the Screen!
Double the serial thrills and excitement . . . WITH THE GREATEST, MOST CELEBRATED ACTION TEAM IN THE WORLD!
NEW ADVENTURES of BATMAN and ROBIN, THE BOY WONDER
BASED ON THE WELL-KNOWN BATMAN COMIC MAGAZINE FEATURE APPEARING IN "DETECTIVE COMICS" AND "BATMAN" MAGAZINES
with Robert LOWERY · John DUNCAN · Jane ADAMS · Lyle TALBOT · Ralph GRAVES
Written for the Screen by GEORGE H. PLYMPTON, JOSEPH F. POLAND and ROYAL K. COLE
Directed by SPENCER BENNET · Produced by SAM KATZMAN
A COLUMBIA SERIAL
Copyright 1949 Columbia Pictures Corp.

OCKET CAR AND PACKAGING (molded plastic, rubber), 10″ long. Japan, 1966

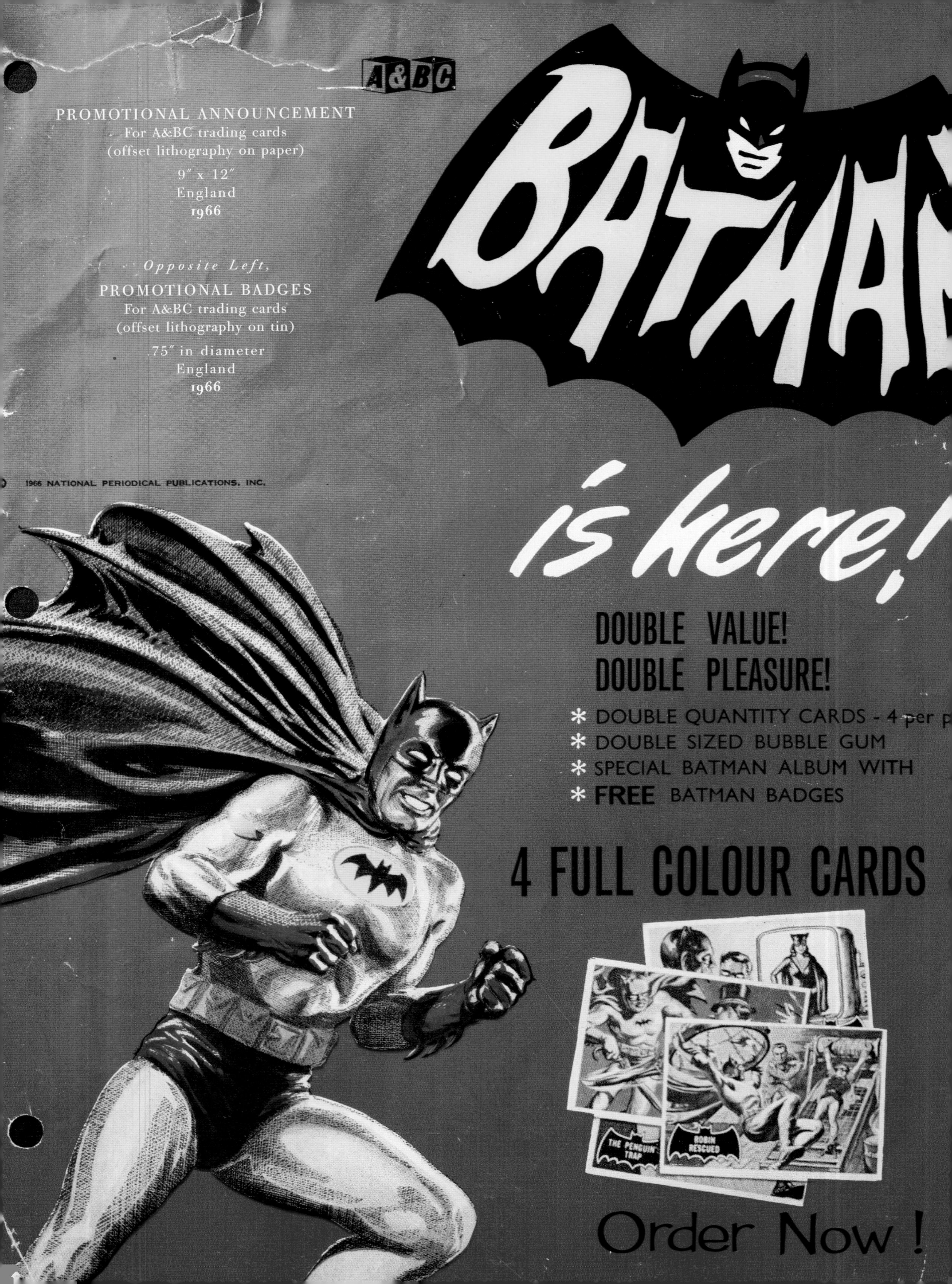

A&BC
1966 NATIONAL PERIODICAL PUBLICATIONS, INC.
is here!
DOUBLE VALUE!
DOUBLE PLEASURE!
* DOUBLE QUANTITY CARDS - 4 per
* DOUBLE SIZED BUBBLE GUM
* SPECIAL BATMAN ALBUM WITH
* FREE BATMAN BADGES
4 FULL COLOUR CARDS
THE PENGUIN TRAP
ROBIN RESCUED
Order Now !

PROMOTIONAL ANNOUNCEMENT
For A&BC trading cards
(offset lithography on paper)
9″ x 12″
England
1966

Opposite Left,
PROMOTIONAL BADGES
For A&BC trading cards
(offset lithography on tin)
.75″ in diameter
England
1966

BATMAN ON A SPRING
(offset lithography on tin, spring)
4″ tall
Japan
1966

COMIC BOOK DISPLAY RACK (offset lithography on tin), 12″ tall. EARLY 1960S

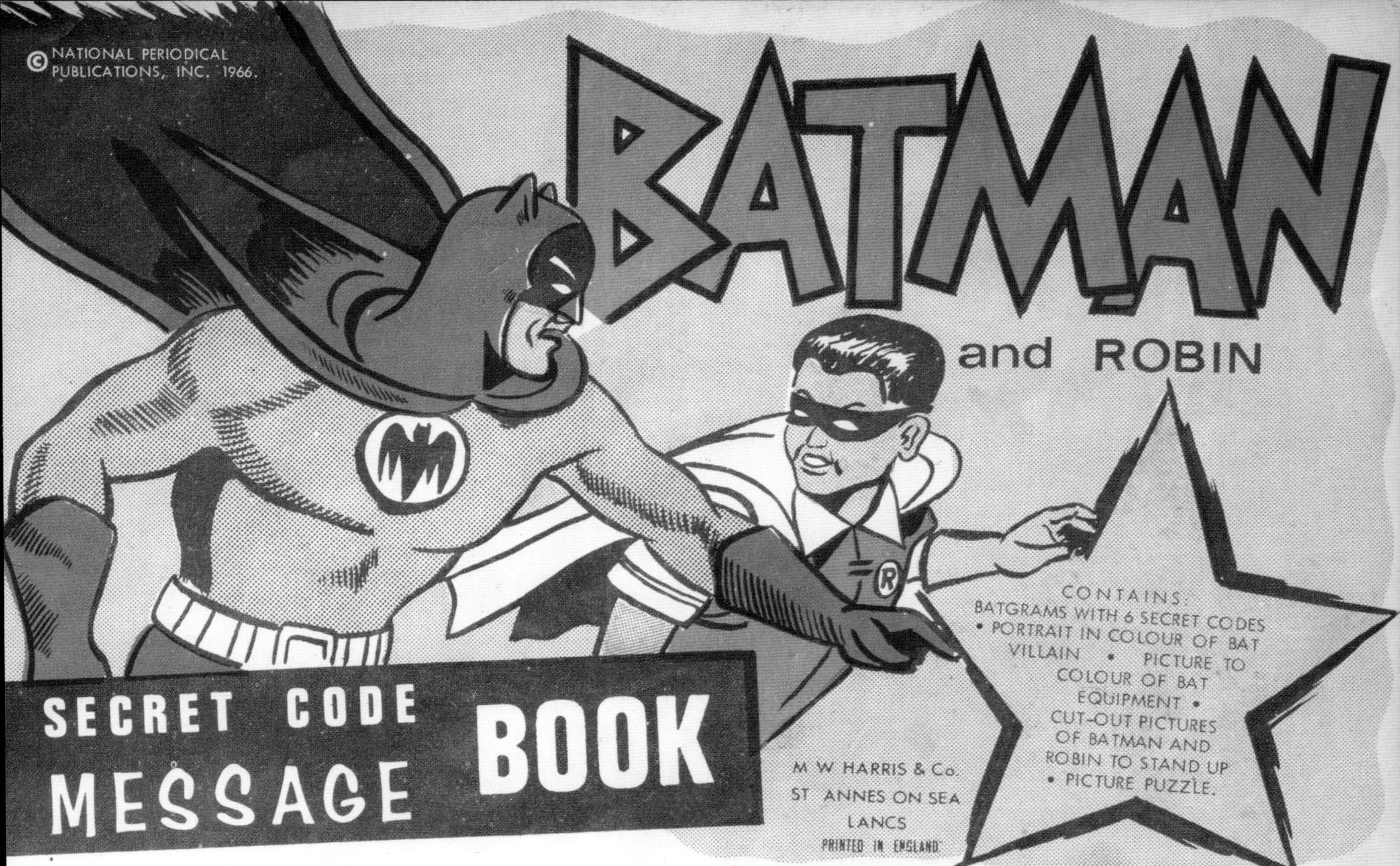

© NATIONAL PERIODICAL PUBLICATIONS, INC. 1966.
BATMAN
and ROBIN
CONTAINS:
BATGRAMS WITH 6 SECRET CODES
• PORTRAIT IN COLOUR OF BAT VILLAIN • PICTURE TO COLOUR OF BAT EQUIPMENT •
CUT-OUT PICTURES OF BATMAN AND ROBIN TO STAND UP
• PICTURE PUZZLE.
SECRET CODE MESSAGE BOOK
M W HARRIS & Co.
ST ANNES ON SEA
LANCS
PRINTED IN ENGLAND

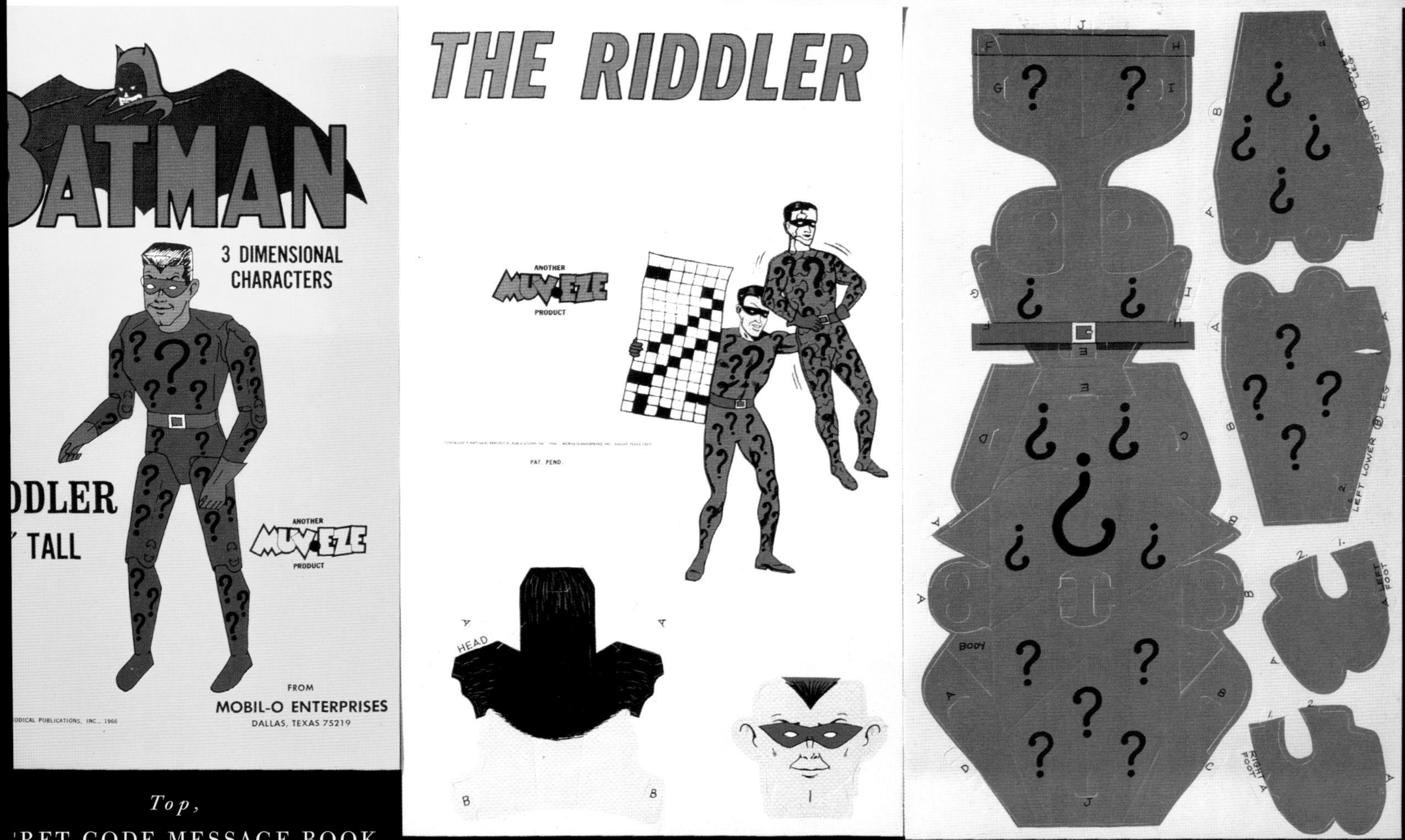

Top,
RET CODE MESSAGE BOOK
(offset lithography on paper)
8″ x 5″
England, 1966

Above, RIDDLER MUV-EZE PAPER TOY
(offset lithography on paper), 11.63″ tall
1966

Left,
BATMOBILE
(offset lithography on tin)
4″ x 2″
Japan
1966

Below,
JELLY LABELS
(offset lithography on paper)
3″ x 5″
1966

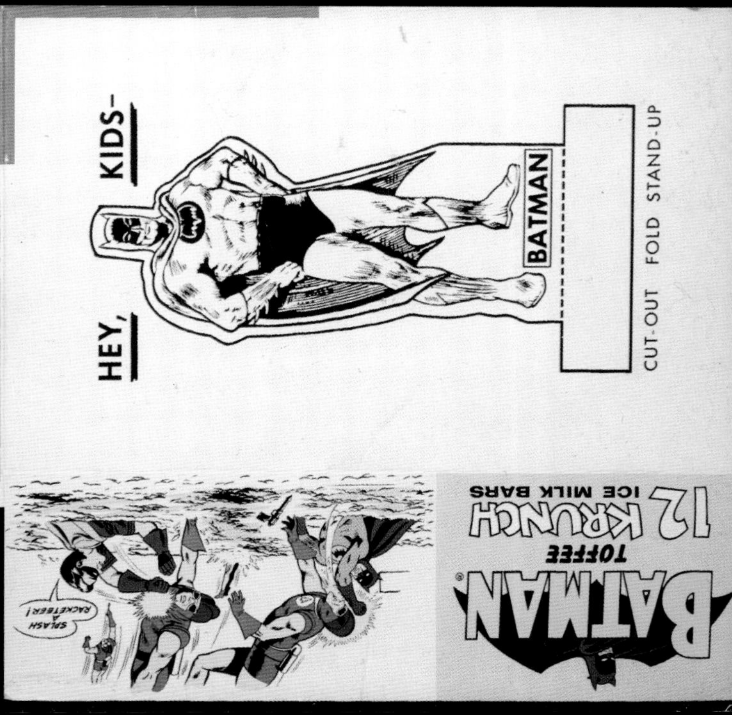

ALL STAR DAIRY PACKAGING
(offset lithography on paper)
2.5″ in diameter; 9″ x 6″ x 3″, 1966

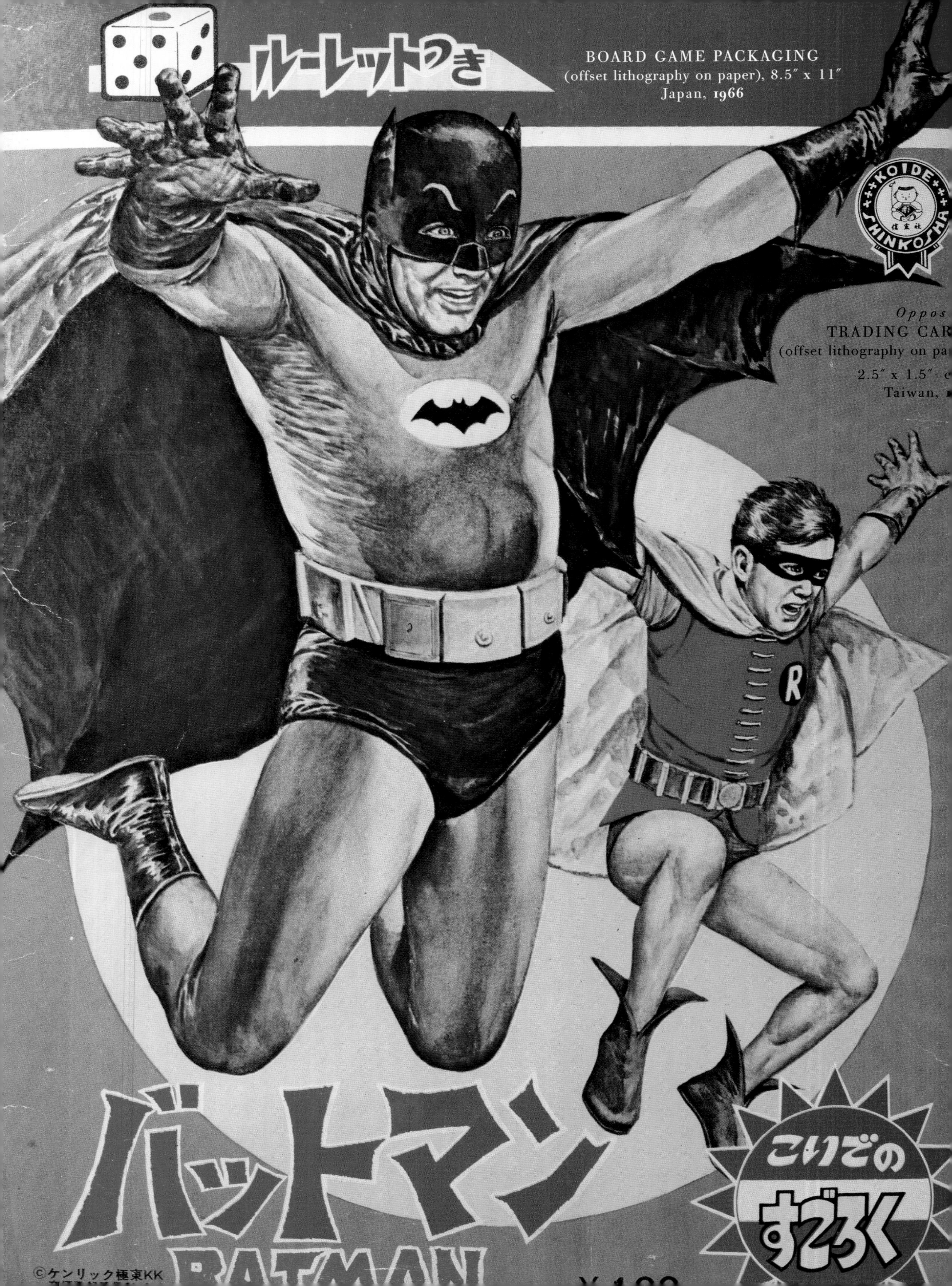

BOARD GAME PACKAGING
(offset lithography on paper), 8.5″ x 11″
Japan, 1966

Oppos
TRADING CAR
(offset lithography on pa
2.5″ x 1.5″ e
Taiwan,

TWIST 'N' FLEX
BATMAN
(molded plastic,
polyester)
7″ tall
England
1966

EXTENDING TELESCOPE
Packaging. (offset lithography on paper)
6″ x 3″. England, 1966

R
BATCODE No Z1.
OBRSN SL RSFCC TBQM BKM TZS LZS.
CLIM SBAR ABTH BILKD MLSSNM IFKN
SL IBHN VLZQ OFTSZQN RSBKM ZO.

PAGE FROM

SECRET CODE MESSAGE BOOK

(offset lithography on paper)

8″ x 5″

England

1966

Overleaf Top,

ROCKET CAR

Packaging.

(offset lithography on paper)

5″ x 3″

Japan

1966

Overleaf Bottom,

BOARD GAME PACKAGING

(offset lithography on paper)

8.5″ x 11″

Japan

1966

PAGE 285 *Top,*

ACTIVITY BOOK

(offset lithography on paper) 12″ x 14″

Holland, **1966**

BATMAN
スピリット号

BATMAN
バットマン
ふくちゃん
©ケンリック極東KK
商標登録番号595225
¥100
KOIDE SHINKOSHA

Below, FLYING JET LAUNCH AND PACKAGING (molded plastic), 12″ x 14″. Japan, 1966

INDEX OF ILLUSTRATIONS

Opposite,
ORIGINAL COVER ART
(detail)
For *Kingdom Come* #3
(acrylic on illustration board)
Alex Ross, artist
1996

This page is perforated for easy removal. Tear it out before you press out the pieces.

Pull the center pages out gently and
then hang up your Batman picture.

Press out all the pieces, trim, open slits, and fold on dotted lines.

Match background colors
of stands and pieces.

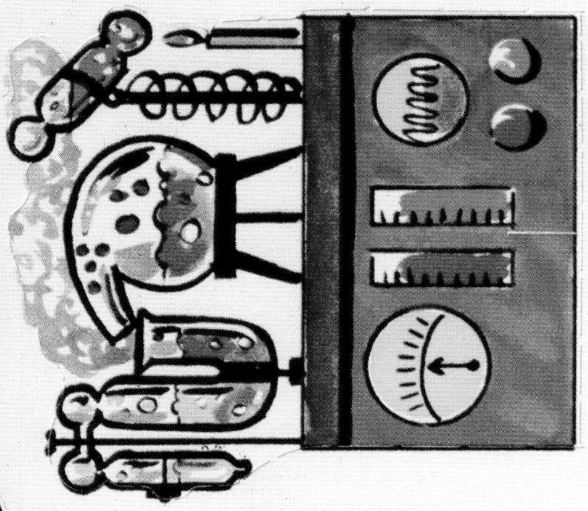

Assemble scenes according
to diagrams.

THANK YOU

To the brilliant and boundlessly patient Geoff Spear, who thought he'd never have to photograph a Bat-anything, ever again. I promise this is the last time! (Although I'm bidding on this really cool thing, and if I get it could we . . .?)

To Steve Korté, my editor and dear friend at DC Comics, who worked harder on this edition than I did. Bless you, Mr. K.

To everyone in my family, who didn't seem to be embarrassed about this at all.

To Saul Ferris, Bat-collector extraordinaire and all-round nice guy, who trusted me with some of the rarest pieces in his collection, many of which make up the "new" section at the end of this book.

To Ali Kokmen, Alison Hagge, Hector Campbell and the wonderful folks at Watson-Guptill, who gave this book a new life and graciously granted me all my production demands.

To Joe Desris, who owned many of the pieces in this book when we shot them and just may know more about Batman toys and comics than anyone else on the planet. I couldn't have done it without him.

To Binky Urban, John Balsamo, Georg Brewer, Bill Bruegman and Toy Scouts, Inc., Calvin Chu, Trent Duffy, Chris Eades, Andrew Elmore, Bob Kane, Chin-Yee Lai, Lev from Toy Tokyo, Jim Makowski, David Mazzucchelli, Frank Miller, Al Serpagli at the Palm Restaurant, Fiona Spear, Art Spiegelman, Michael Stutelberg, Rich Thomas (for the distress!), Paul Dini, Bruce Timm, Thomas Zellers and some guy named Alex Ross.

To the Chinery Collection, for allowing us to photograph the Batcycle and only surviving Batmobile stunt car from the *Batman* TV series.

To John Canemaker, who was the first person to make me think seriously about doing this book.

Love and thanks to Walt for the epigram.

To J. D. McClatchy, who is the only member of the Academy of Arts and Letters who knows my favorite episode of *Batman: The Animated Series.* (And whom I like to watch it with!)

Finally, to Mr. F. C. Ware, who conducts symphonies on the page. May the music never stop.

– C. K.

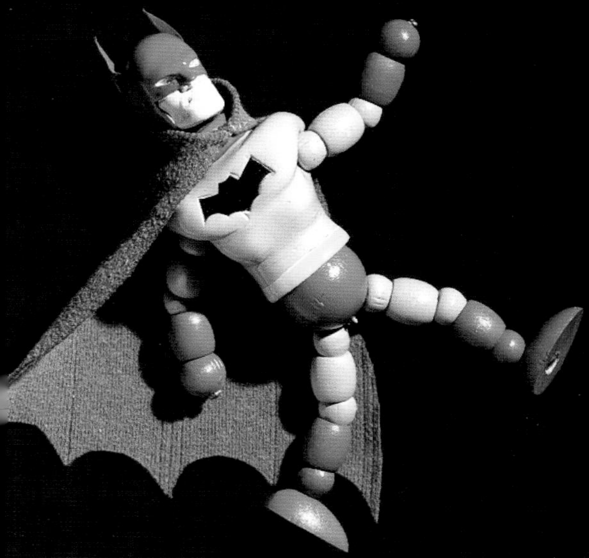

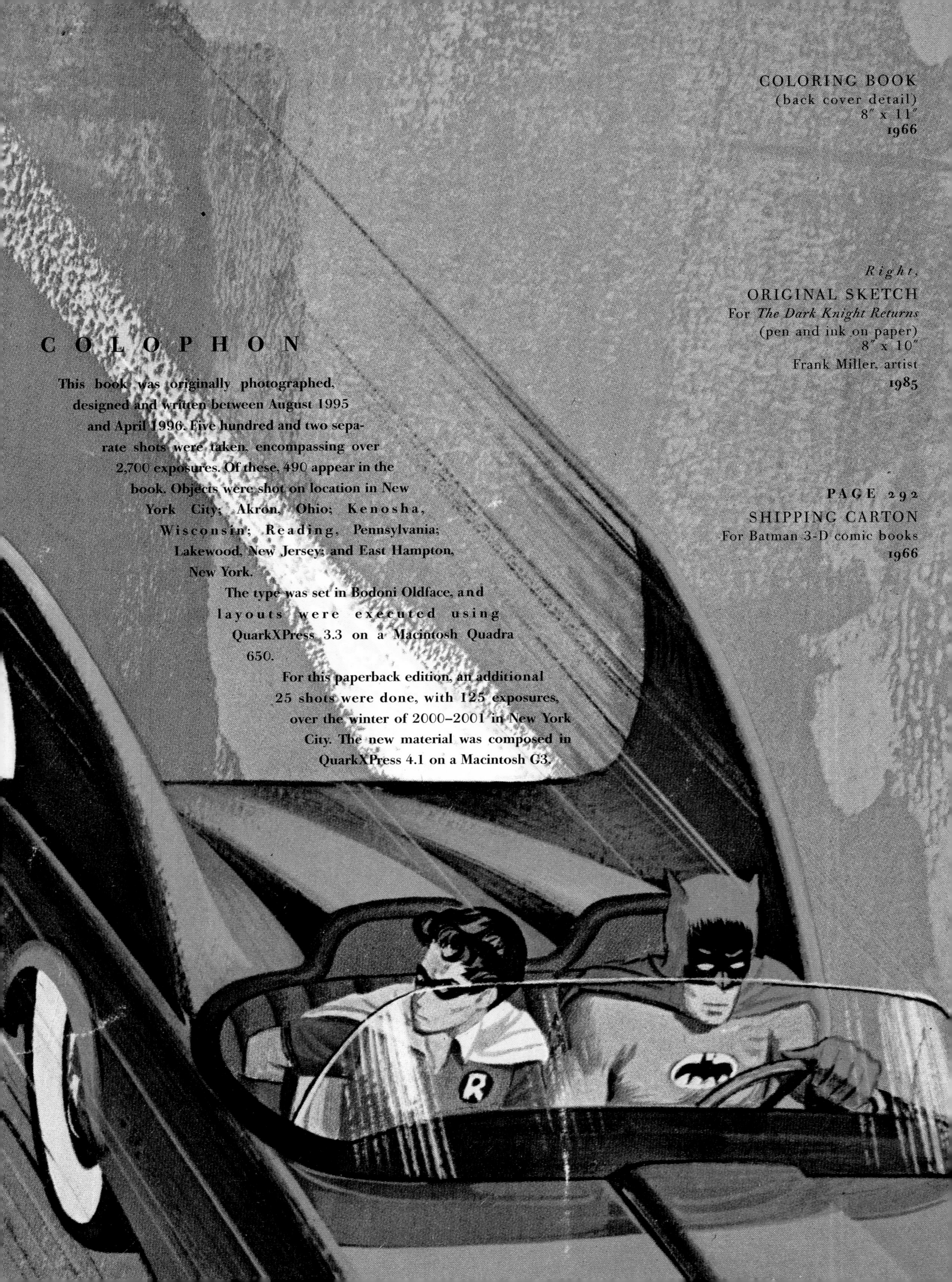

COLORING BOOK
(back cover detail)
8″ x 11″
1966

Right,
ORIGINAL SKETCH
For *The Dark Knight Returns*
(pen and ink on paper)
8″ x 10″
Frank Miller, artist
1985

PAGE 292
SHIPPING CARTON
For Batman 3-D comic books
1966

COLOPHON

This book was originally photographed, designed and written between August 1995 and April 1996. Five hundred and two separate shots were taken, encompassing over 2,700 exposures. Of these, 490 appear in the book. Objects were shot on location in New York City; Akron, Ohio; Kenosha, Wisconsin; Reading, Pennsylvania; Lakewood, New Jersey; and East Hampton, New York.

The type was set in Bodoni Oldface, and layouts were executed using QuarkXPress 3.3 on a Macintosh Quadra 650.

For this paperback edition, an additional 25 shots were done, with 125 exposures, over the winter of 2000–2001 in New York City. The new material was composed in QuarkXPress 4.1 on a Macintosh G3.

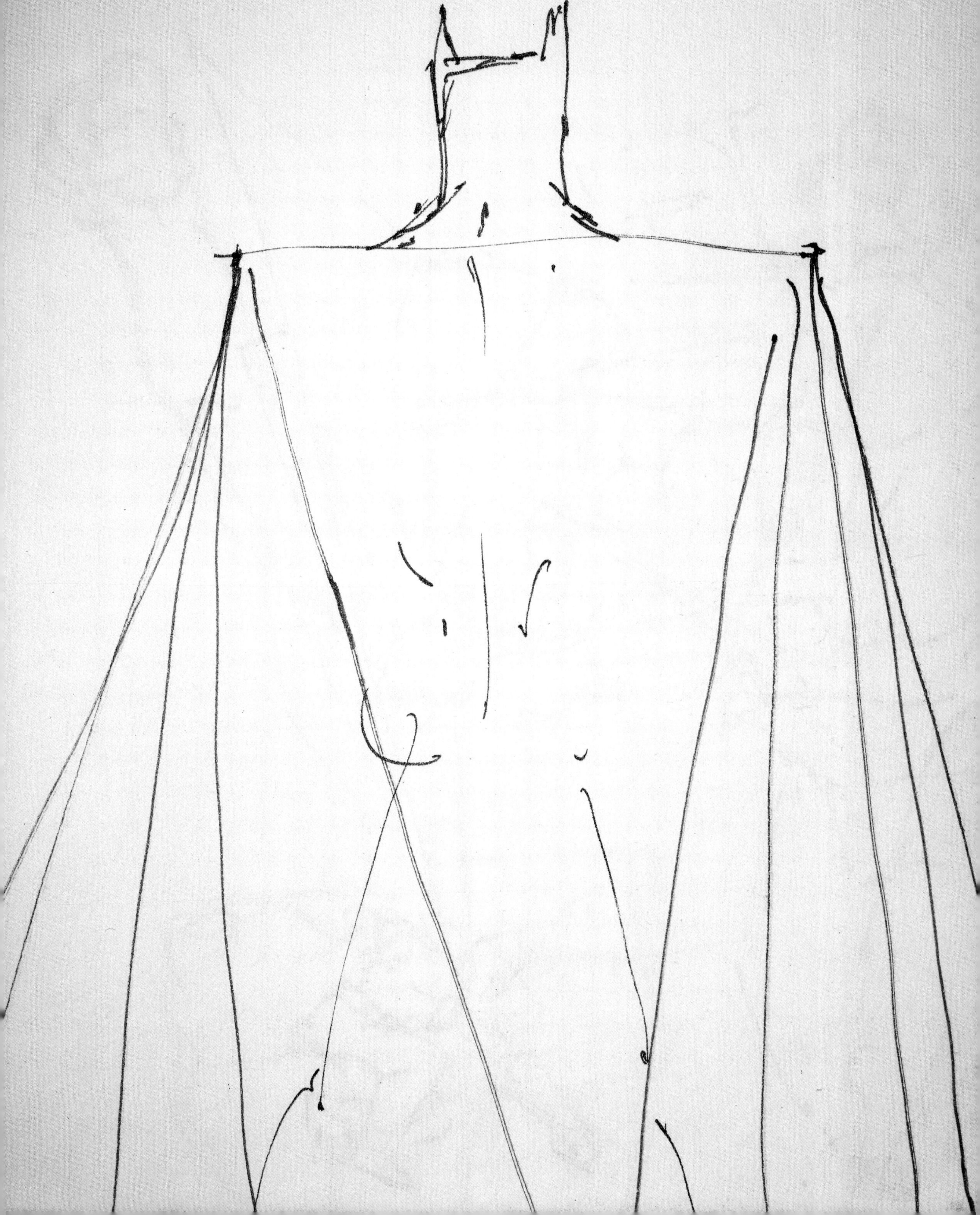

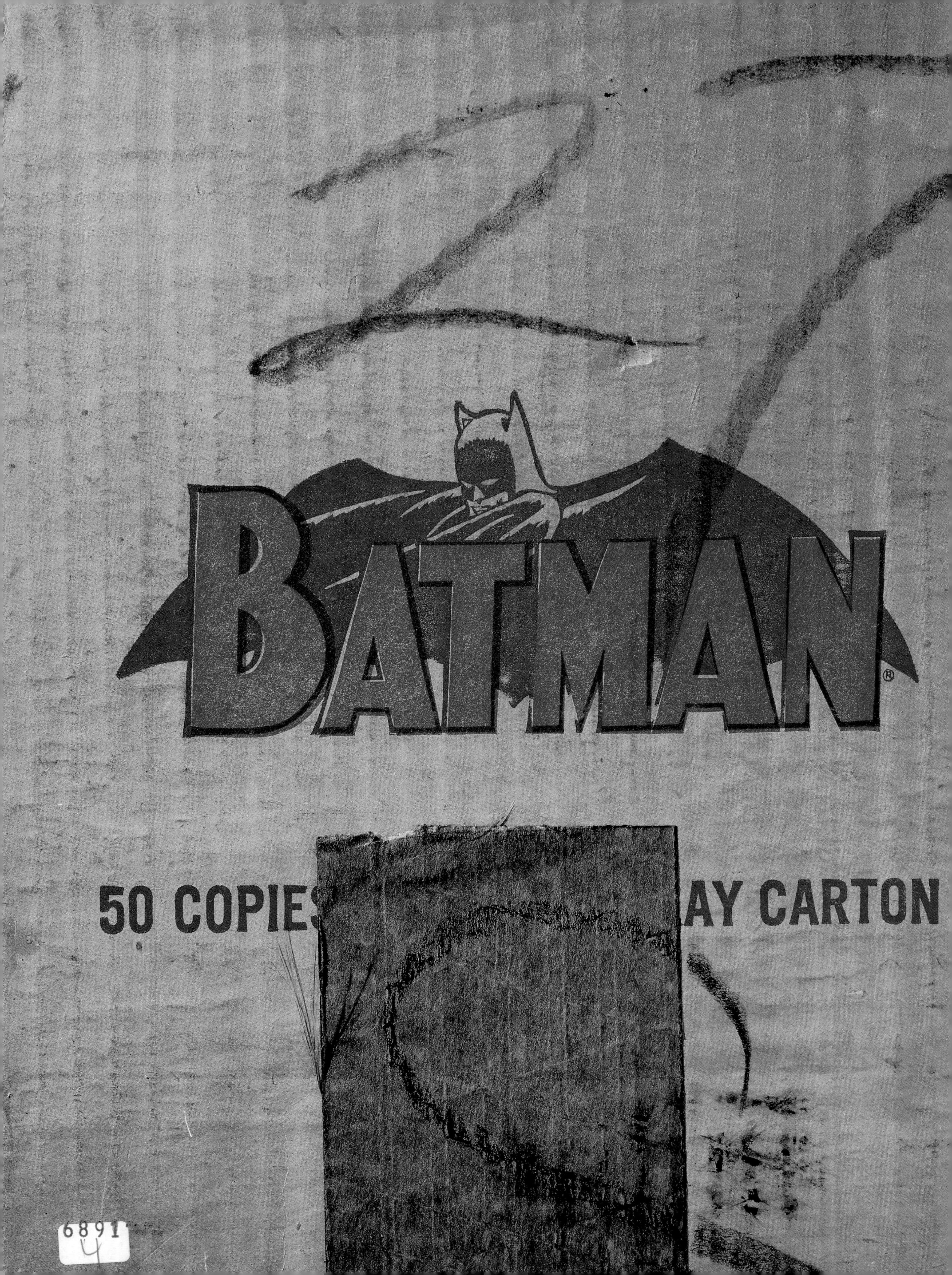
BATMAN®
50 COPIES
AY CARTON
6891